THE MEZCAL RUSH

THE MEZCAL RUSH

Explorations in Agave Country

GRANVILLE GREENE

Illustrations by Jack DeLap

COUNTERPOINT

BERKELEY

Library of Congress Cataloging-in-Publication Data is available

Cover design by Jennifer Heuer
Interior design by Megan Jones Design

ISBN 978-1-61902-844-9

COUNTERPOINT
2560 Ninth Street, Suite 318
Berkeley, CA 94710
www.counterpointpress.com

Printed in the United States of America
Distributed by Publishers Group West

10 9 8 7 6 5 4 3 2 1

for my parents and grandparents

"Mescal," Yvonne said brightly.
The air was so full of electricity it trembled.

—MALCOLM LOWRY, *UNDER THE VOLCANO*

PROLOGUE

ARLY ONE EVENING, Juan and Miguel, landscapers who work in my neighborhood in Santa Fe, stopped by in their pickup. They knew I was writing about the Mexican spirit *mezcal*, and they had a drink they wanted to share with me from their home in the state of Chihuahua. The clear liquid filled about a third of its hand-blown glass bottle, and the men watched me intently as I took a small sip. It was fiercely strong, yet rich with distinctive flavors that took me on several excursions at once. But mostly, it tasted alive.

What was it?

"It's *sotol* from the mountains," Juan beamed.

During my visits to Mexico (which included spending nearly a year in the state of Oaxaca for this book), I had learned that sotol is a distillate of the Desert Spoon plant, *Dasylirion wheeleri*. With its slender, pointed spines, the succulent is sometimes mistaken for the agave plants that are used as the *materia prima* for mezcal distillation. They are related, and like agave, Desert Spoon grows on both sides of the border and has been a valuable resource for indigenous peoples for thousands of years. The strong fibers from the leaves of both plants can be extracted to weave baskets and cord, and their fleshy cores can be baked for food or cooked, mashed, and fermented for distilling spirits. Desert Spoon is named after the base of its leaf, which can be used as a utensil.

Juan and Miguel's sotol had been crafted in and for their community, from local plants, by artisanal methods passed down through generations. Along with traditionally distilled mezcal, *bacanora*, *raicilla*, and other Mexican spirits that use agave, sotol is a labor-intensive drink that historically has been made in small batches and reserved for important events in a village. But it has long found its way across the frontier, and versions have even been fabricated in the U.S. With occasional sips enjoyed along the journey, the men's unbranded bottle had been handed, *amigo* to *compadre*, all the way from the rugged slopes of Mexico's Sierra Madre Occidental, across the international boundary straddling the great Chihuahuan Desert, and up the interstate blacktop partly laid over the ancient Camino Real trade route—until the last swigs were given to me in the Sangre de Cristo foothills.

The guys wanted to hang on to their handsome vessel, so I transferred its contents to a jam jar and put it on a shelf loaded with dozens of other glass containers, every one filled with a handcrafted Mexican spirit that tells an individual story of people, plants, and place. For me, the carefully authored drinks in my small collection represent only a few great books from a vast library that I know I can never fully read, and are written in languages that I'm ill equipped to understand. I'm not a botanist, a

booze pundit, an anthropologist, or any other type of expert—
I'm just an amateur who wanted to learn more. But for Juan and
Miguel, each time they sip their sotol it is as if they are swallowing a liquid version of home. The distillate's unique essences
reconnect them to the culture they remain spiritually a part of,
yet have physically left behind. It doesn't matter if their local
sotol tastes good or bad, or if anyone else likes it. The drink is a
reflection of who they are—and that is something to be proud of.

Moved by their generosity, I found myself wishing that their
gesture had been my initiation into the fascinating world of
Mexican spirits. But the reality was far less memorable. As with
the vast majority of other U.S. consumers, my first experiences
had been with industrially manufactured tequila and cheap commercially made mezcal—the type with a "worm" at the bottom
of the bottle, the "ten yards of barbed wire fence" that the novel-
ist Malcolm Lowry has his alcoholic consul hooked on in *Under
the Volcano*.

I sampled such mass-produced agave products from the early
1980s, during my college years, until 1998, when I encountered a
far more exceptional Mexican drink: a pricey bottle of Oaxacan
mezcal that had been micro-distilled from *Agave angustifolia*,
commonly known as *espadín*. It was handmade by a family in
the remote Zapotec village of Santo Domingo Albarradas, but I
found it repackaged in a gourmet food-and-wine store in Santa Fe.
When I brought it home and tried it, the spirit's delectable flavors
seeped into my consciousness like an otherworldly piece of music.
It tasted completely different from any mezcal I had tried before,

and I became so taken by it that I wanted to learn more about what it was, who made it, and where it came from.

At the time, artisanally crafted mezcal was only just beginning to appear on the radar in the U.S., and there wasn't much information about it. I realized that the best way for me to learn about the spirit was to head to Mexico, where, according to new studies, it has been distilled for thousands of years. My instruction began in 2000, when a magazine sent me to Oaxaca, home to the widest variety of agaves and the mezcals that are made from them. There, I was awakened to the extraordinary diversity of family-produced Mexican spirits.

Manufacturers of tequila use only one type of plant, *Agave tequilana*, and because they generally steam its heart in industrial machines, their product has a somewhat neutral taste. But traditional mezcals celebrate the diverse characters of numerous agave species, which are roasted in underground wood-fired ovens that infuse the drinks with their distinctive smoky notes. The nuanced flavors reflect myriad variations in landscape, soil, microclimates, airborne yeasts, and distillation techniques—not to mention the ingenuity of their makers. On that first visit to Oaxaca, and during my subsequent explorations for this book, I grew to respect the spirit as one of Mexico's most poetic creations. Each mezcal can be an eloquent expression of the alchemist crafting it, even functioning as an unspoken language among the members of a community.

These days, the drink is on the move, finding its way to hip bars from Rome to Tokyo. Mezcal has been adopted by the Slow

Food and craft-spirits camps, and helps to quench a burgeoning thirst for authenticity that has taken hold of many consumers. Yet what is almost certainly the oldest distilled beverage of the Americas remains largely unknown in relation to its hugely popular cousin, tequila, which has skyrocketed in worldwide sales over the past few decades. English-language dictionaries still even spell mezcal in an archaic form: "mescal." Its relative obscurity is due not only to the unsavory image it's been saddled with—"the drink with the worm"—but also, in class- and race-conscious Mexico, to its historically having been identified with the country's marginalized indigenous populations. The diverse peoples who traditionally make mezcal have long been excluded from defining the spirit for Mexican and international markets.

As the price for convenience, we have been conditioned by agro-industry to take for granted a great deal of what we put in our bodies. We've lost touch with our innate ability to wonder about who picked the beans for our coffee, or cut the cane for the sugar we use to sweeten it, or milked the cows for the milk we stir in. But the individual interactions that can arise from getting to know who makes our "stuff" can be profoundly satisfying. And in our fast-paced age of continuous switching between globalization and deglobalization, the truths behind what we purchase are becoming increasingly relevant to the pressing issues of equality and sustainability.

As much as some consumers might prefer to become locavores, most will likely remain globavores—which raises many pertinent questions. In a speech in late 2016, former U.S.

Agave salmiana

PART ONE

DOWN THE RABBIT HOLE

THE FIRST TIME I remember drinking mezcal was in the early 1980s in Baltimore. I was in college, and my friends and I found a cheap bottle in a run-down liquor store near the campus. The high alcohol content served our purposes, but everything else looked dubious. There was a grotesque, crinkled worm lurking at the bottom, and the spirit's yellowy brown color reminded me of water from a rusty faucet. It tasted so awful that swilling it on a dare seemed its best possible use. I didn't think about who made it. I only knew it was from Mexico and distilled from something called agave, which I figured was a type of cactus. And I had heard that crazy things happened when people ate the worm, although I didn't get that far. I probably would have laughed if anyone had told me that tasting notes on body, finish, and terroir would someday be used to describe mezcal.

Many years later, I found myself living in Santa Fe, New Mexico, and becoming more curious about the large country lying across the state's southern border. Echoes of it were everywhere—from chile peppers and mission churches to agaves. The vast desert landscapes now divided between the state and Mexico were once conjoined as a viceroyalty of New Spain. But long before conquistadors came hunting for fabled cities of gold, ancient pathways already traversed the region, walked by Ancestral Puebloan, Mogollon, Hohokam, and other peoples. When I first visited Chaco Canyon in northwestern New Mexico, I was amazed to learn of its archaeoastronomical sites, and the straight, well-engineered roads that once brought turquoise, seashells, and macaw feathers to its beautiful stone-walled buildings. Until then, I hadn't thought much about my belonging to a new culture that had cannibalized the lands of far older and perhaps more sophisticated cultures.

During the era of Spanish colonization, one extremely long indigenous trail was developed into *El Camino Real de Tierra Adentro*, a sixteen-hundred-mile trade route extending all the way from Mexico City to San Juan Pueblo. The grueling wagon and foot journey along it, of which a particularly arduous one-hundred-mile section became known as Route of the Dead Man, brought an influx of Spanish settlers to the newly formed territory of *Nuevo México*. With them came Christianity, disease, guns, and alcohol. A tax record from 1873 for the town of Tequila, where sixteen distilleries were serving a population of twenty-five hundred, noted that three casks of "mezcal wine" were sent all the way to Santa Fe via El Paso, Texas.

One day in the mid-1990s, I climbed into my pickup and drove along several paved-over portions of the Camino Real, as I headed 285 miles south on I-25 to visit some friends in Las Cruces. The highway follows the Rio Grande as it meanders through parched and desolate expanses, bare brown mountains rolling into the distance. El Paso and its Mexican neighbor, Juárez, are only an hour further south from Las Cruces, and we thought it might be fun to spend a few hours on the other side of the border. On a warm Saturday evening at sunset, before Juárez gained its worldwide notoriety as a grisly battleground in the

Mexican drug war, we walked across the international bridge that spans the Rio Grande from El Paso.

Below us, the river trickled through a wide culvert littered with trash. A sagging Mexican flag met us at the middle of the bridge, and we entered the country by passing through a squeaky turnstile. A taxi brought us to a touristy *mercado* several blocks away, where we sat around an outdoor table, swilling ice-cold bottles of Carta Blanca beer. There were stalls selling piñatas, serapes, and other souvenirs, and a mariachi trio serenaded us with mournful ballads while children implored us to buy Chiclets. A guy in a Pancho Villa–style *bandito* outfit was making his way from table to table, with a holster loaded with shot glasses strapped across his chest, a bottle of mezcal in his hand. His target? *Gringos estúpidos.*

It seemed like the right time to give the drink another try, but of course it wasn't. The shot he poured me was so strong and sickly sweet that it gave my body a ghoulish shiver. Just then another man appeared with a small wooden box slung over his shoulder. It had a pair of long wires extending from it with handles attached to their ends. With a naughty grin, he instructed two of us to each grasp a handle with one hand and to use our other hand to hold the hand of our neighbor. As he slowly turned a dial on the box, electricity blasted through the wires, tingled our fingers, and briefly paralyzed our circle in a crude form of shock therapy. This, I thought, was the kind of dumb stuff you get into when drinking mezcal. I was a gringo estúpido.

My head spinning, I was wondering if it would be smart to switch to tequila when we landed in a legendary barroom called the Kentucky Club. One of several establishments in Mexico that claimed to be the birthplace of the margarita, it was on Avenida Juárez, the lively main drag by the bridge. A nondescript facade masked a manly, wood-detailed interior that had been beckoning Americans across the border since Prohibition. The handsomely burnished bar was said to have been carved in France, and Marilyn Monroe had allegedly sidled up to it. The devil-may-care vibe inspired one of the friends I was with to later propose to his girlfriend there, and perhaps inspired her to say yes.

We were served a round of the famous house margaritas by a poker-faced bartender wearing a crisp white shirt and a black tie. As "A Whiter Shade of Pale" played on the jukebox, we toasted a dusty stuffed raptor frozen in action, its wings spread for flight. Then we drank more. Although I liked to think I was as macho as the steely-eyed matadors staring down at us from faded pictures on the bar's nicotine-stained walls, I could barely handle my hangover. I would eventually learn that tequila is actually one of many types of mezcal, but I felt so lousy after our Juárez adventure that I thought it might be better to keep clear of any agave distillate in the future.

SINCE I HAD decided that mezcal could only be cheap rocket fuel, I was surprised when, in the late 1990s, I came across a radically different variation at the Standard Market, a gourmet-food store in Santa Fe. Every bottle of mezcal I had previously seen had an embalmed-looking worm in it. But this brand was elegantly packaged in cylindrical containers that were beautifully woven from palm fiber. I picked up one circled by green stripes and tiny triangles suggesting mountains. A wine bottle inside was labeled with an artful graphic, by the late artist Ken Price, of a yellow pot beside a pink house on a green village lane, below a pair of peaks with dark birds soaring overhead. It was from Santo Domingo Albarradas, a community in the Mexican state of Oaxaca, which a smaller label instructed me to pronounce "wa-ha-ka."

The spirit cost a bracing $45, but I felt strangely compelled, much like Alice when she discovers the tabletop vial with the DRINK ME sign tied to its neck. The clincher, however, was when I found a bottle mispriced for $15. I brought it home and unsealed it by pulling away a thread encased in golden beeswax around the cork—a presentation I had never seen before, and that I imagined must be traditionally Oaxacan. Noting that there was no worm in the bottle, I poured some into a shot glass and held it to the light. Unlike the sickly-yellow mezcals I had previously encountered, it was clear—and smelled both sweet and smoky. Following a directive on the bottle to sip, not shoot, I took a careful taste.

The mezcal was powerful, and its smoke-imbued accents reminded me of the peaty flavors of single malt Scotch whisky. At the time, I was unaware that it tasted that way because the agave hearts had been baked in a firewood-heated pit oven called an *horno*. But as I sipped, the initial smokiness receded and more subtle tastes emerged: something lemon-limey, and possibly peppery—and was that a hint of vanilla bean? As the alcohol warmed my throat and chest, I read more of the label. Like a sommelier recommending a sauvignon blanc, it told me that the mezcal had "a long, dry, smooth finish."

Given my limited knowledge of mezcal at the time, it seemed a stretch to apply an oenophilic vocabulary to "that drink with the worm." Still, even with my unrefined experience sampling fine wines, spirits, and cultivated cuisine in general, I could already tell that this was quite something. Aside from its complex and delicious tastes, it offered a clean, powerful high that seemed to lift me right out of myself. If the drink had a soundtrack, it might have been The Beatles' instrumental "Flying," from *Magical Mystery Tour*. But that night, as I enjoyed my first sips of artisanal mezcal before a crackling fire, it seemed I had tumbled after Alice down her rabbit hole.

The Wonderland to which I imagined myself transported, however, was the picturesque Indian village where the veteran goldminer Howard suddenly finds himself in the 1948 film *The Treasure of the Sierra Madre*. I could almost hear the hearty calls of roosters and burros, and the vigorous trumpet bursts of mariachis. My stunted fantasies of "authentic" Mexican life were perhaps a result of my sheltered childhood in 1960s Baltimore, where salsa was almost unknown as a condiment, and only vaguely as an exotic dance. At that time, Mexico existed for me in the pages of well-thumbed *National Geographic*s, and the records my father played of Herb Alpert and the Tijuana Brass. A Mexican was Mel Blanc crooning the Frito Bandito jingle.

Wouldn't it be great, I thought as I sipped more mezcal, to actually visit Santo Domingo Albarradas and meet the people who distilled this awesome stuff? Not long after that, the free-spirited editors of *Mountainfreak*, a neo-hippie magazine based in Telluride, Colorado, sent me on assignment to Oaxaca to do just that. By the time it occurred to me that they could quite possibly have confused mezcal with the hallucinogenic drug mescaline, I was already on a flight headed to southern Mexico.

ᕙ

WHEN I LANDED in Oaxaca de Juárez, the capital of the state of Oaxaca, in the summer of 2000, Ron Cooper, the American importer of that first eye-opening mezcal from Santo Domingo Albarradas I had tried, greeted me at the provincial airport. He was middle-aged and wore his dark hair in a distinctive top-knot. His fledgling company, Del Maguey (which means "Of the Agave"), exported five Oaxacan distillates to the U.S. Each was from a different village, and he had come up with the term "single village mezcal." In return for what meager publicity my obscure *Mountainfreak* story might generate for his business, he had offered to show me around, put me up, and introduce me to the world of artisanally crafted agave spirits.

Many of us know mezcal as tequila, which is a type of mezcal that was given the name of the town in Jalisco where it's been distilled since the sixteenth century. These days, most tequilas are manufactured by transnational corporations. Although there are plenty of industrially fabricated versions of mezcal, as well, the spirit is traditionally handcrafted in small quantities from the pineapple-esque *piñas* (or hearts) of many different types of agave in multiple regions of Mexico. These small-batch mezcals are known for diverse and intricate flavors, but tequila makers use only one type of plant, *A. tequilana*, and because large-scale distilleries mechanically steam its heart instead of baking it in smoky underground ovens, their products taste relatively bland.

Ron's single village marketing strategy was reminiscent of single malt Scotch. He bottled his micro-distilled mezcals in limited, numbered batches, after purchasing them in bulk from a handpicked selection of small-scale producers known as *maestros mezcaleros*, or *palenqueros*. They created their signature drinks in and for the rural Oaxacan communities where they lived, and Del Maguey presented them to customers like vintners. In a world of worms, Ron's fresh approach to mezcal packaging was innovative. Although his products had only a miniscule share of the spirits market, especially compared with tequila, they were nonetheless winning top awards at tasting events in the U.S., establishing him as a trailblazing mezcal maverick.

He had brought one of the producers along to greet me—Faustino Garcia Vasquez, the maker of Del Maguey's "Chichicapa" mezcal. Vasquez had a dark moustache and wore a cowboy hat, Western shirt, blue jeans, and huaraches (leather sandals). I would learn that his dress is typical of mezcal makers, who are often farmers, too. He and his family lived in a rural village called San Baltazar Chichicapam, which, Ron told me, was "on the other side of that big mountain over there," pointing to a high, rugged ridge looming in the distance.

As we ate breakfast in the airport restaurant overlooking the runway, Faustino seemed completely absorbed by the aircraft taking off and landing outside. Then again, he may have simply felt left out of the conversation. He didn't speak English, and even Spanish was his second tongue, after Zapoteco, a tonal Oto-Manguean language with as many as sixty local versions that sounded, to my untrained ear, like a hybrid of Portuguese and Chinese. My own Spanish at the time was minimal, and Ron spoke it in a laid-back SoCal drawl. His voice reminded me of Dennis Hopper's. Indeed, the late actor turned out to have been one of many prominent friends and acquaintances of Ron, who was a well-established contemporary artist.

꒣

THE HIGH LIFE seemed far away as the three of us piled into the cab of Ron's dusty pickup. Carefully manning the steering wheel, he took us from the manicured, leafy grounds of the airport to a boulevard busy with honking taxis, belching buses, and thunderous trucks battling each other like *luchadores* (wrestlers) in the ring.

Situated at around fifty-one hundred feet above sea level, at the nexus of three valleys, Oaxaca de Juárez is surrounded by formidable pine- and oak-covered slopes that are part of two mountain chains, the Sierra Madre de Oaxaca and the Sierra Madre del Sur. It was early August, still within the annual rainy season that typically stretches from May to September. The air was damp, and the distant peaks were cloaked in white mists.

So I wasn't surprised to learn that some Zapotecs have called themselves *Be'ena' Za'a* (The Cloud People). Around 15 percent of Mexicans identify as indigenous, and about 6 percent speak one of sixty-eight distinct languages. Oaxaca has the second-largest indigenous population in the country, after the state of Yucatán. There are sixteen different ethnic-language groups in the state, and approximately 30 percent of Oaxacans speak a language other than Spanish. The biggest indigenous groups are the Zapotec and Mixtec, who are, respectively, the third- and fourth-largest in the country, after the Nahuatl and Maya. The smallest groups in Oaxaca are the Ixcatec and Popoluca, who together number only a few hundred.

As he fought the traffic, Ron informed me that traditionally distilled mezcal is predominantly crafted by the Zapotec, with the Mixtec coming in a distant second. Although the spirit was slowly gaining respect abroad—in no small part due, he said, to his own crusading efforts to "redefine the category"—it still had an image problem to contend with at home, where it was often looked down upon by elite Mexicans as *campesino* (peasant) swill made by barefoot *Indígenas* (Indians). The Denomination of Origin (DO) for mezcal was established in 1994, and Ron launched his brand in 1995. He had been on a mission to recast the spirit on the world stage ever since.

The city's historic center is famous for its fine colonial buildings, many of them constructed with a locally quarried green stone that has given Oaxaca de Juárez one of its most colorful nicknames—the Emerald City. But here in the less touristy part, the potholed streets were lined with a nondescript sprawl of boxy concrete buildings housing automotive supply and repair shops, an occasional strip club, and simple *taquerías*. Many of these structures were painted in bright oranges, greens, and blues; all were liberally dusted with traffic soot; and some had strips of bare rebar sticking straight up from their roofs, the ends topped with upturned soda bottles.

Even amid the modern hodgepodge, Oaxaca's staggering biodiversity was already in evidence. Over six hundred species of birds have been verified in the state, as well as hundreds of mammals, amphibians, and reptiles, and thousands of species of flowering plants. As we made our way into the city, I could see cacti towering in traffic islands, tropical palms swaying in the breeze, and flowering trees with birds and butterflies fluttering through their foliage.

There were also agaves of many shapes and sizes: a preview of why I had come.

JUST AS A coconut-laden palm tree can bring an idyllic beach memory into soft focus, or a majestic organ pipe cactus will make you picture the Wild West, a round, green, spiky agave almost always springs Mexico to mind. The plants naturally occur in

an expanse stretching all the way from the northernmost countries of South America, up through Central America, across the
Caribbean, and deep into the southwestern U.S. But Mexico,
home to the largest and most diverse agave population in the
world, is their epicenter. Of the approximately two hundred recognized species (there are undoubtedly more), at least 160 grow
in the republic, and about 60 percent are endemic to it.

Although estimates vary, sociologist Sarah Bowen writes in
her authoritative book, *Divided Spirits: Tequila, Mezcal, and
the Politics of Production*, "at least twenty species of agave are
commonly used in the production of mezcal, with some studies finding upward of forty-two species." She cites the ongoing
research of ethnobotanist Patricia Colunga-García Marín, of the
Centro de Investigación Científica de Yucatán (CICY), who has
"found evidence of a history of mezcal production in twenty-four
of thirty-one Mexican states and the Federal District of Mexico."

An agave's circular leaf structure, called a rosette, is similar to
an artichoke's. Its swordlike (and sometimes thorny-edged) *pencas* (leaves), tipped by a single needle that can be wickedly sharp,
are effective armor for its bulbous middle, which can weigh hundreds of pounds, depending on the species. Mankind has presumably utilized the plants for as long as we've lived with them—and
not only for making spirits. The word "mezcal" is derived from
the Nahuatl words *ixcalli* (roasted) and *metl* (agave). The piña's
starchy, nutritious flesh can provide food, when baked, and drink,
when the hearts of some species are scooped out and the vitamin-
rich *aguamiel* (nectar) is allowed to collect within the resulting

hollow. According to archaeological studies of Mesoamerica, pit-roasted agave hearts have been a food staple since at least 9000 BCE. In the U.S., the Mescalero Apache are named after the mescal agave (*Agave parryi*) that they still gather in south-central New Mexico for food. In prehistoric North America, the Hohokam culture farmed the plants.

The thick and powerful *quiote* (inflorescence), which can thrust as high as thirty feet upward from an agave's center in the final act of its life (anywhere from five to seventy years, depending on the species), can also be eaten, along with the succulent yellow flowers crowning it. The blossoms serve bats, birds, and insects, which act as pollinators in return. Many agave species have a symbiotic relationship with a particularly helpful assistant in this regard. For example, the Mexican long-nosed bat (*Leptonycteris nivalis*) is a crucial pollen-spreader for *A. tequilana*.

The stalks have many other uses. They serve as firewood and as material for constructing bamboo-like fences and walls. They've also been crafted into surfboards and didgeridoos. The plant's rigid pencas can be dried and fashioned into crude shelters, and its leaves' strong *ixtle*, or *pita*, fibers can be formed into rope, woven into coarse mats and cloth, or made into baskets and sandals. In the artisanal craft of *piteado*, the agave's fine white threads are intricately embroidered into belts, saddles, and other leather goods for *charros* (cowboys). Its fierce needles have been used as writing instruments, as well as for piercing, poking, or even drawing blood: pre-Hispanic codices depict thorns lancing ears and pricking tongues. As the botanist Howard Scott

Gentry puts it in his landmark book *Agaves of Continental North America*, "The uses of agaves are as many as the arts of man have found it convenient to devise."

Because they are often seen grouped with desert plants, agaves are commonly considered relatives of cacti or aloe. But they are actually unrelated, for a long time having been a part of the subfamily *Agavoideae* of the family *Asparagaceae* before being placed in their own separate family, *Agavaceae*. Genus Agave was first described in 1753 by the Swedish botanist Carl Linnaeus in his groundbreaking two-volume book, *Species Plantarum*, the springboard for modern plant nomenclature.

The Latin name *Agave* is derived from the ancient Greek word for noble or splendid, *agauós*, and that culture's mythology provides a cautionary tale for drinkers: The daughter of the goddess Harmonia and Cadmus, the king of Thebes, was named Agave. While under a spell from Dionysius, the so-called party god, she mistook her son Pentheus for a lion and tore him apart, limb from limb, during a drunken bacchanal. She didn't recognize her mistake until she brandished his head before her father.

In 1492, when Christopher Columbus and his three shiploads of men arrived in the Caribbean on a Spanish Crown–sponsored expedition seeking a new route between Europe and Asia, they noticed that the indigenous Taíno people who lived on the islands called agave *maguey*. The name became part of the Old World's emerging lexicon for the New World, the Taíno's Arawakan language also providing roots for the English words "barbeque," "hammock," "potato," "hurricane," and "canoe."

Twenty-seven years later, when the gold-hunting Spanish nobleman Hernán Cortés set foot on the shores of what's now called Mexico, he discovered the Aztecs using the word "metl" for agave in their Nahuatl language. But the Spaniards ignored this, imposing the word "maguey" as part of their conquest. The plants are now generally known as both agave and maguey inside Mexico, and as agave outside it. But among the country's many remaining ethnic-language groups, they are still identified by a mellifluous assortment of ancient names—*tzaatz* in Mixe, *mai* in Huichol, *tyoo'* in Chatino, *yavi* in Mixteco, and *ki* in Mayan, to name only a few.

The plants can now be found all over the globe. The tough fibers of sisal agaves (*Agave sisalana*) are harvested to make everything from twine and carpets to lumbar-support belts and scratching posts for cats. They are cultivated in Brazil, Tanzania, Java, China, Haiti, and Madagascar. Among other places, *A. tequilana* has made a second home in South Africa, where it's been used to make a non-Mexican version of tequila.

Other species are prized as ornamental plants, particularly in Europe. Agaves bask in the elegant botanical gardens of Nice and Monaco, and in the wonderfully rambling Giardini Botanici Hanbury, which occupies a spectacular forty-five-acre chunk of coastline near the Italian town of Ventimiglia. In the U.S., two of the best collections are found at the Desert Botanical Garden in Phoenix and the Huntington Botanical Gardens in San Marino, California. But the intrepid plants are rooted everywhere, from Miami to Golden Gate Park.

It would be hard to imagine a more striking maguey collection than the one overseen by the botanist Dr. Abisaí Josué García-Mendoza in the magnificent garden of the Universidad Nacional Autónoma de México's Instituto de Biología, in Mexico City. The extensive assortment of agaves thrives among volcanic stone outcroppings, and is probably the most representative concentration in the world. It's an excellent spot to wander, imagining the different plants as spirits.

It's unsurprising that the Zapotec are the largest producers of traditionally crafted mezcal, given that they've been cohabitating with agave for at least twenty-five hundred years. As a people, they number an estimated several hundred thousand, predominantly living in Oaxaca, home to the broadest diversity of maguey species in the world. Mezcals are distilled in the state from at least eight different species of the plant, from many varieties within those species, and from combinations of all of the above. With its deep history of ties between man and agave, and with mezcal-making rooted in its cultural heritage, Oaxaca is the spirit's epicenter.

⌐

AS WE APPROACHED the city's center, Ron nodded at a barren mountaintop to our left, on which, he said, were the legendary ruins of Monte Albán. A mezcal brand had been named after it—Monte Albán—the first large-scale commercial type to be exported from Mexico, in 1975. The pre-Columbian site is thought to date from around 500 BCE and to have been populated by as many as seventeen thousand people. It was a Zapotec stronghold, but was largely abandoned by 1000 CE. I could see that its soaring thirteen-hundred-foot perch would have commanded a strategic and formidable presence. Ahead of us, I caught glimpses of the twin towers of Santo Domingo Church, which was constructed over a two-hundred-year period, beginning in 1570. All around us, it seemed, were stark juxtapositions among the ancient, the old, and the new.

Faustino, who had some business to attend to, stepped out at a busy corner, while Ron and I continued to Mercado de Abastos. One of the biggest street marketplaces in Mexico, it spreads over several city blocks. Ron wanted to begin my introduction to mezcal by taking me to his favorite *pulque* stall. Pulque, he explained, is a mildly alcoholic pre-Hispanic beverage that's made mostly from the aguamiel of the Volkswagen Beetle–size *Agave salmiana*, although other maguey species are also used. The nectar is fermented, like beer, rather than distilled, like mezcal.

Many believe that aguamiel fermentation was as far as indigenous peoples got with agave alcohol before the Spanish introduced them to distillation techniques. But new research debunks this long-held assumption. At the very least, Mesoamericans were enthusiastic experimenters, and their conquerors found them concocting alcoholic beverages from a broad selection of materia prima other than maguey. These included fermented cactus fruit, maize, hog plums, pineapples, coconuts, and honey, as well as various barks and roots—and even chewed tobacco juice and poisonous toads.

As soon as we entered the market, it became apparent that finding the pulque stall wouldn't be easy, even though Ron had visited it many times before. The place felt like a labyrinth. There were no signs or maps to guide you through its dark, close aisles—only row upon row of vendors hawking a mind-boggling array of everything from underpants and stuffed animals to plastic buckets and power tools. It seemed as if anyone could hang out a shingle and do business. Goods hung on the walls, dangled from the ceilings, and were neatly arranged across the tables of makeshift booths.

There were so many articles that it was hard to make out the vendors amid their wares. But if I lingered for even a moment to take a closer look at a hand-carved wooden chocolate stirrer or a plastic bag of deep-fried pork skins, someone would immediately spring from the shadows and greet me with an enthusiastic "¿*Qué tal, güero?*" (What's up, Blondie?) or a "¿*Qué necesitas, caballero?*" (What do you need, Mister?).

There were no price tags, and haggling was expected—which was how I imagined transactions had always been made there. Refreshingly non-corporate, Abastos felt as if the world's most ginormous Walmart Supercenter had been gutted, roasted on a spit, chewed up, and regurgitated into the streets, where it had been reinvented under genuinely human terms. The one thing the market shared with big-box stores was that its various zones had particular themes.

An entire section was devoted to cups, bowls, saucers, plates, and almost anything else that could be made with *barro* (earthenware); another part to the many beautiful flowers of the region;

somewhere else to *zapatos* (shoes) of all shapes and sizes; and yet another area to *licuadoras* (blenders), *tortilladoras* (tortilla presses), and other kitchen gadgetry. But unlike the generic Housewares, Sporting Goods, and Cosmetics sections of box stores, each part of the market had multiple vendors selling goods with their own individualized spins—and one could haggle with them for the best possible prices.

The variety of food items was astonishing: fly-covered cow carcasses; congealed pig heads slow-turning on meat hooks; plucked chickens and glistening hunks of goat; moist mounds of mysterious organs and entrails; pyramids of chiles in multiple shapes, sizes, and shades of red; stacks of brown eggs; earthenware bowls filled with *moles negro y rojo Oaxaqueños* (complex black and red chile sauces, two of seven traditionally made in Oaxaca); balls of string cheese, another local specialty; and an overwhelming selection of fresh breads, fragrant spices, amber honeys, and multihued fruits and vegetables.

Everywhere, hawkers were competing for attention, sticking earth-spackled bunches of onions in our faces, offering us handfuls of roasted pumpkin seeds and ripe tomatoes, or trying to sell us shoulder bags of recycled sugar sacks, in case we wanted to carry anything home. Other vendors called out the names of popular local snacks—tempting us with "*Tlayudas . . . tlayudas . . . tlayudas*" (baked tortillas loaded with refried beans) and "*Nieves . . . nieves . . . nieves*" (ices flavored with everything from avocado to *leche quemada con tuna*—burnt milk and the red fruit of the prickly pear cactus).

Chickens squawked, turkeys gobbled, and boom boxes pumped out ballads crooned over jaunty polka beats as cooks in mom-and-pop food stalls combined the market's ingredients into aromatic concoctions. Their creations were served to hungry patrons, who squeezed together on benches alongside tables covered with brightly patterned oilcloths. Bowls of fresh salsa and sliced limes—their contents eagerly added to everything—sat at the ready, refilled as soon as they were emptied.

Ron asked directions of a girl mixing cacao seeds, sugar, and almonds into a hand-cranked chocolate grinder; sampled a few crunchy, chile-roasted *chapulines* (grasshoppers) from the basket of an elderly woman; and made further inquiries of a vendor selling a pair of forlornly honking geese before we finally, almost miraculously, arrived at a nondescript stall with a hand-painted sign: REFRESQUERIA ANITA, PULQUE Y TEPACHE.

Below the sign sat Anita herself. Completely indifferent to the incongruous pair of *gabachos* (foreigners) who appeared before her, she had the thousand-yard stare of someone who, as Ron cryptically put it, "has seen a lot of people explode into flames."

Two earthenware vessels—one containing pulque, the other *tepache* (a traditional drink fermented from pineapple)—rested on the counter in front of her. She took off the pulque jar's metal lid, ladled a white foamy liquid into two *jícaras* (traditional cups made from halved dried gourds), and passed them to us. The drink felt cool through the hard vegetal skin and smelled mildly acidic. But as I was about to take a cautious sip, Ron stopped me with a light touch to my forearm before carefully tilting his jícara and sprinkling a few drops of pulque onto the ground.

"For the Earth Mother," he said. "She always drinks first."

The libation, which tasted sweet and sour and citrusy, traveled down my throat with a slightly alcoholic kick. From the way Ron was gauging my reaction, I could tell we weren't just having a beer here. So I took my time, slowly drank some more, and soon found out why. Deep into my second pulque, I began feeling decidedly different. It wasn't at all like I had felt when drinking beer, mezcal, or anything else I had tried before. Indeed, with my sensory faculties suddenly heightened, the market now seemed like a vivid Takashi Murakami–Frida Kahlo mash-up.

Ron put it another way: "Pulque is psychedelic, man!"

NO ONE KNOWS exactly when people began making and drinking pulque—only that, when Cortés arrived on the shores of what is now Mexico, it was integral to the religious observances of the polytheistic Aztecs, who were the dominant ethnic group at the time. The sacred drink, which they called *iztac octli* (white wine), was also used by other indigenous societies of the central highlands, where the agaves for pulque-brewing grow naturally. It was particularly prominent in the religious ceremonies of the Mixtec and Zapotec cultures in the region now known as Oaxaca.

The process for making the drink has changed little over the centuries. The agave species harvested for pulque are generally much larger than those grown for mezcal and are also juicier.

When a pulque-producing plant matures, usually at around twelve years, the sprouting of its enormous quiote signals the appropriate time to harvest its bountiful nectar, which surges in volume as the agave directs energy to its center. A hole is cut into the middle of the maguey and the heart scooped out, leaving an open hollow where aguamiel collects. Pulque agaves can yield between one and two gallons of sap per day, and some continue to do so for several months.

The liquid is continuously removed and transferred to vats and other containers. Unlike beer, which requires yeast, pulque is fermented with bacteria. A hundred years ago, when immigrant brewers found their beers in competition with the traditional native drink, they propagandized the superstition that *muñecas* (cloth satchels of feces) were added to pulque to spur its fermentation. Whether this happened or not, there's no doubt that the concoction is highly perishable and must be consumed quickly. When the drink would go bad, the Aztecs called the spoiled, foul-smelling libation *octli poliuhqui* (spoiled pulque)—perhaps this was how the Spanish got the name for pulque.

Although pulque was by far the most important, all sorts of other fermented alcoholic beverages were crafted in Mesoamerica: *matzaoctli* (pineapple wine), *xoco octli* (wine made with the "hog plums" of genus Spondias), *tlaoloctli* (maize wine), and *capuloctli* (wine made from the cherries of *Prunus capuli*), among other potent drinks capable of causing altered states of consciousness.

It has long been assumed that no one there knew about spirits-distillation until the Spanish came and showed them. But in recent years, mezcal-making experiments have been performed using replicas of two-tiered pre-Columbian clay pots, for which the previously assumed use was bean-cooking. A team of scientists, mezcal producers, and archaeologists placed fermented agave mash in the bottoms of the bean-pot "stills," heated them from below, and collected the resulting condensations from the upper halves. The alcohol contents suggested that it was entirely possible that indigenous peoples knew how to distill. A recent ethnoarchaeological study confirms this.

Along with alcoholic beverages, the conquistadors found natives using such mind-altering substances as *peyotl* (*Lophophora williamsii*, or peyote cactus "buttons"), *teonanácatl* (*Psilocybe* fungi, or so-called magic mushrooms), and *ololiuhqui* (*Ipomoea violacea L.*, or morning glory seeds). Yet no substance was quite so venerated in the Aztec world as pulque, which was believed to be a form of divine breast milk.

The Aztecs worshipped multiple gods, who governed many different aspects of their world. There were the feathered serpent-god Quetzalcóatl (ruling the planet Venus, arts, crafts, wind, dawn, and knowledge) and Tezcatlipoca (overseeing sorcery, thievery, and the dark sides of life). Their sacred maguey goddess, Mayahuel, is usually depicted in codices in the company of a flowering agave and a vessel of pulque, much like the one Anita had on the counter of her stall. She is also shown with multiple breasts, for nursing pulque to the Centzon Totochtin, the four hundred rabbit-moon pulque gods who represented the infinite forms that intoxication could assume.

According to one myth, Mayahuel was a lovely maiden who lived in the sky with her grandmother, one of the devilish *tzitzimime* (star-gods) that tried to keep the sun from rising. One day, Mayahuel was swept away by Quetzalcóatl, and as they were entwined in a verdant tree, her angry grandmother sent some of her cohorts to destroy them. Quetzalcóatl managed to escape, but Mayahuel was chopped to bits. After her lover returned and buried her remains, they sprouted into agaves, which is why she was considered the mother of all maguey.

The Aztecs are often considered warlike, superstitious, and legendary for ghoulish human sacrifices, which they performed in the tens of thousands. But they were hardly unsophisticated, and were skilled in astronomy and medicine. The Spaniards were awestruck by their capital, Tenochtitlán, a city of splendid buildings and canals that occupied an island with an altitude of 7,350 feet in the middle of Lake Texcoco. It had a population of over two hundred thousand at the time, more people than in London, and has evolved over the centuries into Mexico City, which now has over twenty-one million inhabitants in its greater metropolitan area.

The Aztecs were wary of the destructive potential of alcohol over their society, and they revered the power of intoxication. Because of the dual nature of pulque—that is, nourishing and damaging in equal measure—its use was strictly regulated. No one younger than fifty-two was allowed to drink it regularly, except for pregnant women, priests, and sacrificial victims. Anyone else caught swilling pulque might be executed.

Yet, with the disintegration of Aztec culture during the Spanish Conquest, pulque found its way into mainstream use. By the nineteenth century, there were pulque bars all over Mexico City, and agave plantations supplied a national thirst for the drink, which was celebrated in art, music, and literature. Just as tobacco, once revered by the Aztecs as a sacred herb, became a source of addiction, so pulque lost its honored place and alcohol abuse became widespread.

⌐

WE BEGAN FINDING our way back through the dizzying market. Ron led me past bustling women in flowered aprons and men hauling handcarts laden with goods. We stopped at a stall where Ron knew the friendly proprietor. She served us steaming bowls of goat stew. We topped them with salsa, chopped cabbage, pinches of cilantro, and squeezes of lime, then wolfed down our *comida* (lunch) with warm corn tortillas that came wrapped in an embroidered cloth napkin tucked inside a straw basket.

"There's an ancient Huaxtec legend," Ron told me between bites of goat, "that warns of the dangers of the fifth pulque. That's the one that gets you really fucked up! After drinking five cups, a chieftain got naked and scandalized his tribe."

Since I was still feeling the effects of just two pulques, I could only imagine what drinking five might be like. Yet it was interesting to imbibe something so deeply rooted in the past of this place. Was I feeling the same way as others had a hundred years ago, or a thousand, or even more? Or had something been lost in translation—certain sensations, or a higher consciousness that one was meant to tune into?

It was impossible to know, but I could just as easily have asked the same questions after eating chocolate, which had also originated in Mesoamerica, possessing its own sacred role in Aztec religion before becoming molded into Hershey's Kisses on assembly lines. But not once during my chocolate-consuming life had it occurred to me to wonder about its history for even a second.

There was something else, too. Looking around, I could see how it might be fun to get to know your favorite chocolate vendor, talk to her about where her cacao beans had come from and who had grown them, and ask her to grind them just so. Here, it seemed, shoppers weren't so much interested in products as in ingredients and the people and stories behind them.

の

OUR BELLIES FULL of goat stew and the pulque still in our systems, we emerged from the darkened recesses of Abastos Market into the blazing sun that pounded the wide boulevard outside. This may have been the rainy season, but it could be incredibly hot anyway. The traffic lanes were clogged with a slow-moving procession of taxis decorated with elaborate floral arrangements and brightly colored crêpe streamers. It was fiesta day for the Oaxacan cabbies, and they were having fun making their way around town, honking the horns of their taxis and blasting salsa music through their stereo speakers.

Ron told me that fiestas are almost a daily occurrence in Oaxaca—mostly held for religious observances. But there were also some esoteric ones, such as *Noche de Rábanos* (Radish Night), which takes place in December. For this annual competition, the crimson root vegetables (a Spanish introduction) are painstakingly carved into saints, nativity scenes, and human figures, then displayed in the town plaza. The winning sculpture appears in local newspapers. I wondered if Ron was pulling my leg—until I came across a postcard of a disturbingly depicted radish-person. That's probably how *I* look to most people who live here, I thought: pink and strange.

Across the boulevard from the market were a couple of *bodegas* selling mezcal. I followed Ron between the taxis to one of them, a dimly lit shop. As my eyes adjusted, I could see a broad assortment of vessels: plastic *garrafones* (jugs, or jerry cans), glass bottles of various shapes and sizes, hand-painted gourds, and crudely made clay vessels. A number of ceramic containers were shaped like *changos* (monkeys), and others had been garishly formed and painted as lactating breasts and ejaculating penises. Ron explained that mezcal is widely considered an aphrodisiac.

There were also bottles of pink, baby blue, and caramel-colored *cremas* (cream-flavored mezcals), as well as expensive *especial* mezcals, like *pechuga* (breast), named after the chicken part traditionally hung in the still vapor during pechuga distillation, and *tobalá*, made from the wild-grown *Agave potatorum*. Ron speculated that both these fancier types were likely fakes. Bottled mezcals of varying shades of brown (*reposados* and *añejos*) were allegedly barrel aged—but Ron said many makers just added dye. Last, but not least, a huge glass jar on the shop counter held brackish-looking mezcal and several inches of what appeared to be wrinkled pinkish-red worms.

Despite my previous misadventures with crummy mezcal, I had managed to get this far without ever having eaten the notorious worm. I was relieved to learn there was no point in ever devouring one. Ron explained that the iconic creature wasn't really a worm at all, but usually the edible larvae of the *Hypopta agavis* moth. It's commonly found on magueys, although sometimes the larva of the agave snout weevil (*Scyphophorus acupunctatus*, or *picudo del agave*) is used instead.

I had always assumed that putting worms in mezcal was a long-standing Mexican tradition. But the idea has been attributed to Jacobo Lozano Páez, a mezcal bottler who had first moved to Mexico City from the state of Coahuila to study art. Instead, he ended up working in a liquor store before launching the brand *Gusano Rojo* (Red Worm) in the early 1950s. The rumored hallucinatory effects of "eating the worm" are unfounded. But new tests have shown that mezcals with worms exhibit higher levels of *cis*-3-Hexen-1-ol. The grassy-smelling, plant-produced, oily compound—used in perfumes—acts as a pheromone for some insects and mammals, although its aphrodisiac effects remain unproven in humans.

According to Ron, larvae were probably the drink's least offensive additives. He guessed that, if tested, most of the shop's mezcal would likely contain more sinister ingredients: food coloring, cane alcohol, fertilizers, pesticides, and other nasty chemicals used to accelerate the fermentation process, kill agave pests, and otherwise mess with what, he insisted, should be an entirely natural process—from the cultivation of the agaves to the making of the spirits.

"A good mezcal," Ron pronounced, "should always smell of sweet roasted maguey!"

As if on cue, the girl behind the shop counter offered me a plastic cup brimming with a yellowish sample from the larvae-filled jar. I held it to my nose and inhaled a bracingly powerful bouquet: a touch of gasoline, hints of paint thinner and fresh asphalt, and what appeared to be a long, dry, smooth finish of airplane-toilet aroma. It smelled just like that first mezcal I had tried in Baltimore.

I handed it back to the girl, and we left.

回

I WAS CURIOUS to see more of Oaxaca de Juárez, but Ron had other ideas. He kept a place in a nearby Zapotec community called Teotitlán del Valle, to which we were now headed. This was where he kept a warehouse, and where he hand-bottled the five varieties of "single village" mezcal he bought for export to the U.S. The community was also where he lived when he wasn't at home in Taos, New Mexico. I gathered, though, that Ron spent much of his time on the road, promoting and selling Del Maguey mezcal. He appeared to enjoy this, although it seemed to be an expensive undertaking.

We drove southeast from the city down a stretch of Highway 190, over what had once been an important road connecting the ancient settlements of Monte Albán, Yagul, and Mitla. Now it was a very tiny segment of the Pan-American Highway, a 29,800-mile route extending all the way from Prudhoe Bay, Alaska, to Ushuaia, Argentina. When the Mexican portion was completed in 1950, an annual speed race was created to commemorate the feat. The grueling La Carrera Panamericana, which followed the road the length of Mexico, was so dangerous that the race was canceled after only five years.

A tamer version of the fabled event was revived in 1988, and two members of Pink Floyd made a film about driving it. The posh race for the classic-car crowd was hard to imagine, however, because the road was a roughly surfaced two-lane blacktop with abundant *baches* (potholes) and *topes* (speed bumps). Even so, its condition did nothing to discourage the evidently fearless *colectivo* (shared-taxi) drivers from darting through the traffic at breakneck speeds, in what for them was a daily road race.

As the strong equatorial sun dropped behind the mountains, we rolled through a vast valley, passing fields of agave, corn, beans, and squash, then strangely shaped hills studded with shrubby trees, cacti, and scrub-covered ruins. Dotted here and there around the plains, small settlements were set against the bases of the steep, cloud-cloaked ridges towering around us. White-walled mission churches with red-tiled roofs rose above the communities: souvenirs of the Spanish colonization. We were now in the Zapoteca—the territory of the Zapotec. Ron pointed out wide swaths, cut straight down the slopes between the trees, that appeared to have been made for power lines but were actually boundary markers between *municipios* (municipalities), communally cleared each year.

Much of Oaxacan land still falls under the *ejido* system. This form of land tenure was established after the Mexican Revolution and was put into practice on a large scale in the 1930s. The idea was to provide a way for landless farmers to establish and communally maintain specific parcels for agricultural purposes, following the takeover of their community holdings by haciendas in the nineteenth century. In 1992, the sale and privatization of ejido land was permitted after an adjustment of Article 27 in the Mexican constitution, and increases in poverty and migration have been attributed to the change.

Mexico's thirty-one states are subdivided into 2,440 municipalities. Oaxaca has 570 municipalities, a very large number—the huge state of Baja has only five. Four hundred and eighteen follow the *usos y costumbres* (traditions and customs) system of indigenous self-governance. The government structure for all municipalities in the country was defined in the constitution in 1917. Every municipio must have an *alcalde* (mayor), *regidores* (councilmen), and a *síndico* (attorney general). In municipalities that choose to follow usos y costumbres, men hold official positions under an unpaid *cargo* (administrative work) system, and perform short-term community projects under an unpaid *tequio* (labor tax) system. In some Zapotec communities, men are required to complete at least fifteen years of unpaid services before they turn sixty. Migrants to the U.S. often pay others to complete their duties instead of returning home.

While driving, Ron gave me some background on his intro-duction to mezcal, using anecdotes that he often shared with oth-ers. He had first come through the area in 1970, when he and two buddies piled into a van to drive the "Pan-Am" from California to Panama on a spur-of-the-moment road trip. "We just wanted to see where the road went," he shrugged. But it was during this journey, which ended up lasting months, that Ron initially visited Teotitlán del Valle. He had liked it so much, he said, he returned two decades later to work on various art projects, some in col-laboration with master Zapotec weavers from the village, which is known for its finely woven *tapetes* (rugs) made of hand-spun, naturally dyed wool.

As a young artist, Ron was associated with the Light and Space movement, which originated in Southern California in the late 1960s and included figures like Robert Irwin and James Turrell. In those days, Ron fabricated sculpture combining light and architectural elements to form contemplative environments. "Growing up in Ojai, light and space were really important to me," he explained. "So I tried to paint on air, with these floating volumes of light made with beams crossing in complementary colors. It was the beginning of minimalism. It was the beginning of not using imagery. I decided to make works related to my experience, and not to art history."

As an art student in Southern California, in the early 1960s, Ron tried a mass-produced mezcal on a foray across the border to Hussong's Cantina, a famous surfer hangout in Ensenada, Mexico. "I was the fool with the bottle upturned in my mouth, swallowing the worm," he laughed. Ron's interest in the traditionally crafted mezcal he began exporting didn't begin until his visit to Teotitlán in 1970, when he first became acquainted with Oaxaca's micro-distilled agave spirits. None were fabricated in the village itself, but as he started exploring the larger region in the early 1990s, he began finding mezcals that spoke to him— some of which he discovered through word of mouth, others by showing up at remote mountain villages and asking around. When Ron tried crossing the U.S. border with several large vessels of mezcal, a customs official allowed him to bring in only a tiny amount, and the seed was sown for Del Maguey.

"This whole thing started because I wanted to be able to share the amazing mezcals I'd found with my friends," he said.

The spirits Ron began exporting under his label in 1995 were not being fabricated on anything close to a commercial scale. Handcrafted by maestros mezcaleros in small batches for consumption in their villages, they were mostly shared at fiestas, weddings, funerals, and other important events. If they were sold beyond their own vicinity, it was more often than not to brokers or bottlers, who bought them in bulk and blended them with batches from other communities. When this happened, both the hand of the maker and the village identity were lost, because the different mezcals were combined to create nondescript products—often with cane alcohol supplemented to stretch them out—which were then sold under labels revealing nothing of their true origins. Hence Ron's coinage of the term "single village mezcal."

As he discovered what pure mezcal expressions could taste like, he reveled in their possible diversity. He found that, aside from each maker's individual touch, which had often been honed over several generations within a family, the flavor of a mezcal, like that of wine, could be accentuated by anything from the microclimates in which the agaves had been grown, to the airborne yeasts that initiated the fermentation process, to the minerals in the local water added to the mash.

I had always imagined importers of spirits as cigar-chomping gangster types cutting shady deals in harbor warehouses—Sydney Greenstreet, or James Cagney. While I knew this couldn't always be true, it seemed safe to assume that Ron must be unusual in the profession, since he viewed his mezcal business as an expression of his art. The transition from creating his light-and-space works to selling mezcal made sense to him—he was interested in the transformative nature of the spirits. By turning people on to mezcal, Ron could transport them to contemplative places that were similar to his light installations in their emotional and psychological effects. At the same time, the drinks he exported brought him attention as an artist-importer, which he didn't seem to mind.

As we turned north from the highway to Teotitlán del Valle, and headed up a road toward the Sierra Juárez soaring in the dusk, I found myself wondering about the people who actually created the spirits in Ron's finely packaged bottles. Who were they, and what were they like? Was the surely difficult work of making mezcal a form of contemporary art for them, too?

எ

THE ROAD CONTINUED all the way up to the remote mountain village of Benito Juárez, named after the beloved Zapotec president who governed Mexico for five terms, between 1858 and 1872. But we would be traveling on it only as far as Teotitlán del Valle, which came into view once we topped a foothill. The community is a cluster of one- and two-story structures of concrete, brick, and stone, with brightly colored metal doors leading into them. Around five thousand people live there. Founded around 1465, the village was originally named *Xaquija* (Celestial Constellation) in Zapoteco. A white church, Preciosa Sangre de Cristo, rises from the center. It is overshadowed by a sacred butte-shaped peak, called *Cerro Gie Betts* (stone brother) in the local dialect.

We passed several weaving workshops displaying tapetes on their outside walls. Many of the rugs had geometric patterns that were inspired by the ancient reliefs carved into the stones of a local Zapotec temple. In the sixteenth century, as part of their imposition of Roman Catholicism, the Spanish tore the indigenous structure down to its foundations and began incorporating its pieces into the church. Construction began in 1581 and was finally completed in 1758.

Ron drove us past the weed-covered temple ruins and parked his truck near a large courtyard, which we walked across to the whitewashed church. There he showed me a beautifully carved pre-Columbian stone motif that had been laid bare amid the plaster. "Check that out!" Ron said, pointing. The Spanish conquerors, he said, "may have forced them to adopt a new religion, but they still haven't forgotten the old one." The ancient glyph was a silent reminder of a complex culture that had been conquered by another and had melded with it, its evolution into something new still going on.

Ron had invited me to stay with him in the village, where he kept a sparse apartment in a nondescript building near the center. He showed me one of his recent artworks, which consisted of a book bolted to a colorful piece of scrap metal from a canning company. The book's cover was a black-and-white photo of María Sabina, the Mazatec *curandera* (medicine woman) who became famous in the 1960s for her ceremonial use of *Psilocybe* "magic" mushrooms—and for the subsequent visits she received from rock stars of the era. The region continues to attract seekers looking for answers via mind-altering fungi, plants, and other substances. To this day, Sabina remains a hippie icon, her image depicted on posters and T-shirts all over Oaxaca.

He had decorated an altar with vases of fresh flowers, pictures of saints, and offerings of mezcal, mostly contained in used plastic water bottles. He picked up one that had TOBALÁ and a date written on it with a black marker. He poured us each a taste into two clay cups that, I assumed, were traditional Oaxacan. They turned out to have been of his own invention: stamped with his company's name, they were used for marketing and promotion.

Sipping mezcal from a neutral-tasting clay vessel, he explained, delivered a more "honest" flavor experience than drinking it from a glass.

"Wait until you taste this," he said. "It's going to blow your mind!"

I had never tried tobalá before, and it was smooth and delicate, like a tear from a mermaid's eye—or so I imagined in my first, cautious usage of booze jargon. I soon felt deeply relaxed and pleasantly tired. As crickets sang and rain began drizzling outside the moonlit windows, Ron offered me an air mattress and a colorfully striped serape blanket. I drifted into deep slumber.

My bed having completely deflated, I awoke, shivering, on the hard, cold floor. My first thought was to warm up with another nip from the altar, but Ron, who was already up and about, handed me a ceramic bowl of strong black coffee instead. For my *Mountainfreak* assignment, Ron had offered to take me to visit the producers he bought mezcal from in Santo Domingo Albarradas. That was several hours away, and I was eager to see where that first artisanal agave spirit I had tasted in Santa Fe was from—and to meet the people who had made it.

◪

WITH ROOSTERS CROWING all around Teotitlán del Valle, we drove to the market in the village center to find something to eat on the road. A miniature version of Abastos, it was already lively. Ron was well acquainted with many of the vendors, most of whom were women wearing aprons and shawls pulled tight against the morning chill. Many were selling tortillas and tamales they had cooked at home and were keeping warm in embroidered-cloth bundles stored in beautifully woven fabric bags. We bought some empanadas filled with chicken and mole negro, and their mouth-watering smell filled the truck cab as we left town and headed farther south on Highway 190.

The rising sun revealed a morning mist shrouding the valley. It slowly burned off as we passed the pre-Columbian ruins of Yagul, which date to approximately 500 BCE and occupy a volcanic outcrop just north of the busy thoroughfare. Here and there were expansive fields of agaves that local *magueyeros* (maguey farmers—also, mezcal workers) had planted for distilling, and we passed a couple of primitive *fábricas de mezcal* (mezcal stills, also called *palenques*), which had been set up for tourists.

"Let's stop and take a look," Ron said, pulling over by one of them.

He briefly walked me through the mezcal-making process. Two men were piling split piñas around a circular, fifteen-foot-deep horno. Once heaped inside it, the agaves would be covered with earth and baked atop wood-fired rocks for several days, until their starchy white flesh was cooked brown with caramelized sugars. The hearts would then be transferred to a circular milling area where they would be pulverized under a *tahona* (a massive round millstone—usually pulled by a horse, a mule, or a pair of bulls). The resulting mash would be transferred to several wooden *tinas* (fermentation vats), where it would stew for perhaps a week or more into a bubbling brown soup.

Finally, the fermented mash and liquid would be introduced to the belly of an *alembique de cobre* (copper still) that was heated from below by a wood fire. The heat would separate the alcohol from the rest of the mixture, so that it would collect as vapor at the top of the still. From there, the alcohol would move, drop by drop, through a long copper *tubo* (pipe) that extended between the still and a water-filled cooling tank. The pipe corkscrewed into the water, disappeared at the bottom, and emerged from the tank's base. When the still was in operation, clear mezcal would steadily drip from it into a container.

To my uneducated eye, the operation appeared dirty, make-shift, and archaic—almost like a rustic display one might find in a living museum—and I wondered if it was hokey. But Ron said it was actually more or less the way most mezcal fábricas looked and worked in Oaxaca, and was pretty much how things had been for hundreds of years.

"Appearances can be deceiving," Ron cautioned. "Some of the distillers around here are amazing artists."

We hit the road again. Turning north, we aimed toward Mitla, a Zapotec settlement featuring a ceremonial site whose oldest buildings dated from 450 to 700 CE. If Monte Albán had been the political center of the ancient Zapotec, Mitla was their religious one. Its ruins are noted for their uniquely detailed mosaics and fretwork, a Mixtec style. After we passed Mitla, the valley narrowed, and we turned and headed north on a tinier road that switchbacked down into a deep green expanse. As we entered a village at the bottom, Ron spotted a semi, its license plate from the Mexican state of Jalisco, loaded with small, prematurely harvested piñas.

"They're taking away our goddamn babies!" he growled.

回

AT THAT TIME in Jalisco, the state where tequila is predominantly produced, there was a major agave shortage, which was partly a cyclical occurrence. When prices for agaves drop, farmers become unenthusiastic about planting them, with the result that the supply of harvestable magueys ceases to match the enormous international demand for tequila. This time the scarcity was largely due to a severe blight attributed to the fungus *Fusarium oxysporum* and the bacteria *erwinia carotovora*, which collectively caused TMA: *tristeza y muerte de agave* (wilting and death of maguey). As many as 40 percent of the country's two hundred million *A. tequilana* plants had been affected, causing a massive crisis for one of Mexico's biggest exports. Unable to compete, many small-scale tequila distilleries shut their doors.

Magueys may appear formidable, but despite their spiky defense systems, there exists a tiny David to the plant's Goliath: the agave snout weevil. The black, inch-long beetle is considered the most destructive vector of blight. First, it uses its needlelike proboscis to burrow a hole into the center of the rosette. There, it both lays eggs and infects its host with fungi and bacteria damaging enough to kill the maguey. As the plant sickens, the beetle larvae chew through its weakened tissues—now made soft and munchable for a hungry grub—and the once-mighty agave loses its color and wilts to the ground like a forlorn gabacho doubled over with a bad case of *turista* (diarrhea).

In the wild, the most disease-resistant magueys propagate and secure the continued survival of their species via an arsenal of methods—through seeds, through small plants growing from their flowers, and through shoots sent out from their bases that develop into baby agaves, which are clones. But when non-resistant plants are cloned and grown in a corporate-scale monoculture, as they are by the tequila industry, they become particularly vulnerable to weevil-borne infections—and disaster can strike.

Ron said the situation was so dire that Jaliscan trucks were coming to Oaxaca from hundreds of miles away to haul off the local maguey crop. According to the legal requirements of tequila's DO, if a spirit is labeled TEQUILA 100% AGAVE, it should have been distilled only from *A. tequilana*. But the Jaliscan semi we saw was filled with piñas of espadín, the maguey species most commonly grown for mezcal. This particular agave is normally harvested within eight to ten years, but much younger plants were now being uprooted to address the needs of the tequila industry. Ron said it was very likely that other regional maguey species were also being ransacked. Furthermore, local agave prices had risen significantly—a turn of events that put Oaxacan mezcaleros in the position of not being able to afford the local maguey, while witnessing the sell-off of their future materia prima.

"Who keeps an eye on all of this?" I asked Ron.

"No one," he replied, shaking his head.

Oaxaca was beginning to feel like the Wild West.

𐂷

WE WOUND OUR way up to, then through, the village of Santa María Albarradas, which clings to a steep slope at around fifty-five hundred feet. From there, Ron steered us onto a muddy track that continued upward into the hills. We were now surrounded by dense forests of pine and oak trees hung with Spanish moss the color of seafoam and dangling bromeliads still dripping with the previous night's rain. The route grew rough with potholes as we made our way up and down hills and around bends, then sloshed through streams rushing faster as it began raining yet again.

After several bumpy miles, I began feeling hungry and unwrapped one of the empanadas we had brought along for breakfast. It was still warm and delicious. But soon after wolfing it down, I felt strange chest pains and an alarming tingling sensation in my left arm. Given my family history of heart ailments, I began to panic.

"Ron," I said, "we need to go back. I'm having a heart attack."

"No way, compadre. We're hours away from the closest hospital. If you're going to die, you're going to die."

"Come on! I'm not kidding!"

"It's just that greasy empanada you ate."

"Empanadas don't make your arm tingle!"

"We just need to get some mezcal in you, and you'll be fine."

"I don't believe this!"

"Look, if you die, I promise I'll bring your parents out here so they can see where it happened."

Just then, we rounded a corner and saw Santo Domingo Albarradas tumbling down the steep mountainside beneath us. A thick white mist, which almost completely concealed the deep valley below, was fingering up into the towering peaks above us, and it seemed as if we must have been significantly higher than we actually were. Indeed, Ron's bottle label said the "pueblo elevation is 8,500 ft." However, according to Google Earth it sits at around five thousand feet. He downshifted as we descended the muddy track into the community, slowly passing a whitewashed mission church decorated with flowers and streamers. A brass band was playing in front, and noisy fireworks were being set off in all directions. Ron had perfectly timed our arrival to coincide with the start of the Zapotec village's annual fiesta. It was an impressive sleight of hand, but all I could think of was death.

"This is straight out of *Under the Volcano*," I moaned. "I'm gonna die here!"

"Then maybe I can have you buried by the church," he joked.

Ron navigated the truck down a steep, winding street and through the village, past fluttering chickens and tethered burros, finally pulling up next to a nondescript one-story adobe. It belonged to Espiridion Morales Luis, who, with his son, Juan, made the mezcal I had tasted in Santa Fe. Espiridion was away performing one of his civic duties for the Zapotec municipio. But Juan came out to greet us, cheerfully ushering us into the family kitchen—a cozy, rustic room with chicks sprinting across its hard-packed dirt floor. His mother was cooking tortillas on a *comal*, a basic wood-fired griddle. She served us each a bowl of hot chocolate, while Ron explained to our hosts that I thought I was having a heart attack. Juan quickly produced an unmarked bottle of mezcal that he and his father had distilled in their fábrica.

"¡Sólo necesitas un poco de medicina!" (You just need a little medicine!) Juan poured me a glass.

I took a sip, Juan's eyes carefully measuring my reaction as the family mezcal calmed my nerves and delivered the familiar clear-headed high I had discovered when I first drank it in Santa Fe. After a few more sips, my chest pains vanished and the tingling in my left arm began to recede. I was cured!

Meanwhile, Ron presented the maestro mezcalero with an official certificate from the San Francisco World Spirits Competition, an annual tasting event where the Luis mezcal had been awarded the platinum prize—the highest honor presented. But the realm of First World arbiters seemed distant. Juan politely accepted the framed document, then set it aside and poured us another round.

A visit to their fábrica—reachable by a treacherous, muddy path down the mountainside—was out of the question because too much rain had fallen. But we could hear music and cheering from the village plaza nearby, so we wandered over to see what was happening. On a basketball court set between government buildings, competing teams from rival villages were duking it out for a grand prize. A brass band serenaded the players from the second story of the town hall, while hundreds of onlookers followed the game with rapt attention.

As I listened to the upbeat polka-infused music, watched the kids play hoops, and gazed into the misty valley plunging below, I realized that this wasn't at all how I had expected Santo Domingo Albarradas to be. It wasn't the romanticized village Howard visits in *The Treasure of the Sierra Madre*; nor was it a fantasy Wonderland populated by smoking caterpillars and grinning cats; and it wasn't as colorful as the picture on Del Maguey's bottle label. It was just what it was, and I knew I had to come back for more.

Agave angustifolia

PART TWO

THEY CALL ME PUEBLO GRANDE VERDE

N EARLY 2011, I found myself back in Oaxaca to begin research-
ing this book—and riding in another vehicle with Ron. He
was nearing seventy, and now drove a white Jeep SUV with a
Del Maguey logo emblazoned on the side. He had also begun
dressing in a daily uniform of Australian work boots, camou-
flage cargo pants, and a white cotton smock that resembled a
pirate shirt. The outfit gave him the air of a *mezcalista* guerilla.
Dusk fell as he steered us through a red metal gate, past a deep,
sooty horno, and up a dirt track to a low-slung mezcal fábrica.
Shadowy peaks loomed in the distance as his headlights panned
across surrounding fields. It was January, the heart of the dry
season, and dead cornstalks stood with their cobs still attached,
nodding like sleeping sentinels.

Besides Ron's new duds and wheels, bigger changes had come
to his mezcal business since I had first tagged along with him over
a decade before. Sales were now on an upswing, as Del Maguey
rode a newfound wave of enthusiasm for micro-distilled spirits.
This was part of a larger trend of consumers espousing micro-
everything—from coffee to beer to chocolate—and paying high
prices for the privilege. In craft cocktail bars, mixologists were
"floating" smoky, small-batch mezcal atop their expensive inventions, as imbibing the once-maligned drink became joining the
"mezcal movement."

According to the Distilled Spirits Council of the United States
(DISCUS), which included mezcal in its tequila data, by 2011

"supplier revenues" for super-premium tequilas had exploded to $641 million from $140 million in 2003. Artisanally distilled mezcal made up a tiny part of those sales, but for well-heeled foodies seeking micro-authenticity through taste, the drink held an exotic and rootsy appeal. At the same time, the increasing thirst for esoteric spirits was beginning to lead consumers to niche mezcals made with rare *agaves silvestres* (wild magueys)—and causing sustainability concerns about the plants.

Del Maguey's tobalá mezcal was now selling in the U.S. for around $120 a bottle, and its midrange espadín mezcals for around $70. By 2011, Ron had been promoting his company on the road for sixteen years. In his de facto role of swashbuckling mezcal ambassador, he moved between the worlds of upscale spirits, gourmet cuisine, and fine art, filling his clay tasting cups from hip San Francisco bars to the Louvre in Paris. Like the actor Jonathan Goldsmith playing The Most Interesting Man in the World in ads for Dos Equis beer, Ron was a white American representing a Mexican drink, and he had become the international face of it.

For many new mezcal fans, as well as myself, Del Maguey spirits were the first traditionally crafted agave distillates they tried. The drinks defined their standards for quality and their palates for what they thought good ones should taste like. Ron's stories about mezcal were often the first ones they heard, too. As more people "discovered" the spirit through him, an assortment of chefs, artists, journalists, DJs, mixologists, chocolatiers, and restaurateurs visited him in Oaxaca, where a tasting ramble through the mountains with the "mezcal visionary" had become a stamp for the spirits-insider's passport. A tequila-industry veteran described the phenomenon to me as "the cult of Ron." He had become an iconic, María Sabina figure for mezcal.

Much of Del Maguey's marketing was accomplished through social media and word of mouth. Ron's visitors listed his mezcals on bar and restaurant menus, flavored cocktails and chocolate desserts with them, and wrote about them in newspapers, magazines, and blogs. Meanwhile, the tasting awards continued to roll in. All of this helped the company maintain its position as the preeminent small-batch mezcal brand, and allowed Ron to hold onto his reign as the world's top impresario for the drink. But Del Maguey now faced competition from a rapidly growing number of other boutique outfits that had followed Ron's lead and were selling handpicked agave spirits made by small-scale producers. Some of these new *marcas* were represented by visual artists who had copied Ron's artist-importer rap.

Spearheaded by Del Maguey, a new and international market had opened up for small-batch mezcal, with enormous potential for benefiting consumers and independent, family distillers alike. But now that the drink had been refashioned as a luxury spirit, there was new money to be made from it, and the gold rush was on for brand owners, distributors, bar owners, brokers, and other middlemen. And just as when Howard, a salty old miner played by Walter Huston in *The Treasure of the Sierra Madre*, cautions, "I know what gold does to men's souls," few seemed to listen.

As hip new companies got launched and stylish mezcal-tasting bars threw open their doors, the marginalized villages where mezcals are traditionally crafted remained largely unchanged—although a brand owner might boast of the tooth filling a producer now had, thanks to them. At least 45 percent of Mexicans live in poverty. The three southern states of Oaxaca, Chiapas, and Guerrero are the poorest, with poverty rates of over 70 percent, and extreme poverty at nearly 30 percent—three times the national average. According to 2011 measurements by the National Council for the Evaluation of Social Development Policy (CONEVAL), Oaxacan municipalities were listed in the top ten for all of Mexico for food deprivation, lack of education, and income inequality.

An estimated 50 percent of Oaxaca's residents live in rural communities of less than twenty-five hundred, where subsistence living is the norm. In its methodology, CONEVAL used a minimum well-being line of 684 pesos (about $50) per month for rural areas, which they estimated as the cost of a basic food basket. In the Oaxacan village of San Juan Tepeuxila, where 57 percent of its 2,773 residents spoke an indigenous language, 97.4 percent of the inhabitants had incomes below the minimum well-being line—the highest in the entire country. Around 75 percent of Mexico's indigenous peoples are considered poor, and the southern states have the largest indigenous populations. A 2010 study from the National Institute of Statistics, Geography and Informatics (INEGI) recorded that 1,165,186 persons aged five and over spoke an indigenous language in Oaxaca, out of an overall population of nearly four million. The records also showed that 16 percent of Oaxacans were illiterate (over six hundred thousand people), more than 20 percent of the state's housing units had no piped water, and almost 19 percent had dirt floors.

With Oaxaca's average per capita income barely enough to buy a few cases of super-premium mezcal, a significant number of Oaxacans regularly leave the state to find work elsewhere. And with jobs scarce at home, many rural village populations depend on money sent to them from relatives who have migrated to other parts of Mexico, and north to *Gringolandia*. But the 2008 economic crisis brought many of these workers back to Oaxaca. To try their hand at entrepreneurship, or just to make ends meet, some families began doing the hard work of growing agave and making spirits to sell beyond their communities. If others could earn a few bucks from the mezcal rush, why couldn't they? It was their traditional drink, after all. The sweat equity cost them time and sore muscles—expenditures they could afford—but getting their wares to the market required them to overcome significant financial and regulatory hurdles as well.

According to a 2012 survey of small Oaxacan producers by researchers Emilia Pool-Illsley and Catarina Illsley Granich, of *Grupo de Estudios Ambientales* (GEA), unbottled mezcals were purchased from distillers "*a granel* [in bulk]" for between "10 and 40 pesos" (at the time, less than $1 to about $3) per liter. The maestros mezcaleros who managed to bottle and brand their "uncertified" mezcals on their own, the study reports, were paid "between 50 and 150 pesos per liter." And mezcals that producers were able to both bottle *and* certify themselves sold for much more, "between 100 and 300 pesos." The most empowered mezcal distillers are those who can somehow find a way to distill, bottle, and certify their own spirits, and then also maintain control of the marketing and distribution of the drinks—but they remain exceedingly rare.

The study also mentions *"mezcales especiales* [specialty mezcals]"—which might be pechuga, tobalá, or other types made from wild agaves—that were sold by producers in bulk for between "20 and 60 pesos" per liter, and for "between 200 and 1,000 pesos bottled." Buyers could export and resell these spirits abroad for hundreds of dollars a bottle. Some brands bought all of their mezcals from distillers in bulk, and subsequently packaged the spirits in 750ml wine bottles, allowing them to sell four bottles of mezcal from every three liters purchased. This practice reduced the amount a maestro mezcalero was ultimately paid per bottle even further.

My own sources informed me that boutique outfits routinely paid producers between 20 and 40 pesos per liter of bulk mezcal, which the brands would then certify and bottle themselves. But there is little transparency in the mezcal business, and privately held U.S. and Mexican companies aren't required to exhibit their financial statements. Although there's no doubt that more small-time producers are distilling more mezcal for the market, and earning more money in terms of the sheer bulk quantity sold, there are no regulated industry standards for what maestros mezcaleros should be paid, and no fair trade practices have been officially applied to the spirit. Despite some well-meaning attempts at positioning mezcal as an engine of regional economic development, independent mezcal makers still operate in an overall arena where efforts at marginalizing mezcaleros have been far greater than those at empowering them.

"Certified producers," Sarah Bowen writes, "are a small but growing (and privileged) group, representing between 10 and 20 percent of all mezcal producers." Their low number is partly because mezcal's Denomination of Origin currently applies to only nine of at least twenty-three states with a history of mezcal production: Oaxaca, Guerrero, Durango, Zacatecas, San Luis Potosí, Michoacán, Tamaulipas, Guanajuato, and Puebla. But mezcal makers in these limited areas who wish to receive legal protection must undergo a rigorous, expensive, and time-consuming process for their spirits to be certified under the DO. This can be particularly challenging for producers with literacy issues and/or economic constraints, regardless of their intelligence, talent, and drive.

"There are thousands of mezcaleros," Bowen writes, who "are unwilling or unable to join the formal market for mezcal. Some are outside the boundaries of the DO for mezcal. Others are within the designated territory but do not want to get certified, because it would require them to alter their production practices, or the costs are too high, or they do not trust the regulatory organizations. These producers exist in a liminal space: outside the legal realm, never captured in industry statistics and governmental records, yet a vital part of local communities across Mexico."

Since the number of certified mezcal producers is low, and the spirit can only be certified in limited areas, the mezcals that are legally available for sale outside Mexico represent only a fraction of the vast, ever-changing kaleidoscope of agave distillates crafted in the country. They also represent the subjective choices of brand owners, who are rarely from mezcal-making communities themselves. "Because small mezcaleros," Bowen writes, "often lack the financial and organizational resources to become certified on their own, they almost always work with intermediaries. The intermediaries help them navigate the process but also capture much of the profit. More specifically, many of the producers who manage to export their mezcal rely on foreign elites or multinational corporations."

〿

RON AND I were on the outskirts of Santa Catarina Minas, a village of around sixteen hundred people, about fifty-two hundred feet high in a broad, mountain-ringed valley. It's near the famous market town of Ocotlán de Morelos—an hour south of Oaxaca de Juárez—and one of the communities surveyed by Pool-Illsley and Illsley Granich for their report. The community doesn't identify with an ethnic language group, and has a small number of households where an indigenous language is spoken. Although "Minas" was founded in 1580 around silver mining, it's far better known for its production of *minero* (miner) espadín mezcals. For as long as anyone can remember, the local spirits have been distilled in old-fashioned *ollas de barro* (clay-pot stills). They are thought to bring a smoother "mouthfeel" to the drink than mezcals made in alembiques constructed of copper or stainless steel.

Del Maguey had been buying its minero in bulk for years from an elderly maestro mezcalero, Florencio Carlos Sarmiento, as well as from his middle-aged sons, Juan Carlos and Florencio, Jr., who operate a tiny distillery of their own nearby. The company also purchased and exported their small batches of pechuga mezcal, which sold for around $200 per bottle in the U.S. At the end of 2011, Eric Asimov cited the Sarmientos' drink in a *New York Times* article, "A Year of Acquired Tastes." In the roundup of elite wines, champagnes, "rhums agricoles," and Islay single malts, Asimov wrote: "I had an opportunity this year to drink one of the rarest and most astonishing mezcals of all, the unbelievably complex Del Maguey Pechuga, produced (I'm not making this up) with the addition of a chicken breast."

Normally, mezcal is distilled two times. But for pechuga there's a special third distillation. The spirit is named for the raw chicken (or turkey—or, sometimes, duck) breast that's suspended by a string over a fruit, spice, and nut mixture that's added to the alembique's earthenware belly along with the twice-distilled mezcal. No one knows who came up with the poultry idea—other meats, such as rabbit, venison, and ham, are also used—but the flesh notes combine with the fruit, spices, and mezcal to create a particularly delicious spirit.

Florencio made a batch of pechuga only once or twice a year, and Ron had brought me to the maestro mezcalero's fábrica to witness the last opening of his clay alembiques—the grand finale of a multi-day distillation process. Ron killed the Jeep's ignition, stubbed out his unfiltered cigarette, and turned to me in the dark. "Are you wearing cologne?" he asked.

"No."

"Good, because Florencio doesn't like *anything* to fuck with the flavor of his mezcal. He doesn't want people wearing perfume around, or animals, or any of that shit—he says mezcal is *muy sensitivo* and can absorb the smell of *everything*. All right?"

"All right."

Unusual for that time of year, fat raindrops began falling as we found our way past a pile of blackened pot shards; a pair of oak *mazos* (grinding clubs) left beside a concrete mashing trough; and a straw cross tacked to one of five wooden tinas. We stepped down and into Florencio's distillery—an open-ended space with a dirt floor and makeshift walls fashioned from corrugated tin and stalks of *carrizo* (cane).

Smoke licked at a pair of bare, soot-covered light bulbs, sent up from the wood fires glowing in shallow pits at the bottoms of two round brick structures. What appeared to be massive cooking pots, molded from reddish-brown clay, were sitting atop them. These were actually ollas de barro—we had passed the heat-shattered remnants of their predecessors outside. Water streamed through black plastic pipes into hammered-copper *cazos* (pans) that rested over the orifices of the alembiques. Mezcal was dripping into the mouths of plastic jerry cans from cane tubes extending out of the earthenware stills' sides.

Wearing a cardigan and a cowboy hat, his hands resting on the handle of a metal walking stick, Florencio greeted us with a nod and a quiet *¡Buenas noches!* from his seat on an adobe *banco* (bench) at the rear of the fábrica. His eyes missed nothing as he peered through large-lensed glasses over his gray moustache. Each element of the distillation process required his attention: There were the sizes of the two fires to consider—perhaps that one needed more wood to heat the still above it? And the audible streams of the water pouring into the copper cazos—were they flowing fast enough to cool the condensers properly? There was also the rate at which the pechuga was emerging from his ollas de barro—"*¡Muy importante!*"

Completing Florencio's directives were two magueyeros, José Velasco and José Sanchez. Both men were bleary-eyed from lack of sleep—and filthy from head to toe. For five straight days and nights, they had been stoking the old man's fires, filling his stills with heavy buckets of mash from the tinas, and enduring bursts of scalding steam as they stood over the hot mouths of the clay alembiques—pitchforking spent *bagazo* (fermented mash) out of them, then adding it to mounting piles.

The workers were near the end of their third, and final, distillation of Florencio's pechuga, which they said they had crafted from the hearts of espadín and "*unos pocos*" (a few) very large piñas of twenty-year-old *arroqueño* (*Agave americana var. oaxacensis*). The entire process, from the harvesting of the agave to the end of distillation, had taken nearly a month.

After baking the materia prima for several days in the horno, the magueyeros hand-crushed the caramelized maguey with the clubs I had seen lying in the troughs outside. Once the mash was suitably fermented for a week or so in the oak tinas, the men had begun feeding it to the bellies of the clay stills. Inside the heated confines of the alembiques, alcoholic vapors slowly condensed upon the water-cooled bottoms of the copper cazos, forming drops that gathered into liquid in the carved wooden *cucharas* (collecting trays) hanging below them, which then finally emerged from the carrizo tubes—as it was doing right now.

回

THE MEZCAL WASN'T a fully developed spirit quite yet. It still required a finishing touch: remixing the batch. Distillation separates compounds through heat. When fermented agave mash is simmered inside a still, its alcohol-rich, lower-boiling-point vapors condense and are collected, while higher-boiling elements, such as water, burn off. This results in a distillate containing a higher ethanol-to-water ratio than before. Congeners, the undesirable leftover compounds (methanol, for example), have different boiling points, and are gradually reduced. The first, roughest mezcal run is known as *shishe* (pronounced "shi-shay"), and exhibits little taste and alcohol by volume (ABV). But when the batch is passed through an alembique for a second time, flavors intensify, and the ABV increases as the spirit reemerges in three distinct portions.

The first part to be delivered from an alembique's womb is called the *cabeza* (head), also known as the *puntas* (tips). It presents the highest ABV (usually 50 to 80 percent—or 100 to 160 proof) and lowest-boiling congeners. Next comes the sweet spot: the *cuerpo* (body), also called *corazón* (heart), which contains less alcohol, exhibits a mellower taste, and forms the lion's share of a batch. The *cola* (tail) is last to arrive. It is weakest in ABV (maybe 20 percent—or 40 proof), and contains the highest-boiling and worst-tasting congeners. After the final distillation, the cabeza, cuerpo, and cola are mixed together for taste and strength in the proportions specific to a maestro mezcalero's personal recipe, or to the requirements set by a buyer, who might have a particular audience in mind for the resulting mezcal. It's an art to juggle the three parts just so.

I stuck a fingertip into a still's warm trickle and touched the spirit to my tongue. It was delectable, even though it was the cola. Over a sweet nose of roasted maguey I could discern other essences. In addition to the fabled chicken breast, the ollas de barro had been packed with fruit, nuts, and spices for the pechuga's special third distillation. Inside the stills were chopped plantains, pineapples, apples, wild plums, and raisins—as well as cinnamon bark, almonds, sugar, and anise.

"Bring us some to taste!" commanded Florencio.

I filled a well-worn jícara and brought it to him and Ron. The artist-importer stuck a two-foot-long *venencia* (hollow cane tube) into the mezcal and sucked some of the liquid into it. He held the spirit inside the tube with the tip of an index finger for a moment, and then released the stream back into the gourd cup.

When mezcal is oxygenated into a vessel—as Ron was doing—its ABV is indicated by the size and number of *perlas* (bubbles) that form and gather in a *cordón* (ring) at the edges. Certified mezcals are permitted ABVs of 36 to 55 percent (between 72 and 110 proof), but most traditionally distilled mezcals—certified or not—commonly stay in a range of between 40 and 50 percent alcohol (80 to 100 proof). A seasoned maestro mezcalero can uncannily ascertain an accurate ABV simply by looking at his perlas: lots of tiny bubbles indicate a lower alcohol level; fewer big ones demonstrate a higher level.

Ron and Florencio peered into the gourd cup and examined the cordón together. The perlas were tiny—typical for a cola, because the alcohol level is always lowest at the end of a batch. The buyer and distiller had agreed upon a flavor profile for the pechuga that needed to be followed for consistency, with an ABV of 49 percent (98 proof). Florencio ordered one of his magueye-ros to fill two more jícaras from plastic containers of cabeza and cuerpo. He added some of each to the cola and handed the jícara to Ron.

"You first," Florencio told him.

Before taking a sip, Ron trickled a few drops on the dirt in the shape of a cross. "An offering," he said, "to the Earth Mother." He worked the spirit around in his mouth, smacked his lips, wrinkled his eyes, tilted his head back, and stared into space as he took his time considering it. Then he passed the vessel back to Florencio, who took a sip.

"*Un poco más cabeza*," the master distiller instructed, with a conviction earned from fifty years of making mezcal. Ron nodded in agreement, adding more cabeza, swirling the mixture together, sucking some of it up into the venencia again, and releasing it back into the jícara to further oxygenate the spirit. He returned the concoction to the maestro, who tasted it again.

"*Un poquito más cuerpo*," said Florencio. Ron splashed in some more cuerpo, and the two men further examined the perlas and took turns sipping the mix. "That's it!" proclaimed Florencio. We passed around the jícara and drank. Raindrops clattered on the metal roof as I stared into the crackling still fires, and time seemed to slow down as my spatial perception gently shifted and my brain tingled against the back of my skull.

In the shadows behind Florencio's ollas, I noticed a round clay shrine with a candle flickering before an image of the Virgen de Juquila—her tiny angelic face floating above her gleaming white triangle of robe. First revered by the Chatino peoples after her effigy survived a fire in the Sierra Madre mountain town of Amialtepec in 1633, she is now held sacred all over Oaxaca as a protector and maker of miracles. Her picture can be found in almost every mezcal fábrica.

Ron recounted how, a few years earlier, when Florencio was suffering from a surgical wound that refused to heal, the old man's family drove him several hours to the remote village of Santa Catarina Juquila. There, Florencio prayed to the famous effigy of the Virgen for *un milagro*. Soon after the pilgrimage, the distiller's wound healed, and he returned from the brink. It's probably a good idea, I thought, to believe in a transformative power if you devote your life to turning plants into drinks.

Bearing plastic mixing bowls, Florencio's middle-aged daughters, Elvira and Plácida, slipped in from the rain. The maestro brandished his cane and ordered a helper to open one of the stills. The magueyero climbed on top of the circular brick structure supporting it. Lifting away the copper cazo, he reached into a white cloud of steam. He quickly pulled up a hand-hewn wooden cuchara with a wizened chicken breast dangling below it by a length of twine. The bird flesh was red from the fruit that had been simmering in the olla beneath it.

Next, the magueyero clawed away the muddy brown mash that sealed the smaller top olla to the larger bottom one. He lifted the upper vessel away, set it aside, and began scooping piles of steaming cooked fruit from the bigger one underneath. He heaped it into the sisters' plastic bowls, and we passed them around. I tasted a piece of banana, a slice of apple, a few almonds and grapes—all cooked together in an aromatic red stew. Amid the mixture, I noticed a cloth satchel tied shut with string. Curious, I asked Florencio what was inside it. "*Un secreto*," he answered, sternly waving a finger at me. His particular methods were his art and livelihood—none of my business.

In the moonlight outside, the magueyeros loaded containers of the pechuga mezcal into battered wheelbarrows. The rain had stopped, the stars were out, crickets and frogs were singing, and a soulful *ranchero* drifted through the damp, earth-scented air from a distant house across the fields. Their days of hard work nearly complete, the exhausted men set into the night, rumbling their loads down the track. They would continue through the red gate, up a quarter mile of rutted dirt road, and store the pechuga at the simple *rancho* Florencio shared with his daughters, before the spirit was trucked to Del Maguey headquarters and bottled for export.

◩

THIS WAS THE first leg of a lengthy, cross-cultural journey that would bring the maestro mezcalero's creation to high-end bars, restaurants, and spirits shops—and eventually into the glass poured for Eric Asimov to taste. When others drank Florencio's pechuga, the focus would likely also be on the novelty of its poultry- and fruit-infused flavor, and the opportunity to imbibe such a rare and extraordinarily expensive drink.

But as I watched the master at work, another aspect of his mezcal's story had come to mind. Although Florencio had made all sorts of personalized tweaks to his setup over the years, his still was nevertheless quite simple, and a handy person could re-create it with clay, wood, and cane. In fact, the Sarmiento family had to regularly remake their stills when they cracked, ordering the pots from a ceramicist in another village.

So, I wondered, since Florencio, his sons, and their magueye-ros could all distill mezcal in ollas de barro constructed with local materials, why wouldn't pre-Columbians have been capable of fashioning similar alembiques and using them to create agave spirits themselves? Certainly the context for making them was already in place. It's been well established that Mesoamericans consumed many types of alcoholic beverages. They were also skilled clay artisans—museum collections exhibit their craftsmanship in wide varieties of ceramic vessels used for cooking, storage, and ceremonial purposes.

It seemed likely to me that a still along the lines of Florencio's would have been easy enough for a pre-Columbian to develop. For example, if one were already heating an olla with something fermented inside it, one would only need to place a cooler, perhaps water-filled, vessel over the mouth of the pot, on the bottom of which ethanol vapor could then condense and subsequently be collected as a rough distillate. However, the commonly perpetuated narrative has long been that even such basic distillation methods—already accepted as having been used in ancient China and the Middle East—weren't introduced to "pre-contact" peoples in the Americas until the sixteenth century, when two sets of "enlightened" foreigners did so.

In this view, the Spanish first brought European techniques via the Atlantic coast: when the colonists discovered natives brewing the mildly alcoholic drink pulque, they began experimenting with agave themselves, eventually applying distillation methods they had learned at home. Then, beginning in 1565, sailors voyaging on the Manila Galleon route between Mexico and the Philippines introduced simple "Chinese/Mongol" clay pot alembiques, used to distill "coconut brandy," to the Pacific coast peoples of what are now Jalisco and Colima states.

Likewise, it's generally believed that before pre-Columbians were actually "taught" distilling, they could ferment only rudimentary "wines" and other drinks brewed with such readily available materia prima as cactus fruits, tree barks, cornstalks, and maguey. Followers of this approach like to think that until the Spanish showed up, *vino de mescal* (mezcal wine, a fermented beverage made of mashed baked agave combined with water) and pulque were as close to mezcal, the distilled spirit, as anyone in Mesoamerica ever got.

After extensive research throughout Mexico in the late 1930s—later recounted in *Alcohol in Ancient Mexico*—the geographer Henry J. Bruman surmised that mezcal distilleries would often originate in places where "an undistilled mescal drink was known in pre-Columbian times," and where agave was also abundantly available as a food source. He guessed that copies of distillation equipment introduced early on were "easily fashioned" from local materials by "the natives," who found "the product of the stills so attractive" that "mescal wine soon came to be looked upon almost everywhere as merely an intermediate stage."

But what if "mescal wine" wasn't "an intermediate stage"? Instead, couldn't it and pulque have both been part of a much broader spectrum of other alcoholic drinks that were also made with maguey? If the European and Chinese/Mongol alembiques were so easy to recreate—using neighborhood cane, wood, clay, and maguey spines—couldn't someone have been distilling already, somewhere out in the boundless nooks and crannies of Mexico? Until recently, no one has known for sure. For one thing, most preconquest indigenous records were destroyed by the Spanish. From the glyphs that remain, there's no way to confirm that each depiction of a sacred vessel held by a god in an ancient codex is filled with pulque, as is generally assumed, and not, for instance, with an agave distillate.

In 2008, Patricia Colunga-García Marín and ecologist Daniel Zizumbo-Villarreal worked with archaeologists and mezcal producers to approach the subject in a way that no one else had tried. As outlined in their article "Distillation in Western Mesoamerica before European Contact," the researchers tested a hypothesis that ceramic "gourd and trifid vessels" unearthed from the Capacha archaeological site in the state of Colima, dating to the Early Formative period of between 1500 and 1000 BCE, "could have been used to produce distilled beverages."

First, the group had replicas made, from local clay, of four different ceramic vessels they found on display at the National Museum of Anthropology, in Mexico City. Although each was slightly different, they were all two-tiered pots—previously thought to be used for steaming or cooking beans. The team also had smaller bowls fabricated from gourds and clay, which they set on top of the mouths of the replicated vessels. These were to function as "condensers." A smaller "recipient" vessel was suspended by string beneath each one to collect any gathered alcoholic vapors.

The researchers placed cool water in the condensers and added agave mash fermented by Macarido Partida, a Jaliscan maestro mezcalero, to the replicas, before proceeding to heat each "still" over a wood fire in a stone pit. After the contents had cooked for two hours at varying temperatures, distillates were collected from the recipient containers and tested in a laboratory. The results showed a 12 to 35.5 percent ethanol concentration among the four replicas used.

"Their archaeological context, and the ethanol yields of the replicas," the group summarized in their article, "suggest that, if used as stills, [the two-tiered pots] were used to produce a prestige product for ceremonial purposes, with high social and cultural relevance." The authors speculated that "this tradition could be thousands of years old." Indeed, in their 2016 book, *El Mezcal, una bebida prehispánica. Estudios etnoarqueológicos* (Mezcal, a pre-Hispanic beverage. Ethnoarchaeological studies), scholars Mari Carmen Serra Puche and Jesús Carlos Lazcano Arce date maguey distillation in Mesoamerica to at least 400 BCE.

Were there inherent forms of racism and classism, I wondered, in the marketing of tequila and mezcal? If not, why was there still a disassociation with the producers of traditionally crafted agave spirits, as well as with the generations of distillers who had come before them? At the very least, I thought, it seemed that business interests—whether small brands or transnational corporations—had been stealing the credit.

᭫

EARLY ONE MORNING in the early spring of 2011, not long after Ron took me to Florencio's fábrica in Santa Catarina Minas, I paid a visit to Del Maguey's new headquarters in Teotitlán del Valle. This was where the company's mezcals were bottled. I rode out to the village by bus from Oaxaca de Juárez, where I had rented an apartment in a small complex that I shared with two baseball players from the local Oaxaca Guerreros team.

I boarded the bus a few blocks away, at a stop by the baseball stadium. The lime-green road warrior was battle-scarred from years of bodywork, its muffler thundering like the pounding hooves of a toro. The burly *chofer* (driver) sat in a custom-made throne crafted from bent rebar and the sort of blue plastic tubing you see on dime-store lawn chairs. *Banda* oompahed from the stereo as we roared off on La Carrera Panamericana. The driver's lanky *ayudante* (copilot) prowled the aisle, collecting pesos from men sporting moustaches and cowboy hats and women clutching bags of goods from Abastos Market, where the bus route began.

At the edge of town, we slowed to a crawl on a bridge by a Pemex oil facility. Several passengers slid their windows open to ogle a wreck. As we crept past it, most of their faces remained impassive while their eyes devoured the scene. Then, as we moved on, many of them solemnly made crosses against their chests. In Mexico, stoicism is a common strategy for coping with the many bumps in life's road that no amount of mezcal could ever cure. The chofer turned up the music and stepped on the gas.

The country can be a tough and unfair place to live for nearly half of its 128 million citizens. A greater middle class may be emerging, but Mexico still has a pyramid socioeconomic structure. One of the richest people in the world, the telecommunications magnate Carlos Slim, remains comfortably positioned at the top, while tens of millions of destitute people form most of the bottom. Oaxaca is so seductively vibrant that it can easily be viewed through the rose-tinted lens of tourism ad copy. Well-heeled visitors fly in to Oaxaca de Juárez every day. They stay at luxury hotels, dine at innovative, high-end restaurants, and shop for folk art and crafts. The reality for most Oaxacans, however, is that navigating police and government corruption, high unemployment, chronically low wages, and the multiple dangers surrounding illicit drug trafficking is the norm, while at the same time government-sponsored healthcare and education are limited resources. Things are so bad in the country overall that a special dictionary has been published, the *Currupcionario Mexicano*. A "chapulín" (grasshopper) is an opportunistic politician who jumps between parties. A *"chayote"* (gourd) is the payment a chapulín makes to a journalist.

Oaxacans are known for getting out in the streets in the tens of thousands to demonstrate for change—even if such disruptions affect the lucrative tourism sector of the local economy. In the years since I had first visited, Oaxaca de Juárez in particular had undergone social upheavals that had placed it in the international spotlight. My last trip to the city had been a weeklong visit during October 2006. I had come there to attend the annual Day of the Dead festivities. But my plans coincided with outgoing Mexican President Vicente Fox's directive to oust a large group of protestors, who had been occupying the city's iconic plaza for several months.

The Popular Assembly of the People of Oaxaca (APPO)—composed of members of the National Union of Education

Workers (SNTE) and other, smaller organizations—was demanding the resignation of their governor, Ulises Ruiz. A scandal-plagued member of Mexico's autocratic, historically corrupt Institutional Revolutionary Party (PRI), he was accused of election rigging and repression of indigenous groups. Altercations between the APPO and police had escalated, and several deaths had resulted.

For a few days after I arrived in Oaxaca de Juárez, the usually charming cobblestone streets surrounding El Zócalo became battlegrounds. Federal and military police, armed with tear gas, clubs, and rubber bullets, fought demonstrators lobbing rocks and Molotov cocktails from behind makeshift barriers spray-painted with political slogans. After the police "liberated" the plaza, Ruiz clung to power until the end of his term, in late 2010. Then, Gabino Cué, Oaxaca's first non-PRI elected governor in eighty years, took office, after a carefully monitored vote.

Although the local political unrest had mostly settled down by the time I returned to the state in 2011, its citizens now faced bigger problems. High U.S. unemployment had taken a toll on the many Oaxacan households depending on remittances sent home by relatives who had emigrated to *El Norte*. It had also become significantly more challenging for the undocumented workers who still wanted to enter the U.S. from Mexico to find jobs. Illicit frontier crossings had dropped sharply. According to U.S. Border Patrol statistics, 327,577 "illegal alien apprehensions" were conducted in 2011, compared to a record high of 1,643,679 in 2000.

Traversing *La Frontera*, already a nightmarish endeavor, was now more perilous and costly than ever. Gangs routinely preyed on migrants traveling through Mexico to the U.S.—not only Mexicans, but citizens of Central American countries, too, many of them refugees. At the border itself, unscrupulous *coyotes* were known to charge crossers exorbitant fees of $3,000 or more, before ditching them in the inhospitable desert terrain of the American Southwest, where many perished. Rape was common. Another frightening deterrent was the escalating violence occurring at the border, where Transnational Criminal Organizations (TCOs) were battling for control of drug-smuggling routes. No one wanted to be caught in the crossfire.

When President Felipe Calderón took office in 2006, he promptly declared war on the vast, shadowy drug network collectively known as *El Narco*. Little progress was made, however, and in 2011 the thugs were still fighting back. The Narcos were also battling each other, using firearms easily obtained in the U.S. and smuggled into Mexico. The stakes were high. Seven Mexican TCOs ran multibillion-dollar operations in both countries: the Sinaloa Cartel, Los Zetas, the Gulf Cartel, the Juárez Cartel, the Beltrán-Leyva Cartel (BLO), La Familia Michoacana (LFM), and the Tijuana Cartel.

The notorious head of the Sinaloa Cartel, Joaquín "El Chapo" (Shorty) Guzmán, was repeatedly listed in *Forbes* magazine's annual roundup of "the world's most powerful people." After escaping prison in 2001, he was finally recaptured in 2014. But in 2015 he escaped again through an ingenious, 1.5 kilometer-long tunnel, dug straight to his cell, before he was recaptured again later that year. Soon after, a popular Mexican actress, Kate Castillo, came under investigation for possible money-laundering ties to El Chapo through her tequila company. In 2011, much of the violence was occurring in bloody turf battles between El Chapo's henchmen and Los Zetas, a ruthless outfit founded by former elite Mexican army commandos.

The TCO bosses aren't the only ones profiting from the drug trade. They spread their wealth to corrupt government, military, and police officials—as well as to many ordinary citizens. The TCOs launder their earnings through banks and a wide variety of business fronts, both in Mexico and abroad. The European bank HSBC has been penalized and sued for processing at least $881 million for the Sinaloa cartel. In 2012, the FBI raided operations in Oklahoma and New Mexico for laundering millions of dollars for Los Zetas through the quarter horse industry.

Although Mexican crime-world figures are ruthless in extracting *cuotas* (tolls), they are often celebrated as heroic Robin Hoods beating the system, their exploits recounted in catchy *narcocorridos* by popular groups such as Los Tucanes de Tijuana and Los Tigres del Norte. At the same time, Mexican newspapers are routinely plastered with photographs of drug-war casualties: decapitated corpses in ditches; bullet-ridden victims behind blood-splattered windshields; and severed limbs arranged like trophies. Lurid articles recount the exploits of henchmen such as "*El Pozolero*" (the stewmaker), who dissolved three hundred victims in acid on orders from a Tijuana Cartel boss.

Although the TCOs' tentacles reach around the world, their biggest market is the U.S. The Mexican cartels supply America's insatiable demand for illegal marijuana, cocaine, heroin, MDMA (ecstasy), and methamphetamine (crystal meth). Whether or not U.S. drug legalization would reduce the enormous flow, American prohibitionist policies have exacted a horrific price. By the time Enrique Peña Nieto, of the PRI party, was elected president in 2012, an estimated sixty thousand Mexicans had been slaughtered in drug-war violence. By 2016, the death toll had risen to well over one hundred thousand, twice the number of American combat deaths in the Vietnam War. Tens of thousands of other Mexicans have simply disappeared and remain unaccounted for. Many compare recreational U.S. narcotics use to genocide.

Dissociative American attitudes toward the challenging realities of Mexican life may have something to do with the spot the country has long held in non-Mexican imaginations as an unrestrictive and nonjudgmental playground for adventuring, partying, hiding, or acting out. Think: Richard Burton and Ava Gardner in *The Night of the Iguana*. In his song "Mexico," James Taylor suggests that it's a place where loads can be lost and minds can be left behind. The mentality has been fueled by the "log off" series of beachy Corona beer advertisements, and by numerous visiting writers (most of them non-Hispanic white males) who have a lengthy history of documenting alcohol and other drugs in Mexico—and of dabbling with various substances themselves.

After traveling with Pancho Villa's revolutionary army, in 1913, John Reed exclaims in his book *Insurgent Mexico*, "I like sotol, *aguardiente* [a spirit distilled from sugarcane], mescal, tequila, pulque, and other Mexican customs!" In the 1920s, D. H. Lawrence mentioned pulque and "the fiery white brandy distilled from the maguey: mescal, tequila" in his novel *The Plumed Serpent*. In the 1930s, the mad French poet, dramatist, and heroin addict Antonin Artaud took peyote (*Lophophora williamsii*) while visiting the Tarahumara people of northwestern Mexico. From 1936 to 1938, Malcolm Lowry's heavy drinking in Cuernavaca and Oaxaca planted the seeds for his mezcal-soaked masterpiece, *Under the Volcano*. And Graham Greene published *The Power and the Glory*, in 1940, about a persecuted "whisky priest" on the lam in the state of Tabasco.

In the early 1950s, William S. Burroughs, a longtime drug abuser, lived in Mexico City with his wife, Joan Vollmer, until he fled the country in 1952 after killing her in a boozy William Tell–style shooting. Mexico features in his novel *Junkie*. Jack Kerouac crossed the border several times in the 1950s and 1960s, and writes of a debaucherous visit to a Mexican brothel in *On the Road*. Timothy Leary first tried *Psilocybe* mushrooms in Cuernavaca, in 1960. And in 1966, Ken Kesey hid from the law in Manzanillo with a Magic Bus full of Merry Pranksters and drugs. His raucous sojourn became the basis for a hallucinatory dramatization, "Over the Border," included in the book *Kesey's Garage Sale*. The episode also played a part in Tom Wolfe's bestseller *The Electric Kool-Aid Acid Test*.

From the late 1960s onward, the controversial Peruvian "anthropologist" Carlos Castaneda sold millions of "nonfiction" books about his mystical encounters with a mysterious Yaqui shape-shifting *nagual* named Don Juan, who introduced him to peyote and jimsonweed (*Datura stramonium*) in the Sonoran desert. However, after Don Juan was exposed as a fictional or composite character, Castaneda was discredited and went into seclusion for the rest of his life. But many of his hippie readers journeyed to Mexico nonetheless in search of similar drug-fueled enlightenment. The country had become a place to "turn on, tune in, drop out"—just as Brazil and northern South American countries have become destinations for taking *ayahuasca*, a mind-altering, indigenous brew made with the *Banisteriopsis caapi* vine.

In Oaxaca, psychedelic tourism has been accessible since at least the early 1960s, when María Sabina emerged as a counter-cultural magnet. Visitors were inspired by a 1957 photo essay about her in *Life* magazine by R. Gordon Wasson, an ethnomy-cologist and J.P. Morgan banking executive, called "Seeking the Magic Mushroom." The article recounted his experiences taking *Psilocybe* fungi with Sabina in a Mazatec ritual in 1955. These days, it's still easy to find "traditional" experiences in Oaxaca with hallucinogenic mushrooms, or with the psychoactive plant Seer's (or Diviner's) Sage (*Salvia divinorum*)—both ritually used by some local indigenous cultures. Cocaine and other illicit hard drugs are also available. Because of its climate and vast swaths of remote, mountainous terrain, the state has a history of marijuana cultivation, and *mota* (pot), though illegal in Mexico, isn't difficult to obtain for recreational use. In the 1970s, a particularly potent strain, Oaxaca Gold, became legendary in the U.S.

In 2011, with many Oaxacans desperate for work and plenty of drug money around to tempt them, there were rumors of agave farmers abandoning their crops and choosing to grow marijuana instead. Some said there were narco-controlled villages deep in the mountains where pot plants or opium poppies were cultivated on a grand scale by farmers who weren't given a choice. Although an unfortunate number of corrupt Mexican police and government officials have a longstanding reputation for accepting *mordidas* (bites, or slang for "bribes") to look the other way, aspiring drug dealers and users might note that the country's judicial system makes it nearly impossible to overturn *any* type of conviction. Certainly, if one should ever want to tap into America's highly lucrative recreational drug market, booze would still be the safest way to go—mezcal, for instance.

リ

THE BUS EXITED the highway and made its way north to Teotitlán del Valle. At the village outskirts, I stepped off by La Cúpula, an inn with a rug-weaving showroom. From there, I walked down a short path to a long building. A *palapa* (palm-frond canopy) towered over one end of the high brick-and-adobe walls. A wooden sign outside read DEL MAGUEY, SINGLE VILLAGE MEZCAL, and an old tan pickup was parked in front. NADIE ES PERFECTO (nobody's perfect) was hand-painted across the windshield—backward. It was one of Ron's artworks. A shepherd came by with his flock, heading to outlying fields for the day. I stepped through the sheep to an imposing set of green metal doors topped with rebar spikes, silhouetted against the blue sky like agave leaves.

Ron stood in the open courtyard, holding a baby maguey plant in one hand and a cigarette in the other. "*¡Bienvenidos!*" he said with a smile. Although Del Maguey sales were climbing fast, you wouldn't have known by the look of its rustic headquarters, where Ron slept upstairs on the bare concrete roof of the warehouse. A tarp on his bed protected him from the wayward droppings of an owl roosting in the palapa rafters.

Ron's longtime business associate, Francisco "Pancho" Martinez, cracked jokes with a wild cackle as other men from the village worked. A young man, Xenon, knelt before Ron in a little garden, planting a nursery of baby agaves harvested from a recently hacked quiote. Across the courtyard, next to a round brick well covered with pink bougainvillea, another employee, Nerio, sat on a low wooden chair, rinsing wine bottles by hand. One by one, he placed them upside down on a circular metal drying rack. The area was contained inside high, thick walls—except for one corner, where there was latticed brick. Through the open spaces left between the blocks, I could see the surrounding valley and mountains.

I followed Ron into a single-story building that the palapa sat on top of. In a cool room inside, two other men, Andres and Cosmito, were using a crude wooden form to align and attach Del Maguey labels to bottles of mezcal. The men were numbering each label by hand with a stamp they pounded into a dusty inkpad. Before slipping the bottles into cardboard shipping cartons, they dipped the cork-filled tops into a pot of melted, honey-colored beeswax. Ron said the wax was recycled from leftover church candles.

He introduced me to the workers in Spanish. From their befuddled looks, it was clear my name wasn't one they had heard before, or knew how to pronounce.

"Granville is a French name," Ron explained. "It means *pueblo grande*."

Cautious nods of recognition: "*Sí . . . pueblo grande . . . claro.*"

"And his last name means *verde*."

"*¿Sí? ¿Pueblo grande . . . verde?*"

"*¡Oye!* He looks like a *pueblo pequeño* to me," winked Pancho. Everyone had a good laugh and went back to work. From then on—to my face, at least—my Oaxacan *apellido* (nickname) was Pueblo Grande Verde.

A large room by the bottling area functioned as both warehouse and office. From a simple wooden desk, set against a whitewashed wall, Ron ran his enterprise using a laptop and a smartphone, coordinating with employees in a satellite office in Taos and the Del Maguey tasting room in Oaxaca de Juárez. The desk was surrounded by blue plastic barrels, stainless steel kegs, and white plastic vats encased in metal frames.

Although the company was awarded Distiller of the Year at the 2011 San Francisco World Spirits Competition, the actual distilling of Del Maguey mezcal was done entirely in the individual *fábricas* of the maestros mezcaleros Ron bought from.

The spirits were trucked to Teotitlán del Valle in bulk containers from the communities of Santa Catarina Minas, Santo Domingo Albarradas, San Luis del Río, and San Baltazar Chichicapam (Del Maguey called it "Chichicapa")—and from an additional village that Ron kept secret, along with the identity of the tobalá maker who resided there. Otherwise, Del Maguey identified the maestros mezcaleros it purchased spirits from on its website and in its marketing materials. In 2013, the company began exporting mezcal from small-batch distillers in three more Oaxacan villages: San Pedro Taviche (near Octolán de Morelos) and two remote villages in the Mixteca region—San José Río Minas and San Pedro Teozacoalco.

The walls were decorated with a pin-up calendar from a local auto parts store; a mock-up image of a rally car with the Del Maguey logo emblazoned upon it; a brown map of local mountain ranges and nearby villages; and several artworks Ron had created from crushed plastic water bottles he had found on the road to the village. One of these sculptures had a lot of dead wasps glued to it. Some were inscribed with *rótulos* (hand-painted sign lettering). A piece of scrap metal was painted with a rabbit glyph and the words MEZCAL CON AGUA NO ES MEZCAL, a reference to the unscrupulous practice of diluting a spirit with water to stretch it out.

Ron was preoccupied with designing a light-and-space art installation for an exhibit to be held at the same time as the fifty-fourth Venice Biennale. The show, called Venice in Venice, was to feature the work of SoCal artists. Ron said that, in previous

years, there had been talk of his possibly re-creating an entire
functioning mezcal fábrica for the official juried exhibition, complete with horse and millstone, but the plan had never come to
fruition. While in Venice, in addition to presenting his sculpture,
Ron was planning to pour Del Maguey mezcal for the art crowd.
I asked him if he was going to bring along one of the maestros
mezcaleros he bought from in Oaxaca. He said that instead he
was arranging for a couple of young American mixologists to
join him.

Given Ron's approach, it was unsurprising that Del Maguey
headquarters felt more like an art-fabrication studio than an ordinary bottling facility. In fact, he now described his mezcal company as "my sixteen-year art project." His artworks are found in
major museum collections, so an assertion like that wasn't sur-
prising. I had noticed a big metal piece hanging on a courtyard
wall, with the inscription TODO ES MI OBRA (everything is my
work). Looking around at his busy employees, I wondered if the
statement said something about Ron's sense of artistic license—
was everyone involved with Del Maguey aware that Ron considered their work part of his art? It was tempting to cast him as
an appropriator. Yet, there I was, taking notes, doing my own
appropriating for this book. I, too, was tapping into a culture I
wasn't a part of. I was now Pueblo Grande Verde, on an adventure of my own.

By this time, Ron had been highly successful at elevating
mezcal's profile, and he had been equally skilled at keeping Del
Maguey in the spotlight. Concurrently, in some ways his business

felt like a stage set for him as an artist. I recalled a visit to *Las Pozas* (The Pools), the surrealist jungle gardens the aristocratic English poet Edward James (a patron of Salvador Dalí) had constructed near the mountain town of Xilitla, in the Huasteca region in the state of San Luis Potosí, beginning in the early 1960s. Old photographs show the magnificently bearded eccentric in flowing white robes, or in a loincloth, and sometimes with a large parrot, posing on strange concrete pillars and weird stairs to nowhere. In a manifestation of Ron's art, he was photographed around the world with celebrity chefs and mixologists, wearing his own iconic garb. In mezcal, Ron had found a win-win for himself as a businessman and as an artist.

ᗡ

A SHRINE WAS set up at the end of the storage area, decorated with candles, flowers in vases, and bottles of mezcal. It also held a green ceramic incense burner, bearing a fragrant, smoking hunk of copal resin. A gilded frame, with an image of the Virgen de Juquila inside it, hung on a *petate* (straw mat) behind the shrine. On either side, industrial metal shelves stood loaded with dozens of mezcal samples—an archive of agave spirits. Many were in plastic water bottles with hand-scrawled inscriptions; others were in glass vessels of various shapes and sizes.

Several of the containers were sealed with official labels from the Mezcal Regulatory Council (CRM), the advisory organization that certifies mezcals and tests them for compliance with the quality standards set by the NOM (Norma Oficial Mexicana, or

Official Mexican Standard). These were established in 1994 at the same time as the DO for mezcal. The DO delineates where an agave distillate can be produced and called mezcal, and the NOM sets the standards for its production. The CRM began certifying mezcals in accordance with the NOM in 2005.

Over the years, Ron had taken Del Maguey through the processes of the USDA and the Mexican and American organic-certification systems, which allowed him to label his mezcals organic. Meeting those standards was important to him, as he had long been an advocate of pure, undoctored mezcal. But the brand's spirits were also required to meet the specific standards and testing requirements of the NOM. For a company to market mezcal legally under the DO, its bottles must be labeled with an official NOM registration number. Del Maguey's is NOM-O41X.

The DO and NOM for mezcal have been controversial since they were first created, in part because they reflect the business interests of the large-scale commercial mezcal companies that spearheaded them in the first place. Mezcal's DO was closely modeled on the DO that was established in 1974 for tequila. The first DO outside Europe, it was also backed by powerful, corporate brands. The small-time producers who have historically crafted agave distillates as part of their cultural heritage were powerless in defining the DOs for either mezcal or tequila.

"In Mexico," Sarah Bowen writes, "the system that protects and regulates DOs is based on a fundamentally neoliberal model: one that aims to protect markets for Mexican producers while creating as few barriers as possible." In 2016, Proximo Spirits, owned by the family behind tequila behemoth Jose Cuervo, added mezcal to its portfolio. Likewise, the international spirits companies Bacardi, Diageo, William Grant & Sons, and Pernod Ricard have also made moves into mezcal.

Mezcal's DO initially covered only five states: Oaxaca, Durango, Guerrero, San Luis Potisí, and Zacatecas. Over the years, certain areas of Guanajuato, Tamaulipas, Michoacán, and Puebla also received DO protection. There is no DO for raicilla, but separate DOs have been established for bacanora in Sonora and for sotol in Chihuahua. Although for centuries, the word "mezcal" has been applied to a wide range of distillates across Mexico, agave spirits crafted in non-DO areas must now be called *destilados de agave*, and a proposal has been submitted to revise that to "*aguardiente de agave*," which makes even less sense. In theory, DOs are implemented to protect intellectual property rights for regionally specific agricultural products and foodstuffs, such as Gorgonzola cheese, Armagnac, and Melton Mowbray pork pies. In practice, the DO for mezcal has marginalized a far greater number of producers than the comparatively small number of certified ones that it has protected.

Two categories were established for mezcal under the NOM. The purest is Type I mezcal, which must be distilled from 100 percent agave-plant sugars. Type II mezcal may contain a minimum of 80 percent agave sugars, and up to 20 percent of its other fermenting sugars may be derived from non-agave sources. Three aging categories for mezcal were also defined: *joven* (young), reposado, and añejo. Joven mezcals are meant to be clear. Reposado (rested) mezcals can be colored—whether naturally, from a wooden barrel, or from additives—and are stored from two months to a year. Añejo (aged) mezcals can also be artificially colored, but must be stored for at least twelve months in oak containers. Any of these three mezcal categories may be *abocados*, with *abocantes* (additives) such as artificial colors, sweeteners, and flavorings. Some abocado mezcals contain "worms" or scorpions, while others may be sweetened, viscous cremas with coffee or mint flavorings added—or artificially colored in various hues.

The NOM allows certified mezcals to contain from 36 to 55 percent ABV (between 72 and 110 proof), and prohibits them from being exported in bulk from Mexico. Mezcals should leave the country only when certified and bottled. Tequila follows a different set of rules. It may be shipped to the U.S. in separate bulk batches, where it can then be blended and bottled as *mixto* (mixed). It is also permitted to contain only 51 percent agave sugars. (Any tequila not labeled 100 PERCENT AGAVE is mixto.)

In 2011, two proposals were submitted to amend the NOM, both backed by corporate interests. One called for the branding of the word "agave," which would then be exclusively used by DO producers. "The proposal," Bowen writes, "was as if France had granted exclusive use of the word 'grapes' to winemakers in the Bordeaux region." The second proposal asked that mezcals be permitted to contain as little as 49 percent agave sugars, and that non-DO producers must label their distillates with the word "*Agavacea*" instead of using the word "agave." In 2016, a similar proposal was submitted, this time requesting that producers of all non-DO mezcals must call their spirits "*komil*"—an obscure, Nahuatl word for "intoxicating drink."

These proposals were tabled after an international public outcry, proving that the murky dealings that have long surrounded the mezcal business are becoming harder to hide. As consumers have grown more passionate about mezcal, they have also become more aware of the socioeconomic realities and traditions of the peoples who have historically crafted alcoholic maguey expressions. New aficionados have become increasingly active in nonprofit organizations such as the Tequila Interchange Project, a consumer advocacy group for distilled agave spirits. Another organization, Mezonte, seeks to improve biological and cultural awareness. Even small actions like signing a petition or sharing a story online can demonstrate views and concerns to both the Mexican government and the corporate interests that would like more control of the popular drink. One proposed regulation asked that mezcal be divided into the categories of ancestral, standard, and artisanal, causing discussion about whether that action would benefit or further marginalize distilling families.

Mezcal is now available in over forty countries, and its future could fall in the hands of consumers around the world who make it clear what they will and won't purchase, and why. The spirit will be made as long as agaves grow and producers distill them. But down the road, the most successful brands could be those that offer the most transparency—from ingredients and processes to wages and other costs. It's not inconceivable that mezcal could equally benefit consumers and producers alike. But so far, maestros mezcaleros—the true guardians of the spirit's cultural heritage—have been given very little say in defining their creations for both the Mexican and international markets, when instead they might be celebrated as national, living treasures who craft thoughtful expressions of plants, people, and place.

Aside from whether or not they are eligible to receive DO protection, or if they even should want it, maestros mezcaleros are liquid poets, handcrafting their small batches with highly individualized techniques, using plants they have often lived among for years, sometimes decades. Much like skilled French *parfumiers*, maestros mezcaleros are adept at reducing botanical ingredients to particular notes, which, similar to vocabulary in a language, add up to spirits with flavors developed over time by community consensus. In this sense, they are master storytellers—their poetic concoctions the drinkable folklore of their cultures, and the transcendent articulation of dreams. Mezcal goes way beyond tasting notes, or a cool-looking brand image, or whether a mezcal is certified or not. As writers of a liquid language, mezcal makers deserve our respect for their authorship. Certainly, one of the great joys of mezcal is that, much like listening to songs or reading books, drinking the spirit can bring you deep into someone else's consciousness—one of the precious delights of being human.

"Saving mezcal won't save mezcaleros," Bowen writes. "And as long as the market dictates how to regulate and protect mezcal,

it's always going to privilege mezcal over mezcaleros. We can—
and should—choose mezcals and tequilas made from diverse,
sustainably produced varieties of agave, according to the practices that have developed in particular places. But we also need
to consider how agave farmers, workers, and small producers are
treated. That means pushing companies to be more transparent
about their labor practices and the prices they pay to agave farmers and mezcaleros."

Likewise the future of agaves also needs to be rewritten.
In an article included in the compendium book *Mezcal: Arte
Tradicional*, biologist Catarina Illsley Granich writes that the
manner in which the DO for mezcal is currently structured is
"likely to lead to a loss of diversity in magueys and mezcals."
As a cautionary example, she cites the DO for tequila, which
specifies that the drink must be exclusively produced from only
one type of agave. The resulting monoculture has "nearly led
to the complete disappearance," she writes, "of local varieties
of *A. tequilana* that now only survive in certain more isolated
fields, and only thanks to some small producers who conserve the
plants because they like the distinctive taste of spirits made from
these agave varieties."

So rather than establishing arbitrary rules and regulations for
mezcal, why not celebrate the spirit's incalculable expressions
of plants, people, and place? Wouldn't it be better for producers, consumers, and agaves if maestros mezcaleros were encouraged to experiment, and not be chained to the required unifor-
mity of the haphazard DO? The NOM standards for mezcal

are like grammar imposed on an ancient language. Why would artists allow themselves to be restricted—if not out of economic necessity?

In the current universe of officially sanctioned mezcal, brand owners have the most power to experiment freely. I noticed a pair of wooden casks near the shrine. Ron said they were made of French oak and he had been using them to age mezcal. He took a bottle from one of the casks and poured me a half inch. The spirit was light, reddish-brown, and very smooth. "Notice anything different?" he asked. There was an unusual sweetness beyond the agave and smoke, but I couldn't quite place it.

"Candy corn?" I asked.

"Bourbon!" he said with delight.

The mezcal had been stored in a cask previously used for the classic Kentucky spirit, and Ron was tracking its flavor progression month by month. He poured me a slightly darker, more recent sample, and I now detected the familiar bourbon taste. It was a North American fusion—the continent's oldest distilled spirit imbued with the hint of a newer counterpart. The drink also exemplified where rarified spirits were headed: arcane subgenres of artisanal mezcals aged in bourbon, rye, or wine casks; small-batch bourbons aged in tequila barrels; and so on. The potential for cross-cultural pollinations was huge. But I felt I was landing at the end of the story when I wanted to be closer to the beginning. Ron understood. "OK," he said, "let's hit the road."

A GOOD-HUMORED YOUNG man appeared at the bodega: Arturo Ramírez Zenteño. He was the quality-control inspector for Del Maguey. The three of us climbed into Ron's Jeep and headed southeast on Highway 190. We were going to the village of San Luis del Río to visit maestro mezcalero Paciano Cruz Nolasco, who made three types of mezcal for Del Maguey at that time: Vida, Crema de Mezcal, and San Luis del Río.

Ron scowled as we cruised past a new mezcal factory, Casa Armando Guillermo Prieto. The 34,120-square-foot cream-colored plant was plopped alongside the road, looking like a hacienda on steroids. The company is part of Grupo CIMSA, a regional bottler of Coca-Cola, and produces a 100 percent agave mezcal called Zignum. Inside the compound, thousands of oak barrels were stored for aging reposado and añejo versions. The business also distributes El Recuerdo de Oaxaca, a blended, 100 percent agave mezcal with a worm; and El Señorio, a 100 percent agave mezcal that has won awards at the San Francisco World Spirits Competition.

Eschewing the complex and smoky-hued flavors of tradition-ally distilled, small-batch mezcals, Zignum targets palates attuned to neutrally flavored tequilas. The drink is certified as Type I (100 percent agave), but it's manufactured using industrial equipment that grinds raw espadín, extracts its juice, and cooks it in giant autoclaves. After fermentation in enormous tanks, the spirit is created through column distillation, a more efficient method for industrial purposes than the pot-still techniques used for mak-ing traditional mezcals. Casa Armando Guillermo Prieto can produce up to 14,000 liters per day, and in 2013, it entered a distribution agreement with Bacardi. Did the strangely named Zignum, I wondered, represent the future of mezcal?

We continued on, passing mezcal bodegas set up for tourists, a burning pile of trash, and an old pickup with a cactus growing in its bed. We stopped for gas at a Pemex station in Tlacolula. The sprawling market town is locally nicknamed "Tokyolula" for the profusion of multihued plastic wares and other Asian-made goods for sale in its lively weekly mercado. The streets were swarming with loud yellow-and-green *moto-taxis* (three-wheeled cabin cycles) ferrying women with woven shawls pulled tight against the blowing dust.

As the gas tank filled, Ron checked his smartphone, and shared the news that country music superstar Toby Keith had just launched a brand of worm-in-the-bottle firewater called Wild Shot Mezcal. It was produced in the state of San Luis Potosí from "green agave plants," and no one could figure out what those actually were. On the company's website, fans were encouraged to submit "worm warrior" selfies. Ron's social media network of anti-worm purists was buzzing with outrage over Keith's new product. But it wasn't all bad news for them. As Kelefa Sanneh once observed in the *New Yorker*, in a story about coffee obsessives, highbrow products attain their position only in relation to lowbrow stuff, like Keith's mezcal. "In order for connoisseurs to exist, they must be outnumbered by philistines, and if the connoisseurs are honest, they will admit that they enjoy this state of affairs," he said.

After Ron turned right at another Pemex station, farther east and past the ruins of Yagul, we began to see great fields of espadín reaching into the valley around us. In Santiago Matatlán, we passed under a sign extending across the road with a copper alembique atop it: BIENVENIDOS A STGO. MATATLÁN, OAX. "CAPITAL MUNDIAL DEL MEZCAL" (WELCOME TO SANTIAGO MATATLÁN, OAXACA, "WORLD CAPITAL OF MEZCAL"). Although this was a debatable claim, a variety of mezcals are fabricated in and around the town in both small artisanal and larger commercial distilleries. The main drag was lined with bodegas hawking a broad assortment of types—from jovens to cremas. There was a time, however, when there had been many more mezcal operations in Santiago Matatlán.

The surrounding region had a deep history of small-scale, community-oriented mezcal-making, but when the national railroad came through Oaxaca in 1910, it opened up possibilities for more commercialized applications. A station opened in nearby Tlacolula, allowing producers to ship their wares more easily to Mexico City and the coastal port of Veracruz. Because Mexico's industrialization came more slowly to Oaxaca than to other states—largely because of its physical geography and the great number of indigenous peoples and indigenous-held lands—mezcal producers had generally been left to their own devices over the centuries, untouched by the type of large-scale mechanization and foreign investment that reshaped tequila production in the state of Jalisco. In fact, tequila may have been aggressively developed into Mexico's emblematic drink because it was perceived as less "encumbered" than other mezcals by indigenous cultures and the dire poverty associated with them.

Certainly, traditional-mezcal makers were fiercely resistant to outsiders tampering with the unique distillation methods their families had developed over time. They had little interest in industrial agave steamers and baking ovens or in their drinks tasting un-smoky and bland. Furthermore, in response to onerous periods of prohibition, severe taxation, and other forms of government and corporate suppression, they would routinely distill their spirits in clandestine stills hidden deep in the mountains, far from the reach of meddling authorities, using whatever wild-grown, mezcal-making magueys were at hand. But as demand for the spirit increased, the supply of these agaves silvestres steadily dwindled, and farmers began cultivating large fields of espadín in the 1930s. They sold their crops to local mezcal makers, and by the 1940s Jaliscan producers were also buying them during tequila agave shortages.

Santiago Matatlán had more than fifty distilleries in the 1950s, from small palenques to large facilities owned by the Chagoyas and other powerful mezcal-making families. Production steadily increased into the 1980s, until a cyclical shortage of Jaliscan maguey caused prices for Oaxacan espadín to rise astronomically, and tequila makers began buying the plants illicitly. "Over a thousand palenques in Oaxaca went out of business as a result of the high agave prices, shortage of labor, and economic problems in Mexico more generally," writes Sarah Bowen. "Many of the remaining palenques began adding low-quality cane alcohol to mezcal to cut

costs. This led to unfair competition between traditional mezcaleros and those who were mixing in cane alcohol, because it cost
about five times more to produce mezcal than cane alcohol. By the
early 1990s, the industry was in crisis—and at a crossroads."

After the deaths of forty people attending a fiesta in the state
of Morelos were attributed to bad mezcal, in 1994, the drink
became the subject of widespread health warnings and boycotts.
Although everyone agreed that sweeping changes needed to be
made in the mezcal business, no one could concur on how to
make them. When the DO for mezcal was established, it over-
whelmingly reflected the interests of a few large mezcal companies that pushed to technologize production to compete with the
tequila industry. This was accomplished despite intense oppo-
sition and a 1980s government-funded study by the industrial
engineer Alberto Sánchez López. He concluded, writes Bowen,
"that following the path adopted by the tequila distilleries would
jeopardize the quality and taste of mezcal; instead, he emphasized
the need to support the thousands of families involved in the production of mezcal, stating that development strategies needed to
go 'beyond technical and financial solutions and consider social
and ecological variables.'" His conclusions still ring true today.

Before the modernization of tequila in the late nineteenth
century, which began a steady overshadowing of mezcal, small-
batch agave distillates were highly regarded throughout Mexico.
Like fine wines, they expressed the country's creativity, craftsmanship, and untold expressions of peoples and flavors. Now
that a similar understanding of mezcal was reemerging, along

with a swelling appreciation for the type of small-scale wares that Ron bought and sold, Santiago Matatlán was home to several artisanal distilleries, such as Los Nahuales and El Rey Zapoteco. Local competition continues to foster different marketing angles. For example, one brand, Fidencio, produces a mezcal *sin humo* (without smoke) that is distilled from agave baked in a special oven. This gives it a more neutral flavor, like tequila.

As we drove on, the road began to twist sharply as it ribboned into the mountains. Every now and then, Ron pointed out a tobalá or *tepeztate* (*Agave marmorata*) agave intrepidly growing on the rocky cliffs rising alongside us. As we shifted through microclimates, clusters of organ pipe cacti appeared on steep slopes, and dramatic roadside drops offered spectacular rippling-ridge vistas. Highway 190 is an important thoroughfare between Oaxaca de Juárez and the lush isthmus lowlands—and a steady stream of buses, semis, and piña-teeming trucks chugged uphill from the opposite direction. The route is also a well-known corridor for conveying illicit drugs. At the outskirts of a sleepy village, San Pedro Totolapa, we slowed to cross a series of speed bumps at a military checkpoint, where a gun-toting soldier gave us an appraising glance.

About twelve miles beyond, we turned left from the highway and followed a narrow mountain road that soon changed from asphalt to dirt. Arturo pointed out a field ahead, lined with neat rows of espadín. Soon there were maguey plots all around us. On a slope high above, cowboy-hatted magueyeros were harvesting the plants. One of the men kicked a spike-shorn piña to the road, adding it to an impressive pile. At the top of a hill, the community of San Luis del Río came into view, stretching ahead of us against the side of a steep-walled valley. A river coursed through the bottom, garden plots scattered here and there along the banks. The river was low because it was the dry season. But the flattened brush and trees up the slopes on either side indicated that it had run strong during the rainy months.

The village was a hillside tumble of plain houses made of brick and concrete, seemingly deserted in the midday heat. Although Ron's bottle label said "the pueblo elevation is 8,000 ft," Google Earth puts San Luis del Río at around thirty-two hundred feet. (In later years, Del Maguey stopped putting altitudes on its bottle labels.) Snoozing dogs lay in the dusty road, barely acknowledging the Jeep as we crept past. Ron turned uphill to follow a steep track between rows of dwellings. He parked by a two-story home behind a row of tall pines, and Paciano Cruz Nolasco came out to greet us. The sturdy maestro mezcalero wore a battered felt hat, a pale green T-shirt, khaki pants, and huaraches. It was a self-styled uniform, like Ron's—Paciano would have it on every time I saw him.

"¡*Bienvenidos!*" he called.

Paciano ushered us to a shady concrete patio amid the cluster of simple buildings where he and his family lived. We sat on wooden chairs at a dining table covered by an oilcloth bearing an image of a red poinsettia. Surrounding us were a corn cob pile, a stack of soda bottle cases, fat turkeys gobbling in a wire enclosure, a well-worn rifle, several squashes piled by a rolled-up hammock, a green coconut heap, and ducks and chickens wandering at large. There were also several blue- and red-colored plastic barrels and enormous white plastic vats filled to the brim with the family mezcals.

Arturo unscrewed the lid from one of the smaller containers, inserted a length of rubber tube, and sucked its end until some spirit emerged. He siphoned the liquid into a glass chemistry beaker and dropped in an alcoholmeter. The fragile instrument looked like a colossal thermometer, but was actually used for measuring alcohol levels. While Arturo made careful notes in a ledger, I sat at the table with Paciano and Ron. One of Ron's artworks was propped up in the window above us: a crushed green plastic bottle with the inscription NACIO CON ESTRELLA (star born) affixed to a green plastic tray.

Looking up between the buildings, I could see vultures slowly circling in an air current high above. The wind whistled through the pines. One of Paciano's two daughters, a young woman named Mary Lou, emerged from a nearby room holding a baby. He was the son of her older brother, Marcos, and his girlfriend, Imelda, who appeared in the doorway behind them, smiling shyly and holding a broom. The baby was wrapped in a blanket, and wore a cap, a bracelet, and a tiny gold ring. He flexed his fingers and sleepily blinked at his grandfather, who eagerly took him in his arms.

"My new worker!" laughed Paciano.

PACIANO WAS ONE of the first palenqueros Ron had bought mezcal from to export. They had met nearly two decades before, when Ron and Pancho showed up in San Luis del Río, in search of mezcal. Paciano had spent most of his life in the village, and through years of hard work had established himself as a prominent man, raising three children with his wife, Asunción. He grew tens of thousands of agaves, which he distilled into three different espadín mezcals for Del Maguey. San Luis del Río (47 percent ABV) was his signature spirit. Vida (42 percent ABV) was mostly intended for cocktails. And Crema de Mezcal (40 percent ABV), sweetened with agave syrup, was marketed "for women only, and a few strong men." For a time, Paciano had also made an espadín mezcal for *Sombra* (shadow), a brand cofounded by Aspen-based sommelier Richard Betts and Brooklyn-based "wine innovator" Charles Bieler. Sombra is now distilled in Santiago Matatlán.

Paciano had recently begun experimenting with a new mezcal for Ron, which he was crafting with the hearts of *A. tequilana* that he had planted during the last maguey shortage many years before. He had recognized a business opportunity at the time, when Jaliscan trucks were creeping down to Oaxaca, in search of espadín piñas. With a nod to the disastrous monoculture approach to agave cultivation affecting the tequila trade, Paciano and Ron decided to develop Azul—a spirit tasting the way tequila might have before the cloned cores of the "blue" maguey were steamed in large-scale manufacturing processes, rather than roasted by small-scale artisanal mezcal methods.

"Do you want to try *un poco*?" Paciano asked me.

"Of course!" I replied.

He produced a battered soda container filled with mezcal, then poured some of it into clay tasting cups for Ron, Arturo, and me. Paciano said he almost never drank alcohol himself. I would learn that this is not atypical of maestros mezcaleros, who spend much of their lives working closely with spirits and hold great respect for their power. As we sipped his new creation, Paciano played with his grandson. Unlike neutral tequila, the Azul placed sweet notes of caramelized agave hearts front and center, and I could taste hints of citrus and nutmeg. The maestro mezcalero was still fine-tuning it. But as he and Ron discussed the new mezcal's alcohol content, the fermentation process, and various other details, I could see that Ron's role wasn't passive. Although Paciano actually distilled the spirit, Ron was concerned with bringing out its best aspects, like an editor working with a manuscript.

Asunción, wearing a pink dress, her dark hair in a braid, emerged from the kitchen carrying a tray of white bowls. She set them before us with a basket of homemade tortillas wrapped in an embroidered cloth. Mary Lou poured us plastic cups of warm orange soda. Looking into my bowl, I saw chunks of meat in white-and-gray speckled skins floating in a rich broth. I bit into a chunk, and found it somewhat like pork or chicken—although riddled with tiny bones. Asunción had flavored the soup with chiles and avocado tree leaves, which gave it a delicious, licorice-like taste.

"Do you like *sopa de iguana?*" Arturo asked me, sitting down to lunch.

"I do now!" I replied.

"Look!" said Paciano, picking up a white cloth sack. He reached inside and removed a pair of live iguanas by their tails. They were about two feet long, and their mouths were tied shut with blue raffia strips. It was mating season for the reptiles—they were easier to catch as they roamed the surrounding hills, seeking *amor.*

"*Es un afrodisíaco,*" Arturo assured me, tilting his bowl for every last drop.

In a narrow passageway by the house, a pair of redheaded parrots squawked in a cage, a cue for Paciano to recount the brief time he and his family had lived in Mexico City many years before. One of his jobs there was working as a water carrier, lugging five-gallon jugs on his powerful shoulders.

"One day, when I was making deliveries," he laughed, "I heard an old lady call down from a hill: Bring me two! But after I'd carried those heavy jugs all the way up there, she turned out to be a parrot talking to me."

After lunch, Paciano left us to return to some unpaid civic duties he was required to perform for a community project. He had already spent much of the day axing a dead tree and making other improvements along a local road. We said goodbye, and I climbed in the Jeep with Arturo and Ron. We were going to see Paciano's son, Marcos, who was manning the family fábrica.

We wound our way through San Luis del Río and down to the river. Ron drove the Jeep straight into the waterway, turned right, and headed down the center, splashing between shallow

stretches and exposed bars of gravel and sand. A few small mezcal fábricas were set among palm and banana trees along the
banks, and I could see hodgepodge agave patches planted on
even the highest slopes above us. In the distance, a man slowly
led a piña-laden burro down a steep path that shimmered in the
waves of heat.

ꆜ

THE NOLASCOS' FÁBRICA was set in a hollow carved out of a rocky
hillside. Agaves were planted in rows above it, much in the style
of a vineyard. Paciano had relocated the distillery there not
long after a flood swept it from a spot closer to the river. But
it appeared to me to have been there forever. Dead tree trunks
supported a tin roof sheltering a pair of copper alembiques. The
stills were contained in adobe-brick structures built on either side
of a cinder-block cooling tank. A wood fire was burning under
each alembique, and mezcal was trickling from copper pipes into
plastic jugs.

Outside the fábrica, there was a circular milling arena, with
a massive horse-drawn *molino Egipcio* (an "Egyptian" millstone
molded from river rocks and cement). On the other side of that,
next to a rock-lined roasting pit, a brawny magueyero was splitting fat espadín hearts with an ax. Behind the stills, Marcos was
standing on a ladder propped against one of several wooden fermentation tinas, scooping out bucketfuls of a sloppy brown mash.
The fábrica was hot, filthy, and swarming with bees and flies, but
it was also an efficient production line. Piñas were baked in the

horno, then pulverized under the slow-rolling molino Egipcio. The mash was then fermented in the tinas, and finally distilled in the alembiques.

Marcos wiped his hands on his GABINO CUÉ T-shirt and came over to greet us. He was in his mid-twenties and had the lean build of a basketball player. He wore jeans and a Yankees baseball cap.

"What's up?" he said in perfect English.

A year earlier, Marcos had been living in Louisville, Kentucky. He had returned to Oaxaca to help his father expand the family mezcal business. Marcos said that he had been happy in the U.S., where he spent several years working a succession of jobs in roofing, fast food, and bricklaying. He was initially reluctant to return to Mexico, so his parents sent his two sisters north to bring him home. Marcos said he was nineteen when he had crossed the border from Mexico into the U.S. by himself. The ordeal took him five grueling days on foot. He didn't talk about it much, revealing only that "we walked at night and saw lots of snakes." It wasn't any easier for his sisters, and one of them ended up staying in the U.S. and starting a family. But Mary Lou eventually returned to the village with Marcos. First, though, she worked long hours for a year and a half stocking fruit in a grocery store.

One of the stills was emitting its final drops, indicating that it was time to switch out its contents. Marcos gently removed the tubo from between the alembique and the cooling tank. Then he knelt over the hand-hammered copper *sombrero* (still top) and clawed away the *masa* (a muddy residue left from spent maguey mash) that had been placed around the sombrero's edge to seal it to the alembique's belly. Setting the still top aside, he stood in a cloud of steam bursting up from the wide opening below. He then began pitchforking the spent mezcal mash onto a heap of softened maguey fibers where a dog was curled up asleep. It stood up, shook itself, and wandered off.

When the still was empty, Marcos unplugged a side drain and rinsed the alembique with pails of clean water from the cooling tank. The tank was gravity-fed by a black plastic pipe extending several hundred yards upstream in the river. Finally, he resealed the drain and replenished the still with several buckets of fresh mash before reassembling the apparatus and stoking the fire. The routine would be repeated every few hours, around the clock, until the tinas were entirely emptied. This would take several days. There were hammocks and petates for anyone fortunate enough to grab a few winks, although an eye was always needed on the fires so that temperatures would remain consistent and a still wouldn't explode.

After slugging down some water and wiping the sweat from his brow, Marcos unscrewed a lid on a plastic barrel and inserted a venencia. He sucked some mezcal into the cane tube, held it in with a fingertip, and released the liquid into a jícara. He handed it to me to taste. The drink was rough and strange.

"Do you like it?" he asked me, with a funny look.

"It's . . . interesting."

"Ha! It's the cola! When you drink that, you can't even kiss a girl."

Arturo explained that Paciano's cabeza was typically 60 to 65 percent ABV, with *muy fuerte* (very strong) flavor. His cuerpo usually came in at 45 to 55 percent ABV, and tasted strong, too. His cola normally measured only 20 to 25 percent ABV, and, obviously, didn't taste as good as the others. But it was necessary to combine portions of all three to achieve the proper flavor profile for Del Maguey.

"Mezcal has lots of curves," winked Marcos. "Like women!"

Balancing a batch requires fine-tuning, but I could already see that getting the spirit to that point would require enormous amounts of manual labor. Magueyeros do most of the tough stuff—everything from planting, tending, and harvesting agaves, to packing and building hornos, grinding the baked piñas into mash, gathering and cutting firewood, and emptying and refilling stills. None of these tasks are easy, and some of them—such as working with heavy tahonas drawn by large working animals, and handling extremely hot and potentially explosive stills—are dangerous. In Oaxaca, an emergency room can be several hours away. Marcos told me that his magueyeros typically earned from 100 to 120 pesos (less than $10) per day. A migrant farm worker in Napa Valley can earn more per hour. Yet given the local economy, people were lucky to find such employment in their communities, and of course that only happened if a maestro mezcalero could afford to hire them at all. If not, he would try to shoulder as many of the backbreaking tasks as he could himself.

Throughout the agave regions of Mexico, there were thousands of other small-scale operations similar to the one I was standing in, many of them even smaller. I wasn't privy to how much Paciano was paid for his mezcal per liter, but given Ron's bulk buying power and global reach, I knew Paciano was in a far better financial position than most maestros mezcaleros in terms of the large quantities of mezcal he was able to continuously sell to Del Maguey. He also grew his own agave, so he didn't need to purchase his materia prima from someone else. I had noticed that he had running water, a TV, and a truck—things that many other people in the village didn't have.

But would an American small-batch distiller, vintner, or brewer toil under such grueling conditions? I wondered. And was there another expensively priced, top-shelf spirit, anywhere in the world, that was crafted in a similarly disparate socio-economic dynamic? I couldn't think of one. I asked Marcos which steps are toughest.

"All of them," he shrugged. "Come back sometime, and I'll show you."

Agave potatorum

PART THREE

WARM ORANGE SODA

A COUPLE OF WEEKS after my first visit to San Luis del Río, I stood on a steep mountainside of espadín agave, grasping a machete and cursing in pain. A sharp, nasty maguey thorn had pierced my pant leg, penetrating deep into my thigh as I hacked at the fifteen-foot-high, six-inch-thick quiote thrusting skyward from the plant's rosette. I was in one of Paciano's many agave plots near the village, surrounded by dozens of towering asparaguses swaying in the breeze.

When agaves are grown for mezcal-making, their once-in-a-lifetime stalks are removed to prevent the plants from expending a last burst of reproductive energy up and into them. If they are not removed, the plants will flower and die. After their quiotes have been severed, *capón* (castrated) agaves are then left in the ground for varying periods of time—sometimes years—allowing their internal sugars to intensify for stronger mezcal flavor. In the course of the afternoon, I had managed to take down only ten stalks, needing thirty to forty strong hacks to sever each one. But far below me, I could see Marcos and two magueyeros, Lionel and Rufino, speedily working their way downhill through the plants. They were wielding their machetes like ninjas, efficiently toppling each quiote with only a few deft strokes.

At around thirty-one hundred feet, the seemingly vertical landscape was covered with a loose combination of crumbly tan-colored earth and gray sharp-edged rocks. This type of steep arid slope provides the right sort of drainage for agaves, which typically require little water. They don't do well in damp earth, where puddles can form and lead to rot. The hardy plants, which have very shallow root systems, conserve moisture through crassulacean acid metabolism, opening their stomata (pores) at night to absorb carbon dioxide and closing them during punishing daytime heat.

The terrain, soil, and climate of the hills surrounding San Luis del Río contribute to the unique *goût de terroir* (flavor of the earth) of the local mezcal. The French winemaking concept of terroir, or *terruño* in Spanish, is increasingly applied to agave spirits, just as it's been used with such other drinks as wine, tea, and coffee and such foods as cheese, tomatoes, and chocolate. An intrepid maguey battling a cool mountain climate and tough mineral-rich earth at a high altitude could supply a mezcal with quite different flavor aspects than an agave thriving in volcanic terrain and warmer temperatures at a low altitude—conditions that might lead to a mellower, earthier taste.

Other than quiote removal, along with planting and weeding a few times a year, the most labor-intensive chore in maguey cultivation is harvesting. A *coa* (a long wood-handled knife with a sharp rounded blade) is often used to pry the plants from the earth and chop off their pencas. Sometimes the tool is also used to split a piña in two so that the agave can be more easily strapped to pack animals and transported from a field.

I had done a little gardening, and had limited experience picking corn, grapes, berries, and apples—but that was all child's play. When I spotted the other men cruising back up the mountainside,

dodging the thorn-tipped magueys with fleet-footed ease, I speculated that working with agaves requires not only excellent physical coordination, but also an intimate understanding attainable
only from living among them. At least, that's what I told myself
when Marcos appeared before me, utterly unscathed. As for me,
blood was dribbling from an ugly puncture wound in my forehead, and there were deep scratches crisscrossing my ankles and
forearms.

I had barely begun to learn, but everything to do with mezcal-
making already seemed daunting. I thought about what Howard
says in *The Treasure of the Sierra Madre*: "An ounce of gold,
Mister, is worth what it is because of the human labor that went
into the findin' and the gettin' of it." Somewhere very far away,
someone would pay $70 a bottle and several dollars a pour in a
bar for the mezcal that would be made from these plants. I was
feeling resentful already.

"How many quiotes did you guys cut?" I asked Marcos.

"About four hundred," he said, looking me up and down.
"Does that hurt, Pueblo Grande?"

"Well, just a little," I lied.

"The real pain comes later, where the spines went in."

"Real pain?"

"It only lasts for a while," he laughed. "You'll see. I'll show
you what to do."

The two others joined us, and we began making our way back
to the truck parked at the top of the slope. "Look at how healthy
our magueys are," said Marcos, gesturing at the thriving plants

around us. Ron had just taken him on a trip to Jalisco, where they had visited sprawling tequila haciendas and observed large-scale agave cultivation. "I learned that we've got the best mezcal and the best maguey in the world right here," Marcos said. "In Jalisco, I saw how a fábrica could grow into a company. Maybe one day I'm going to have the biggest one of all."

Reaching the crest of the hill, we scrambled under a rusty barbed-wire fence bordering the dirt road from Highway 190 to San Luis del Río. Marcos and I climbed into the cab of his father's red pickup, and Lionel and Rufino jumped in the bed. The proverb DIOS TARDA PERO NO OLVIDA (God is late but doesn't forget) was inscribed in white rótulos above the windshield.

On the way back to the village, the men kept an eye out for iguanas to hunt. Soon, Rufino banged on the roof and shouted for us to stop. He aimed a rifle at an iguana asleep on a tree branch. At the sound of his shot, it dove to the ground and scampered into the brush. Farther down the road, when Rufino fired at a brown hawk perched on a cactus, the regal bird had the opposite reaction. Marcos explained that the men wanted to stuff the bird and make a trophy of it. But as the bullet whizzed past, the hawk merely shrugged its feathers, turning to give us a dirty look.

"It's saying fuck you!" Marcos laughed.

I remembered the dusty bird of prey at the Kentucky Club, back in Ciudad Juárez.

回

AT PACIANO'S COMPOUND, Mary Lou and Imelda had swept out an empty upstairs room, where they had kindly strung a blue-rope hammock for me to sleep in. The walls were of unfinished brick and cinder block, and large windows presented grand views of the valley and mountains. Sinking into a beat-up old car seat outside, I looked up at a huge thunderhead boiling above the village. Following a massive clap of applause, sheets of rain suddenly dropped like stage curtains. I slipped inside and watched the storm from a window, inhaling the fresh scent of water-dampened earth as mists slithered up ridges dotted with agave plots.

The torrent soon slowed to a drizzle, and the community came alive as soaked men returned to their homes from toiling in fábricas and surrounding fields. Gray smoke plumes snaked up from kitchen fires, and a burro brayed for its dinner under a tall fruit-laden cactus by the path below. Nearby, an old man in a straw cowboy hat stood in his doorway, trimming his luxuriant white moustache with a large pair of scissors.

When the rain stopped, I went downstairs to join Paciano's family. It was early evening, and Mary Lou offered to take me on a tour of San Luis del Río before dinner. She led me through a web of narrow roads and paths, passing lime and orange trees, more towering cacti, and a medicinal Cuachalalà tree (*Amphipterygium adstringens*). A *carpintero* (woodpecker) was vigorously attacking the strangely wrinkled bark, which has been traditionally used as a treatment for cancer and malaria. Through an open window, I could see an armadillo hide tacked to a dark blue wall. Several other houses were shuttered and appeared devoid of life.

Mary Lou told me that about eight hundred inhabitants normally lived in the village—but perhaps only five hundred or so were around now, the others having left to work in the U.S. or elsewhere in Mexico. We didn't see many people until we came to the village church, which was packed for its evening service. The faithful were praying aloud in unison, between soft-spoken remarks by the priest. Farther ahead, kids were shooting hoops on a basketball court surrounded by purple-flowered jacaranda trees.

As we had walked through the village, I had heard various names announced through a scratchy loudspeaker. I hadn't understood why this was happening until an officious voice called out "Margarita Perez . . . Margarita Perez . . . Margarita Perez," and a frantic woman came rushing past us. Mary Lou explained that the announcements were for telephone calls. Cell phones didn't register in San Luis del Río, so most people shared a landline located at an office near the church. When a call came through, the name of the intended recipient was broadcast, and the caller was instructed to phone back in fifteen minutes. This would allow the summoned villager enough time to hustle from any part of the community to answer. Mary Lou said it usually took her about ten minutes to get there from home. "Sometimes I'm out of breath when I pick up the phone," she laughed. Life became a little easier for the family when they had a line installed in their home the following year.

There were TVs in the village, but to the best of my knowledge no Internet. Although it would have given everyone stronger ties to the outside world, and better access to information, I noticed that the isolated, "offline" residents were actually communicating with one another—chatting, laughing, and having leisurely and intimate conversations. This type of elemental human interaction is increasingly rare in the U.S., but in San Luis del Río, no one was glued to smartphone screens—all social networking was done face-to-face. As we walked along, each person we met greeted us with a polite "¡*Buenas tardes!*" that we heartily reciprocated. Another Oaxacan custom I enjoyed was the common practice of telling fellow diners "¡*Buen provecho!*" (Enjoy your meal!) as you passed them in a restaurant.

From the village center, Mary Lou led me down to the river. On the way, we passed a fábrica, where a boy was leading a plodding horse that was drawing a tahona over fresh-baked maguey hearts. On the riverbank, several women were conversing as they washed clothes on wide flat rocks. Frogs hopped in the shallows as I followed Mary Lou across a line of stepping-stones set in the flow. Downstream, a girl sat in the current, singing and shampooing her radiant hair. I was reminded of a scene in the film *The Night of the Iguana*, when Richard Burton—playing a disgraced reverend turned alcoholic tour guide—stops his bus on a bridge overlooking an idyllic riverside, where women merrily scrub their washing and children frolic.

"What are we stopping for?" asks a passenger.

"A moment of beauty," he answers. "A fleeting glimpse into the lost world of innocence."

That romanticized world—if there had ever really been one—was very lost by now.

Reaching the opposite side of the river, I followed Mary Lou a short way uphill for a view of San Luis del Río. Suddenly, the loudspeaker called "Paciano . . . Paciano . . . Paciano!" and Mary Lou sprinted off, nimbly making her way back across the torrent. The mezcal business was calling.

ᗉ

AS DARKNESS FELL over Paciano's house, I helped Mary Lou feed Cinnamon, the family donkey. Then Asunción served Marcos and me boiled rabbit in a spicy red broth, corn-and-chicken tamales, and glasses of warm orange soda. After supper, Asunción showed me her kitchen—a smoky outbuilding with a dirt floor. She had cooked the hearty and delicious meal on a basic wood-fired comal.

Imelda was heating a pot of water there, which she emptied into a large plastic basin. Her baby was feverish—a warm bath might help. Before she slipped the boy in, I was surprised to see Marcos open a bottle and add some mezcal. He explained that this was a traditional remedy; the combination of toasty water and spirits would be soothing. Indeed, the boy smiled up at Imelda as she gently cradled him in the bath. Then Marcos poured some mezcal into a plastic cup and handed it to me.

"Rub this all over before you go to sleep," he said. "It will help ease the pain from those maguey thorns."

I went upstairs, peeled off my clothes, and covered myself with mezcal. It seemed to melt into my skin, and I soon felt a powerful heat dulling my aching wounds. I climbed into the hammock, burrowed into my sleeping bag, and immediately drowned in a bottomless sleep. I had been out for only a few hours when a neighbor noisily saddled a donkey and trotted into the star-studded dark. For the rest of the night, I lay listening to roosters crowing, burros hee-hawing, and the breeze whispering softly through the pines.

As the morning sun glowed red and purple from behind the mountains, I found Mary Lou and her mother in the kitchen, kneading balls of corn-flour dough, pressing them into tortillas, and baking them on the comal. Imelda was grinding fresh pears in a blender for the baby to eat. Marcos appeared, and Asunción fried us a couple of *barbudos* (catfish) caught in the river. She served them with the tortillas and warm mugs of cinnamon-flavored *atole* (an indigenous corn-based drink).

After breakfast, Marcos and I piled into the truck to head down to the fábrica, where Paciano was waiting for us to help him fill his horno with agave. On the way through the village, we picked up Lionel and Rufino, then stopped at a tienda for gas. There weren't any gas pumps in San Luis del Río, so Marcos siphoned fuel from a jerry can to the tank. At the fábrica, we found Paciano standing at the edge of the pit oven, eyeing a pile of white-hot rocks lying on top of glowing embers.

The horno was ringed by some three hundred piña halves, waiting to be thrown in and baked. First, a magueyero pitchforked damp mash across the heated rocks to protect the agave from searing. Then, eight of us began heaving the plant hearts on top. They were unwieldy and hefty, with hard white insides and tough pineapple-like skins. By the time Paciano cautioned that the maguey sap could irritate my skin, it was too late: I had already gotten some on my forearms. A rash quickly developed and started to itch.

"Just put some mezcal on it," Paciano said. I did and it worked.

When the piña stack was about six feet tall, everyone stepped aside for Paciano and Marcos to cover it. The maguey would need to bake for four days, until its starchy flesh was perfectly caramelized into sugars, so the idea was to trap as much heat inside the pit oven as possible. Working quickly, the father and son quietly spoke to each other in their local dialect as they wrapped the agave pile with worn tarps and soot-covered petates. Then they shoveled dirt over the entire mound, laid down several logs to hold things in place, and sealed spots where smoke was leaking through with more earth.

When the horno was packed to their liking, there was one more pressing task to address. Something was wrong with the waterline between the fábrica's cooling tank and the river. It was blocked by an air bubble. Water is crucial for mezcal-making—aside from its use as a coolant, it contributes flavor when added to the mash during fermentation. The unique minerality of the water from a spring, creek, or well can be reason enough to situate a fábrica nearby.

I followed Paciano and Marcos upstream as they lifted the black plastic pipe, yard by yard, and jiggled it. It was impossible to hear anything over the roar of the flow, so the men communicated with hand signals. After much tinkering in the hot sun, they were at last able to clear the air bubble from the line. "*¡Mucho trabajo!*" said Paciano, wiping his brow. "*¡En todo momento!*" (A lot of work, all of the time.)

As we walked back to the fábrica, I asked him about a gold prize the Vida mezcal he distilled for Del Maguey had just won at a U.S. spirits-tasting event. "*¿Oro?*" he guffawed. "What gold? Where's *my* gold! When we have money, the dogs dance—without money, we dance like dogs."

🔲

I SPENT THE remainder of the day with Marcos and Lionel, gathering another necessity for mezcal production: firewood. The fuel is used for heating hornos and stills, as well as kitchen comals, the woodsmoke contributing to many serious health problems. Firewood was in such high demand in San Luis del Río that we had to venture far beyond the village outskirts to find any. Marcos drove the pickup deep into the mountains. We wound our way through a valley, crossed a bridge over an upper stretch of the river, and finally stopped at a thicket on top of a high ridge covered with agave fields.

Marcos filled a chainsaw with an oil-and-gas mix, and Lionel
and I followed him into the brush. As Marcos handily sawed up
dead tree trunks and branches, Lionel and I carried them back
to the truck and piled them in the bed. When it was half full, he
and I climbed into the back, leaned against the cab, and held on
for dear life as Marcos confidently navigated the twisty dirt road
back to the village, careening past plummeting drops.

We unloaded some of the wood at Paciano's compound,
where Mary Lou and her mother sat side by side in a hammock,
crocheting colorful blouses to sell on market day. Asunción
offered us cool watermelon slices and round, brown *chicozapote*
fruits, inside of each a big black seed surrounded by yellow-
green, sweet-and-sour flesh.

Our next chore was delivering the remaining wood to the
fábrica. First, we stopped at another tiendita to buy a couple of
cases of ice-cold Coronitas. We came upon Rufino alongside the
road, and he climbed into the truck with a battered guitar. It was
dusk when we finally arrived at the stills. An older magueyero,
Ignacio "Nacho" Ortiz, was manning them, a felt hat pulled low
over his seasoned face. He told me that he had grown up in the
village and had been making mezcal there for sixty years, since
he was fifteen. His teenage son, Abraham, was stoking one of
the alembique's fires. Another magueyero lay sprawled in a hammock, dully leafing through pornography crudely published on
black-and-white newsprint.

Using a flashlight, Marcos checked the horno for escaping
smoke, shoveling dirt over telltale cracks. Frogs bellowed from

biological sense. Still, as Vanderbilt writes, to "acquire a 'conditioned taste aversion,' a visceral dislike of a food, one must generally vomit after consuming it." I had definitely done that after drinking lousy, industrially manufactured mezcal in Baltimore and Ciudad Juárez. Those versions of the spirit also occupied a peculiar niche. Everything about them looked bad, but I had still wanted to drink them.

Now that I was older and presumably wiser—and with that "conditioned taste aversion" firmly in place—why was I still crazy about mezcal, even if it was for a clearly superior version of the spirit to the ones I had swilled when younger and dumber? "All tastes are, in essence, 'acquired tastes,'" writes Vanderbilt. "Flavor conditioning helps us to like or dislike flavors." The more we become assimilated to new tastes that meet our expectations, the better we like them. When I was a kid, I refused to eat mushrooms because of their flavor and texture; now I forage for mouthwatering *Boletus edulis* (porcinis) in the local mountains. Vanderbilt uses coffee as an example. "Tell people a coffee is bitter," he writes, "and they will think it is more bitter than if you had not told them. The opposite can happen as well, with our brains, neuroscientists have suggested, actually 'suppressing' our response to the bitter when we are not told to expect it."

My expectations for what the Luises' mezcal would taste like began with my picking up Del Maguey's beautifully packaged bottle in Santa Fe, and reading the alluring label that evocatively described its contents. Everything about it appealed to me—not only the tasting notes, but the exotic and adventurous quality, too—even though my negative feelings about mezcal were quite strong up to that point. "When our expectations are violated," writes Vanderbilt, "interesting things happen." I bought the spirit, sipped it, liked it, then loved it the more I drank it, and realized that mezcal could be something entirely different from what I had previously thought. My perception of the drink underwent such a readjustment that now I was writing a book about it—and did I like the drink even more because I wanted that book to succeed? It's hard to say.

Another reason I liked the Luises' mezcal much more than the ones I had tried until then was that it smelled better. Its tantalizing aromas sparked all sorts of pleasant olfactory sensations when I inhaled them and took me to a broad spectrum of places—which was fun. Likewise, I couldn't imagine my sister and brother-in-law, both enthusiastic oenophiles, not sniffing their favorite glasses of wine. "Here is that thing," writes Vanderbilt, "that is so easy to forget yet never fails to startle when we experience it firsthand: Most of the action when we are tasting something comes from the nose." Without the smell of coffee, would we still enjoy its bitter taste? In fact, we often use sweeteners and dairy products to cover it up. But good scents can lead to good feelings, too—realtors use the aroma of freshly baked cookies to sell homes; coffee gives us a lift.

Obviously, one of the basic selling points for mezcal is that it contains alcohol. The drug, like exercise, stimulates the release of feel-good endorphins. I got high from drinking it—a pleasing reward for my brain. This is the major reason why we enjoy consuming alcoholic beverages—until we drink too much. But I knew that sometimes I drank mezcal not just to feel good, but to escape my current reality. Reading neurologist Oliver Sacks's book *Hallucinations*, I was relieved to discover that I was merely satisfying a fundamental biological requirement.

"To live on a day-to-day basis is insufficient for human beings," he writes. "We need to transcend, transport, escape; we need meaning, understanding, and explanation." And, in order to fulfill such needs, "We seek a holiday from our inner and outer restrictions, a more intense sense of the here and now, the beauty and value of the world we live in." Of course, there can be a dark side to a mezcal-induced "holiday" too. In his essay "Why Do Men Stupify Themselves?" Leo Tolstoy writes, "When a man is sober he is ashamed of what seems all right when he is drunk. In these words we have the essential underlying cause prompting men to resort to stupefiers."

The satisfaction I received from sipping mezcal had deep roots. The Iroquois crafted an alcoholic drink from maple syrup, rice liquors were distilled in ancient Asia, red algae was turned into a Siberian spirit, and beer and wine were made by pharaonic Egyptians. Prehistoric cave paintings depict hunter-gatherers collecting honey, possibly for fermentation into a type of mead. In his book *Intoxication*, psycho-pharmacologist Ronald K. Siegel notes that "beer, known to early Neolithic agriculturists, is probably the oldest alcoholic drink," and that the "earliest appearance" of distilled spirits was in "ninth-century Arabia."

Siegel describes an ongoing thirst for alcohol by other animals, too. He cites a 1545 trial in the French village of St. Julien, when a legal complaint was filed against drunken insects getting hooked on the local grapes. He also mentions an unruly incident in West Bengal, when "a herd of 150 elephants broke into an illegal still and drank copious quantities of the moonshine mash." He provides many other examples of enthusiastic animal drinkers—including parrots, chimpanzees, hamsters, and raccoons. By drinking mezcal, I realized, I was participating in a universal animal act of transcending reality via intoxication. So I was making, I felt, a connection with nature.

But when I drank the spirit in Mexico, I was also adding to a lengthy history of alcohol consumption there. Before the arrival of the Spanish, the drug was revered as a powerful intoxicant, and its use was largely reserved for ceremonial purposes. When pulque, mezcal, beer, and other alcoholic drinks became more widely available during colonization, a pattern of heavy, regular binge drinking developed that persists today. As Tim Mitchell writes in his book *Intoxicated Identities: Alcohol's Power in Mexican History and Culture*, "The Spanish word for a binge— *borrachera*—encapsulates its episodic nature, its status as a special event. The borrachera patterns that concern epidemiologists were already well established by the end of the eighteenth century. Heavy drinking was promoted by powerful vested interests, both rural and urban."

Recent studies have shown that alcohol can cause cancer of the liver, breast, colon, larynx, esophagus, oropharynx, and rectum, and that heavy drinkers are at the highest risk for contracting these diseases. Cirrhosis is also a significant health problem in Mexico, particularly among males. "Alcoholism and Spanish imperialism went hand in hand," writes Mitchell. "But only because alcohol possessed a number of subversive powers, for the indigenes, that the colonizers did not anticipate: the power to unleash ecstatic self-experiencing; the power to assuage or numb distress of all kinds; the power to help people cope with loss of life from disease and exploitation, perhaps to keep survivors from sliding into full-blown dissociation; and, most striking of all, the power to serve as a continuing template for the emergence of new cognitions, new identities, and rekindled hopes for the new redress of grievances. It seems likely that Mexican 'problem drinking' began as *solution* drinking."

⧉

ONE MORNING I rode out to Santo Domingo Albarradas with Arturo. We began our journey by colectivo, one of the inexpensive shared taxis by which I usually traveled in Oaxaca, unless I was taking a bus or hitching a ride. Nearly always four-door Nissan sedans, colectivos were Arturo's principal mode of transport for his regular rounds to Del Maguey's maestros mezcaleros. Three customers usually sit abreast in the back, and two others often share the front passenger seat. The taxis can also be hired by a single rider, but the driver will often charge more.

Colectivo companies typically have specific routes, and each taxi is inscribed with the name of its final destination and painted with identifying colored stripes. Drivers shuttle between towns and villages that are often several hours apart, maximizing profits by cruising at breakneck speeds. It's a tough way to make a living: I was never charged more than a few dollars per trip—perhaps covering my share of the gas. And accidents are all too common. The more saints I saw on a driver's dashboard, the warier I became.

I met up with Arturo at dawn in Oaxaca de Juárez, in a dusty side yard not far from Abastos Market. We cracked pistachios and waited for enough passengers to fill the other seats in a two-saint colectivo headed for Ayutla. The town is located several hours south in the remote, mountainous Mixe region, but we needed to go only as far as the village of Santa María Albarradas, where a Luis family member would meet us.

Finally, we squeezed into a backseat with a rotund farmer. Then, a girl slipped in front with an elderly Mixe woman wearing the intricately woven costume and headdress of her people. The driver fired up a speedy salsa to set the pace. Even so, every passenger other than me fell asleep within minutes of setting off. Arturo's head snored against my shoulder, the farmer farted, and I took in the passing scenery as we retraced the circuitous route I had first taken with Ron many years before.

In Santa María Albarradas, Armando, the youngest member of the Luis family, picked us up in an immaculate white pickup. He was in his early twenties and wore a crisply creased cowboy hat, the beginnings of a moustache, and a T-shirt from Tommy's Mexican Restaurant in San Francisco, which read:

OUR TEQUILA BAR CAN KICK YOUR TEQUILA BAR'S ASS. As we slowly followed the dirt road through the mountains to Santo Domingo Albarradas, he cued a popular ballad on the stereo, "*Dos Botellas de Mezcal*." It was a lovelorn plea from a man to his sweetheart, asking her to leave a couple of bottles of the spirit on his grave, because he missed her so much that he would surely die of a hangover. Armando sang along.

The village looked just as I had remembered it—but without the rainy mists that had obscured the surrounding valleys before. I could now see how deeply the mountainsides plummeted below. We passed a school with a lively group of uniformed students out front. Then we continued past the whitewashed church, made our way through the village proper, and drove halfway down the great slope below it.

Armando parked the truck at the base of a footpath, and Arturo and I followed him a hundred yards up it, navigating a steep grade to the Luis fábrica. It occupied a thirty-foot-wide, 150-foot-long perch, surrounded by small plots of agave and corn. High up the mountainside above us, a massive butte, locally called "*piedra de zapato*" (shoe rock), jutted into the clear blue sky from alongside the village.

Juan, now in his late thirties, greeted us with glasses of warm orange soda. He and Armando were chronic gigglers—within minutes, their rippling chortles had us all laughing without knowing why. It was a good thing the brothers had strong senses of humor, because their fábrica wasn't in an easy spot for making mezcal. Everything had to be laboriously carried in and out by hand, or strapped to the backs of pack animals. But there was a reason for the location: a clear spring bubbled from the earth nearby. The water cooled the Luises' mezcal as it emerged from their single copper still and provided unique flavor elements to the spirit when added to the tinas during fermentation.

Their fábrica offered excellent views. A jacaranda tree bloomed purple farther down the hillside, where the road disappeared deep into the valley. It then crossed an unseen river before switchbacking up the opposite incline to a great cut across the facing escarpment. A big red truck was chugging along it to a bend around the mountain, looking like a child's toy in a diorama. To the east and west, verdant ridges undulated from the sides of the tree- and rock-covered pitch.

The Luises' simple setup consisted of a small milling arena with a tahona attached to a rig made of tree trunks, an open-sided adobe structure with a tin roof sheltering the single alembique, three wooden tinas, and an horno. At the edge of the fábrica's plot, four horses were hitched in the meager shade offered by a scraggly cluster of *guaje* trees. There were also a mango tree, a lime tree right next to the still, and a vegetable garden teeming with tomatoes and peppers below it. All of these surrounding plants could potentially contribute notes to the Luises' spirit.

The most important factors for making mezcal are the species of agave used, along with the altitude, soil, and microclimate where the plants were grown; the minerality of the water added to the mash in the fermentation process; and the airborne yeasts that convert the baked maguey's sugars and carbohydrates into alcohol. Although large-scale distilleries will control the fermentation process by adding specific yeasts to their mash, small-scale maestros mezcaleros traditionally allow their roasted maguey to gather yeasts that spread naturally through the atmosphere from nearby plants. For this reason, it's often thought that mezcals exhibit the flavors of a fábrica's botanical neighbors—the Luises' lime tree, for example.

As the yeasts go to town on the bagazo, like college kids at a keg party, they release gases that float to the top of a tina and bubble. During fermentation, you can hear the fizzing if you put your ear to a vat's wooden side. Maestros mezcaleros decide when it's time to distill partly by tasting the brown fermenting liquid, and partly by monitoring the appearance and sound of the bubbles. But yeast activity also increases temperature, another important factor. José Garcia Pacheco, an artisanal distiller from the village of Yogana, once explained the importance of fermentation temperature to me.

"For a good mezcal," he said, "one of the secrets is knowing the perfect time to add water to a tina. When the bagazo starts to get hot after two or three days, the tina is asking for water. Most of the increase in temperature happens overnight, and, at its peak, even if it's one in the morning, is when you have to add water. A lot of people don't care, but it makes all the difference to put it in at just the right moment."

Now that Arturo and I had arrived at the Luises' fábrica, there was work to be done: over two hundred massive, freshly halved piñas were arranged in a ring around the horno, ready to be heaved in and baked. They were so big they looked like dinosaur snacks. But first, each part needed to be weighed and recorded. Juan and Armando lugged an unwieldy metal scale from the fábrica to the pit oven. Then, as Arturo took careful notes in a ledger, the brothers hoisted the agave on and off the scale. This was very demanding but the easiest task they'd had in a while—Armando explained that they had brought all of the maguey to the fábrica by horseback from fields several kilometers away: sixty-eight round-trips in five days.

The weighing complete, Arturo announced that the heaviest piña (measured when the brothers held its two halves together) was an impressive 137.55 kilos (303.24 pounds). Collectively, all of the agave weighed 8,178.65 kilos (18,030.83 pounds). To celebrate, we retreated to the shade of the fábrica, where Juan opened an old soda bottle of their mezcal. He rinsed out a plastic cup in the alembique's cooling tank, then poured some of the spirit for all of us to share. I couldn't believe it. Here I was at the very source of the fascinating drink that had first brought me to the village long ago—sipping it not only in the fábrica where it had been distilled, but with the family who had crafted it. It was a perfect moment . . . except something tasted different.

"¿Es su espadín mezcal?" I asked uncertainly.

"¡No, Pueblo Grande! Es mezcal tobalá!"

They made a small batch each year with wild agaves from the surrounding hills.

"Es un afrodisíaco," Arturo assured me.

The brothers chortled, and we drank some more. The tobalá was exquisite. If anyone puts dos botellas de mezcal on my grave, I thought, I want them both filled with this one.

ꔰ

I RETURNED TO Santo Domingo Albarradas on my own a few days later, arriving at the family compound just in time to meet Juan and Armando's father, Espiridion, as he and Juan were saddling a pair of horses. The men were about to ride the animals down the valley and collect loads of firewood for the family comal.

Espiridion was around seventy, and he had the same infectious laugh as his sons. He told me there had been three generations of maestros mezcaleros before him, and that he now left most of the mezcal-making to Juan and Armando. Until only a few decades before, he said, when Santo Domingo Albarradas had been far more isolated, his family had always distilled their mezcals in clay alembiques. Espiridion shared that he had never imagined anyone beyond the community drinking his spirits, and that he was proud of their entirely local ingredients.

"¡Nuestro mezcal es legítimo mezcal!" he exclaimed. "¡Es puro, puro mezcal!"

Espiridion saddled up another horse so I could ride with him and Juan. The saddles were crudely fashioned from wood and burlap, and lacked stirrups. I clumsily climbed onto my mount, Soldado, from a low rock ledge, as the father and son flew into their saddles with acrobatic ease. As we trotted from the village, I was relieved to find Soldado surefooted as we quickly made our way along a twisting trail with sickening cliffside drops. On the opposite mountainside, a battered school bus was grumbling up the switchback, its muffler echoing through the valley.

"*La banda*," said Juan. "They're going to the next village to play at their fiesta."

We continued riding past parcels of cultivated agave, as well as many wild tobalá magueys, growing in the shelter of scrubby oak trees. At one point, Espiridion reined in his horse and signaled for us to halt. We dismounted, and he took me through several verdant rows of thriving espadín agaves. He had planted the magueys himself, he said, tending them through the years.

"Look," said Espiridion, proudly stroking a plant's long green leaves like the shoulders of an old friend. "*¿Bonita, no?*"

Remounting the horses, we followed the trail farther into the narrowing valley. Finally, we came to a clearing, where Espiridion and Juan had heaped a pile of dead limbs and branches they had gathered from a surrounding thicket. We tied the wood into six hefty bundles, strapping two to the back of each horse.

"This will be enough wood for a month of tortillas," Juan called over his shoulder as we led the loaded animals single file to the village.

▣

ON MY NEXT visit to Santo Domingo Albarradas a few days later, one of Espiridion's many daughters, Esther, served some of those tortillas to both me and Armando for breakfast. Armando had started his day at 5:00 AM, his current community *servicios* requiring him to man the village corn grinder early enough for the local women to make tortillas for their families.

In addition to helping her mother with the consuming daily chores of women in traditional Zapotec households, Esther operated a dry-goods tiendita by the road at the edge of their compound. I bought a toothbrush from her, since I would be staying the night. Juan and Armando had invited me to spend twenty-four hours in the fábrica while they showed me how they crafted their mezcal.

I grabbed my sleeping bag and followed Armando down the steep trail to the Luises' distillery. The valley was filled with acrid smoke that had blown in from forest fires burning in faraway mountains, the air so hazy it appeared almost white. We found Juan manning the alembique. The brothers were just beginning five around-the-clock days of distilling three tinas of fermented espadín mash for a batch of the Santo Domingo Albarradas mezcal that Del Maguey regularly purchased from them in bulk.

Shishe was already dribbling from a copper pipe into a twenty-liter plastic jerry can. This would later be combined with the cuerpo and cola, to create a final mezcal with an ABV of 49.2 percent. Each run would make up the contents of about two of the containers. Distilling was at least a two-person job for the Luis setup, requiring a series of continuously repeated steps. First, one of the brothers would clamber over a tina side, step into its fermented caramel-colored stew, and scoop up five-gallon bucketfuls of mash for the other brother and me to slosh into the still. Then, when the alembique was loaded to the brim, either Juan or Armando would kneel atop the structure containing its base, form a ring of masa around the edge of the still's mouth, and reattach the copper sombrero with U-shaped clips. After that, the tubo was replaced, and its joints were covered with tightly fastened cloth strips. Finally, the fire was stoked with fresh wood. Between each batch, the still was rinsed out with spring water.

At mid-morning, by which time the alembique had been humming along for an hour or so, Juan held a clay bowl under its warm trickle of shishe, filled it to the brim, and passed it around. Although the drink wasn't a fully developed mezcal, it already exhibited some eloquence. "Wowww," said Juan, using one of the few English words he knew. We shared three or four more bowls in quick succession. Slipping into a collective torpor, we slumped against the adobe walls of the fábrica. To perk us up, Juan mixed *refrescos* of spring water, sugar, and limes squeezed from the tree outside.

Every now and then, someone would appear on the nearby path. A farmer stopped by for a *copa* (cup), sprinkling a few drops on the ground as an offering before he drank. A woman waved hello with her machete on the way down the mountain to tend a field. An elderly couple slowly trudged uphill from the river, leading a horse laden with firewood they had gathered from its banks. As the day grew hotter, a kettle of *zopilotes* (vultures) circled above, their shadows sweeping across us like a second hand on a clock.

In mid-afternoon, Esther came down the steep path from the village, carrying our comida in plastic pails. They contained rice, black beans, jalapeño peppers, sliced carrots, and a warm stack of tortillas wrapped in an embroidered napkin. For a table, we laid a plank across two crates. As Armando, Juan, and I ate, Esther harvested limes and tomatoes from the garden, piling them into her apron. As she left the fábrica to go home, she offered me a sprig of a pungent herb she had picked. It tasted minty, and for a moment it lifted me from the haze.

Later, when Armando hiked down the mountain to feed and water the family's horses and bulls, it was my turn to help change out the still. Juan kept an eye on me as I gingerly removed the tubo, climbed on top of the alembique, lifted away the sombrero, and began emptying the bagazo from inside with a pitchfork. Then we flushed it with fresh water, and Juan hopped into a tina, wearing a straw hat to protect him from the sun. He passed me dripping buckets of liquid and mash, which I poured into the alembique, and then I used wet masa to make a new seal for the sombrero.

Before adding more wood to the fire, Juan spread a tortilla across the coals and spooned some refried beans on top, making us a crispy tlayuda to snack on. When Armando returned later on, the three of us ate a light dinner of *anamilitos* (animal crackers) dumped in bowls of weak coffee. We unrolled three petates on the hard ground to sleep on. But there was very little shut-eye to be had—now that the copper still was consistently hot, each batch was taking only a couple of hours to complete.

Because there was no electricity, every time we emptied and refilled the alembique, the brothers propped up burning sticks to illuminate our work. Their orange glow silhouetted whoever was standing over the still with the pitchfork, making him look like a blacksmith working a forge. At some point in the wee hours, I was given a new duty: scooping the mash from a tina. Rather than ruin the only set of clothes I had brought with me, I stripped to my *ropa interior* (underwear) before climbing into the barrel. Juan and Armando found this hilarious, roaring with laughter as I stood waist-deep in the café-au-lait-colored bagazo. They were more modest, and always climbed into the tinas fully clothed. When the next batch of shishe emerged, Juan tasted it and made a pretend sad face.

"Wowww," he joked. "*¡Sabor de Pueblo Grande desnudo!*" I felt like the Huaxtec chieftain Ron had told me about who had bared all after drinking too much pulque.

By the time it was my turn to keep watch, the cool night air had settled the smoky haze, stars were out in the thousands, and a new moon had formed a thin orange smile. Fireflies twinkled through cornstalks, a breeze swept through the lime tree, and a gurgle of springwater chilled the still, its fire crackling to a chorus of snores.

At dawn, I was startled awake by exploding fireworks overhead, fired from the village to announce a celebration. At the same time, the alembique began sputtering at the edge of its sombrero. Juan jumped up from his petate and quickly added daubs of wet masa to seal the leak. Then, with a weary yawn, he began his day by scrubbing his clothes on a flat rock. Armando was long gone, having already hiked uphill for his corn-grinding chores. As the sun peeked over the mountains, I rolled up the petates, tied them with string, and laid them in a corner of the fábrica. After hanging his laundry out to dry, Juan set a pot of tomato-and-scrambled-egg soup in the fire. We devoured it with beans and tortillas. Then we enjoyed a sip of the family's espadín mezcal.

"What makes yours taste so good?" I asked Juan.

"*Mis manos*," he shrugged, showing me his hands.

ONE EVENING SOON after, I stopped by Mezcaloteca, a tasting room I had heard about in Oaxaca de Juárez. It was on Calle Reforma, a cobblestoned thoroughfare in the Centro Histórico. Across the street, a high wall surrounded the Santo Domingo Cultural Center's expansive Jardín Etnobotánico (ethnobotanical garden). More than a thousand endemic plants were growing there, among them a selection of magueys.

Mezcaloteca was one of few spots in the world where a significant selection of Mexico's diverse agave flavors—and their innumerable combinations—could be sampled in one spot. Behind the polished wooden bar, shelves were neatly arranged with dozens of handsomely labeled wine bottles filled with small-batch maguey distillates, many of them uncertified, that had been sourced from all over Mexico. For decoration, there was a miniature copper alembique, a large *grabado* (woodblock print) of Oaxacan-born President Porfirio Díaz, and dried quiote blossoms propped about. Though the place looked as if it had been there forever, it had opened the year before.

The young proprietors, Marco Ochoa and Silvia Philion, had previously worked in marketing and advertising in Mexico City.

Marco was descended from five generations of mezcal distillers in San Antonio Mangoli, a tiny farming community three hours south of Oaxaca de Juárez. He and Silvia were eager to give traditionally crafted Mexican spirits the respect they thought was long overdue. Their approach was radically different from that of a typical Oaxacan mezcal bodega, where gyrating girls in skimpy outfits were often stationed out front, pushing colorful crema shots on tourists. Instead, the tasting room's atmosphere was subdued, even reverential, as aficionados quietly sipped from their jícaras, sampling Mexico via their taste buds and comparing mezcal flavors in earnest whispers.

Fittingly, the establishment's name was a fusion of mezcal and *biblioteca* (library). Each bottle was labeled with extensive details that included the name of the producer, the village and region where the spirit had been distilled, the ABV, and the maguey species used—as well as the size of the batch, the type of alembique, the kind of horno, the mashing method, the style of tina, and so forth. Such transparency is unusual: few mezcal brands even identify the maestros mezcaleros who make their spirits on their bottle labels. But Marco and Silvia wanted that to change. They were also enthusiastic educators. While charging patrons for copas and botellas of their offerings was their business (and they now have a brand, Mezcalosfera, available in the U.S.), they freely shared their extensive knowledge—drawing on an assortment of maps, charts, and books to introduce the vast mezcal world to anyone interested.

Although mezcal bars have opened in many cities abroad, none outside Mexico can offer anything close to the arcane selection on hand at Mezcaloteca, because they are able to sell only the comparatively few certified mezcals that can be legally exported from the country. The tasting room gave an idea of how things might be different for consumers abroad, if maestros mezcaleros throughout all of the mezcal-producing regions in Mexico were able to bottle, market, and export their small-batch spirits. Similar to a wine bar, Mezcaloteca was a place where you could learn about producers, their drinks, and methods, while beginning to understand which agaves you preferred for mezcal—like grapes.

The choices seemed infinite. Stepping up to the bar, Silvia poured me a jícara of wild-grown *serrano* (*Agave americana*). "This one tastes like cheese and leather," she noted, and, bizarrely and wonderfully, it did. Then Marco brought over a bottle of wild *cenizo* (*Agave durangensis*), and pineapples and blackberries tap-danced through my mouth. Next I tried a wild *tobaxiche* (*Agave karwinskii*), then a tepeztate, an arroqueño, a *mexicano* (*Agave rhodacantha*), a wild-grown espadín, and a hybrid of *madrecuixe* (*A. karwinskii*) and *bicuixe* (also *A. karwinskii*), followed by several more spirits fashioned from other combinations of agaves silvestres.

As the *degustación* (tasting) went late into the night, Marco and Silvia explained that, similar to vintners, maestros mezcaleros employ techniques tested over generations of working with agave.

All steps in the distillation process, and the instruments used along the way, can affect the unique flavors and potency of an individual mezcal. Agave mashed with oak clubs in a hollowed-out tree trunk, for example, can make a mezcal taste different from one distilled with maguey that's been ground in a metal machine. A bagazo fermented in a cowhide draped over wooden supports may supply notes absent in one developed in a stainless steel vat or a plastic drum.

In my mezcal explorations so far, I had mostly encountered espadín agaves and the spirits crafted from them. But after tasting the shape-shifting pops of flavor delivered by other types of magueys that evening, I was curious to see more species in person.

"Why don't you visit my family's rancho?" suggested Marco, walking me to the door. "They grow many different agaves there for their mezcal."

"I will!"

"*Bueno*. My cousin Ramiro will show you around."

॒

A FEW DAYS later, I extricated myself from a jam-packed minibus in Miahuatlán. Marco's cousin, Ramiro Cortés, picked me up in a Suburban, then drove me out to the family's ranch four miles away in San Antonio Mangoli. Ramiro was in his early thirties, curly haired and shy. Every now and then, as the parched hills rolled past us, he would gesture at an agave growing along the road. At one point, he showed me an eight-foot-tall *cuixe*

(*A. karwinskii*). It looked like a cross between an agave and a palm, the plant's narrow trunk topped by a spiky crown.

Ramiro explained that cuixe, which only grows wild, takes fifteen years to mature, unlike its wider-leafed cousin, madrecuixe, which can be cultivated and is typically harvested after ten years. He said that an increasing interest in mezcals made with agaves silvestres was creating pressure on the plants. Wild magueys were being harvested for distillation without a long-range strategy, willy-nilly, when instead careful planning was needed to sustain them, beginning with responsible management of the ones still left.

As we drove through the 125-acre property owned by his family, Ramiro pointed out some of the thirty thousand magueys they were growing for mezcal, many of them wild ones that they were "tending." Out the window, I could see more cuixe, as well as arroqueño, *maguey de coyote* (*A. Americana var. oaxacensis*), tepeztate, madrecuixe, espadín, mexicano, and *verde* (*A. salmiana subsp. crassispina*).

Ramiro told me that, although his family considered itself to be stewards of maguey, mezcal was its livelihood—a delicate balance. For 140 years, Rancho Mongoli's mezcaleros had followed an annual cycle of distilling from February to July, spending the rest of the year tending the agave and farming squash, corn, and beans. The family also brewed pulque and harvested wild tobalá from the nearby mountains. "We grow crops to eat, and make mezcal for money," said Ramiro.

We pulled up to the fábrica, set next to a cluster of adobe houses on a rocky ridge overlooking a small valley. Around us were horses, mules, ducks, chickens, a pair of lemon-lime parakeets in a wire cage, and an enormous pig tied to a tree. The voices of goatherds echoed from the riverbanks below, and I could see a little church with a red dome and two turrets on a distant crest and cuixe- and cacti-speckled slopes rippling into the beyond.

Cicadas were singing their slow-rising song, and a hot wind rustled a tree where three dogs—Pirata, Tucán, and Mezcalito— were napping together in the shade. Near them, a quiote had blasted eighteen feet up from the center of a broad-leafed pulque agave. Ramiro told me they would eventually transplant its "*bulbilos*" (asexually produced flower-clones genetically identical to the parent plant), as they already had done with its "*hijuelos*" (root-produced sucker-clones, also genetically identical to the parent plant).

In the milling arena, Ramiro's father, Felipe, was driving a pair of massive bulls that were pulling a hefty tahona over baked madrecuixe piñas. As Felipe commanded the toros with guttural sounds, another of his sons, Ajeo, stood at the center, raking the mash left in the team's wake as it slowly circled past. From a pile to the side, Ramiro picked up a caramelized chunk of a long madrecuixe heart. He hacked off a morsel of the bee-covered flesh and offered it to me to sample. It was like gooey, fibrous candy, tasting smoky-sweet.

Just down the ridge stood four weathered tinas, lurching from age. One of them contained madrecuixe bagazo that had been fermenting for several days. Ramiro's uncle, Margarito, had just finished emptying a copper still inside a redbrick structure nearby. His son, Levi, clambered into the vat and began filling raffia sacks with mash. He passed each one up to another magueyero, who then hoisted it over to the alembique and emptied it into its mouth.

Once the still was refilled, reassembled, and chugging away, Margarito offered me a jícara of mezcal. He had distilled the spirit from madrecuixe, and infused it with a handful of cacao beans in its second distillation. He watched me intently as I tasted breathy hints of chocolate. As I sipped more of his uncommon mezcal, it struck me that creating agave spirits isn't a skill one walks into—it's a multidimensional process one has to fully live with to understand.

曰

THE MOST LEGENDARY wild maguey used for mezcal-making is tobalá. Although cultivating *A. potatorum* should be done to a much greater degree in order to preserve the species, the plant's flavor is commonly considered best when collected from its natural mountain habitat. It seems to enjoy the company of scrub oaks on high rocky slopes.

One day, I paid a visit to Del Maguey's secret tobalá-mezcal producer, whom I'll call Eugenio Ramírez. Eugenio was a master distiller descended from three generations of mezcaleros, and he had offered to let me come along with him to harvest wild tobalá maguey in the mountains. He lived in a village at around fifty-five hundred feet near Santo Domingo Albarradas, where he shared a simple adobe home with one of his sisters. I found him there at their kitchen table, waving flies away from a basket of breakfast rolls and watching the morning show *Hoy* (Today) on a little TV. He was a slight, soft-spoken man in his early sixties, who always wore a plaid cowboy shirt and huaraches. Spirits pundits lauded his tobalá mezcal as a near-magical drink, and it sold for around $120 a bottle in the U.S.

We drank mugs of hot chocolate, dunking rolls into them. The kitchen had a tin roof, unfinished walls, and a dirt floor. On the table was a clay vase of purple, orange, and yellow flowers. A carved wooden cross hung above a doorway, and an altar was plastered with religious imagery culled from expired calendars. Eugenio's sister ran a tiendita next door, where she sold such basic necessities as eggs, bread, milk, beans, and matches. Every now and then, a face would appear at the kitchen door, and she would step out to assist.

At one point, she returned with a slender young magueyero named Leo, whom Eugenio and I followed through a flower-and-herb garden and past an orange metal gate set in the compound wall. Leo's muscular brother, Ricardo, was waiting in the road outside with five burros, a horse, and a mule. He wore a tight T-shirt with mirrored silhouettes of the curvy, reclining woman I had seen on semitruck mud flaps. Both men carried machetes in leather holsters and wore colorfully striped cloth satchels over their shoulders. Leo handed me a straw sombrero to protect me from the high-altitude sun, and we all waved goodbye to Eugenio's sister and started up a steep red-shale track.

Leo's stocky black dog, Oso, raced alongside us as our route arced over the village below, a green-and-blue municipio and red-and-white church rising from its center. An enormous ridge arched ahead of us, reminiscent of Sugarloaf Mountain in Rio de Janeiro, and Leo said it was a *monte sagrado* (sacred mountain). Tall agave quiotes bearing crowns of bright-yellow flowers swayed above an orange cliff high on its side.

The men kept the team going at a brisk pace. Not long after leaving the community behind, we came to a bend in the road where a cool brook coursed through gray boulders. We stopped so the animals could drink. Then we left the track, following a path up into a pine grove. There we passed a small group of people from the community, who were clearing brush from the bases of saplings for a reforestation project.

Ascending higher, we arrived at a woodland of short, twisty oaks dripping with Spanish moss and bromeliads, where Oso darted among the trunks. As we crossed a ridge, a great valley opened beyond us, with a pair of mountains looming in the distance. We descended a short way into the expanse, and I soon began noticing squat tobalá magueys sheltered here and there beneath the oak branches. They were tiny in comparison to espadín, with wide, spike-edged pencas extending from reddish soil littered with curiously shaped hunks of flinty-gray rock.

As the brothers tied the pack animals to some trees, I followed Eugenio through the dappled forest; he whistled as he crunched his huaraches over leaf-covered animal trails. We passed several stacks of basketball-sized piñas, which he and the magueyeros had left for the men to pick up later. Stopping at a mature tobalá maguey, Eugenio pantomimed how he could neatly separate the plant from the earth with his machete, hack off its leaves, and leave them on the ground to rot. But he said he would allow this one to send up its quiote and flower, which, he explained, usually happened in autumn.

Eugenio told me that the species propagates through seeds, and is pollinated at night by bats. He said his community had appointed him guardian of the wild agaves, which require careful management to ensure their survival. They are fast becoming an endangered and precious resource as international demand for tobalá mezcal increases. He told me he paid the village twenty pesos per piña and distilled mezcal for its annual fiesta in addition to the batches he made for Del Maguey. The plants were so small that I could see how it could require an enormous number of them to make much mezcal. And it was difficult to know how sustainable Eugenio's practices actually were.

I helped the brothers carry the hearts, one by one, through the forest and heap them beside the pack animals. There were so many piles scattered about the slopes that I couldn't see how the men kept track of them all. But they knew the land well. Leo used special hand signals to communicate with Ricardo, who was hard of hearing, as the men nimbly leaped between rocky ledges.

Stopping for a break, Eugenio opened a package of sugary pink-and-white cookies, and we shared them with a liter of warm orange soda. Then we loaded some of the agave in rope-net sacks, and the magueyeros strapped them and the remaining loose piñas to the backs of the team with cord. When all eighty-five hearts were securely loaded and balanced, we began to descend. A brisk wind rose up and beat our faces with grit.

Below a tree near the dirt road we had taken out of the village, we unloaded the agave for a truck to retrieve later. The brothers rewarded the animals with a snack of dried corncobs. Then we squatted in the shade and passed around a simple comida of cold tortillas with a can of chipotle peppers, a moist chunk of queso blanco, and a plastic container of fried eggs and beans. Afterward, it was time to head back up the mountain again to fetch another load of wild maguey.

As we approached the village, three of the burros broke loose and bolted downhill. Ricardo and Leo raced after them and disappeared. I continued on with Eugenio and together we brought the remaining animals to a paddock. As he fed and watered them, I listened to a mournful clarinet solo broadcast through the community's crackly public speaker. Back at the house, Eugenio's sister served us cool brown refrescos of pureed squash to drink. Then Eugenio turned on the TV, settled himself in his chair, and slipped into a saucy *telenovela*.

回

WHEN I RETURNED to Eugenio's village several days later, there were hundreds of tobalá piñas stacked around the edge of his six-foot-deep, twelve-foot-wide, rock-walled horno—all ready to be baked. Several yards away, his red-painted fábrica was tucked into a lush hollow, below a two-lane blacktop at the village's edge. On either side of the road above us were shops selling candy, cigarettes, sodas, Coronitas, and the ubiquitous junk food peddled by the Mexican conglomerate Bimbo.

Eugenio, Leo, and Roberto were waiting by the pit oven with three magueyeros: Wenceslas, Malecio, and Malecio's teenage son, Crispin. Joking and working quickly, the men began piling leafy dead branches around a wooden pole erected in the horno's center. Then they added dried cane, lengths of firewood, and smooth gray stones. Leo used a machete to split a fat stick into several skinny shards. After drawing up the pole from the middle of the pile, he lit the splintered lengths of wood and dropped them into the narrow hole left behind. He then inserted a skinny tree branch and stirred it until a plume of smoke emerged. We added more rocks to the heap before stepping away to allow Eugenio to place the last few as he wished.

Half an hour later, a dense column of smoke was pouring from the pit oven. We sat on our heels in the shade of a mango tree, watching the flaming tongues lick up from below the stones. As the fire settled, we walked up to the road, where Eugenio, Wenceslas, and I climbed into Malecio's ancient black Dodge Dart. The men wanted to give me a tour of their village, but the car was out of gas. Malecio stepped into one of the tienditas and returned with a fuel-filled plastic jug.

The car sputtered uphill, following steep red-dirt roads. Bougainvillea blossomed red alongside us, and an empty potato-chip bag skittered ahead in a gust. Eugenio and I got out at his home, where his sister fed us spinach soup and bowls of fried egg and squash. While a chicken pecked at our tortilla crumbs on the earthen floor, I tried to distract Eugenio from a peculiar TV show involving a man wearing a red tartan cape and a red Sherlock Holmes hat who was laying green lettuce over a red spaghetti pile. But Eugenio, I had already learned, was a man of few words.

"What do you enjoy about making tobalá mezcal?" I asked him.

"Drinking it! It's *suave* (smooth), it's *rico* (tasty)—I like it!"

"What makes yours different from others?"

"Mine's better because I know how to make it well and I only use wild maguey. Cultivated tobalá tastes different because the magueys aren't growing where they want to—in the forest under the trees."

When the TV show ended, Eugenio brought me to a dark shed, where he kept plastic barrels of mezcals made with tobalá, espadín, and wild-grown tepeztate agaves. He unscrewed the top of a barrel containing tobalá mezcal, sucked some of the spirit into a venencia, and released it into a jícara.

"Look at my perlas," he said. "See how pretty they are?"

Eugenio's bubbles were somewhat large, and he told me that his mezcal's ABV was around 45 percent. The cordón glistened in the sharp ray of sunlight piercing the tin roof. I took a sip, imagining myself transported back to the mountain grove where we had collected the piñas. As I sipped some more of the drink, Eugenio watched me with a playful sparkle in his eye. Then, before we started walking back to his fábrica, he poured some of the mezcal into a half-liter water bottle and sold it to me for 120 pesos—just about ten bucks.

ㄹ

I FOLLOWED EUGENIO downhill through the village, passing a little cemetery with crosses listing over bouquets of plastic flowers. From a position high on an exterior wall of the village church, a soulful face carved in red sandstone watched us. Through the open door of the church, I could see a statue of the virgin. She was dressed in white, with strings of orange and red lights blinking around her. From deep in the apse, behind the effigy, a Cyclops-sized, yellow-and-blue stained-glass eye stared straight through me. A dog was barking in the distance, and a buzzard circled high overhead.

Back at Eugenio's horno, the smoke had died down and the gray rocks were glowing white, though some were still red-hot. Leo and Roberto appeared and tossed a few more stones on the pile. One of the rocks popped into the air and exploded with a loud crack. "Be careful, Pueblo Grande!" cautioned Leo. "¡Es muy peligroso!" (It's very dangerous!)

Wenceslas and Malecio showed up, just as a syrupy ranchero floated down from a comedor (small restaurant) on the route above us. We all stood aside as Eugenio began puttering about his enormous pile of tobalá piñas, occasionally brushing one with his fingertips: the master at work. Using his palms to gauge the horno's heat, he finally said it was time to throw in the maguey. First, Leo and Roberto laid metal sheets over the hot rocks to protect the agave hearts from searing. Then we all gathered around the pit oven and began hurling the piñas into it. They flew through the air like cannonballs, crisscrossing paths until they eventually grew into a six-foot-high stack.

The hearts now piled inside the horno, the men proceeded to hose down several blackened petates before wrapping them around the agave. Then they added a layer of threadbare plastic tarps and covered the entire mound with dirt. As I had seen Paciano and Marcos do in San Luis del Río, the magueyeros slowly circled the pile, quickly containing escaping smoke with extra shovelfuls of soil.

A heavy rain began falling, so we all took shelter inside Eugenio's fábrica. There, we sat around drinking glasses of warm orange soda, eating biscuits, fighting off relentless attacks from squadrons of mosquitoes, and eyeing the horno for further traces of smoke. Behind us, white roses bloomed beyond the dormant copper still. Lizards chased one another over the massive tahona in the milling arena, which would remain empty for an incredible thirty days while the piñas slowly baked in the pit oven.

All around us, misty shrouds mingled with wood-smoke twists, and rain coursed through red rocks and red soil. Water flooded the road in a crimson torrent—the mountains bleeding from the hundreds of wounds where their tobalá agaves had been cut in the days before. How soon would new ones grow on those slopes again?

Agave karwinskii

PART FOUR

AUTHENTIC AUTHENTICITY

ONE EVENING IN Oaxaca de Juárez, I attended an elegant mezcal-pairing dinner in the Centro Histórico. It was held in the handsome courtyard of Azul, a chic boutique hotel occupying a refurbished colonial compound. In addition to a gourmet restaurant, there were an art gallery, a rooftop bar, and guest suites designed by the esteemed Oaxacan painter and sculptor Francisco Toledo and other prominent artists. Agave distillates made with espadín—and also from wild-grown tobaxiche, madrecuixe, tobalá, *largo* (*A. karwinskii*), and *papalote* (*Agave cupreata*)—were poured to complement inventive dishes by Alejandro Ruiz Olmedo and other rising local chefs. Their plates featured colorful edible flowers and the blue-black corn smut *huitlacoche*, a regional speciality.

I was seated with a middle-aged dentist from Guanajuato, who grandiloquently described each spirit presented to us, and the dapper young scion of a powerful mezcal-making family in Santiago Matatlán, who spent most of the meal on his cell phone. Serving mezcal at a swanky dinner was typical of the moment— just as several of the well-to-do women around us wore designer versions of the indigenous, traditionally embroidered *huipil* tunic, so too had artfully packaged versions of the spirit become fashionable. But after spending time in rural fábricas, passing around beat-up jícaras with unpretentious maestros mezcaleros, it felt odd to be sipping the drink with well-heeled diners pontificating on mouthfeel, complexity, and terroir. However, I was learning that once a distillate leaves the hands of its maker, anything goes.

Two of the brand representatives introducing the event's mezcals belonged to the families that had created them. One was Marco Ochoa, whom I had already met at his tasting room, Mezcaloteca. The other was Graciela Ángeles Carreño, who was in charge of marketing for *Real Minero* (Genuine "Minero" mezcal), her family's artisanal distillery in the village of Santa Catarina Minas. Using locally grown maguey, her father, Lorenzo, and her brother, Eduardo, fabricated several types of mezcal in the signature earthenware alembiques of the Ocotlán municipality, the brand's labels featuring a black silhouette of an olla de barro. Her mother, Florentina, was in charge of bottling. Their spirits are now available in the U.S. The Ángeleses remain one of the few mezcal-making families who are able to control all aspects of their business.

At the Azul dinner, Graciela presented a spirit they had crafted from wild largo agave, which was paired with *tiradito*, a Peruvian sashimi appetizer. Later, I was curious to hear more of her thoughts on mezcal after reading two articles she had written—one on traditional medicinal uses for the drink and the other about the lesser-known role of women in selling it. So, one morning not long after the event, I took a colectivo out to Santa Catarina Minas. There, Graciela and her husband, Mario, welcomed me into the Ángeles family compound. It was situated near the sleepy village square and catty-cornered from the municipio, where Eduardo was busy performing his duties as current community president.

ㄹ

THE REAL MINERO distillery was located at the village outskirts, but I followed Graciela through a leafy inner courtyard to her home office, which had a red tile floor, a ceiling inlaid with carrizo, and a wooden desk surrounded by antique glass jugs inside sturdy wicker baskets. Although higher education is unusual for most mezcal-producing families, Graciela and Eduardo both went to college, where she had studied sociology and he engineering. A woman working in the male-dominated mezcal business is also uncommon. "It's not something you're going to see much of in other places," she said. "But in Santa Catarina Minas, women have been very important in the commercialization of mezcal, because they were usually the ones who sold it."

The family enterprise had been passed down from her father's side. Both of his grandfathers had been maestros mezcaleros and his two grandmothers were *mezcalilleras* (female mezcal sellers). Graciela said that, in the early twentieth century, when for a time severe government restrictions had been imposed on the production and sale of mezcal—and operations had slipped into the shadows as fly-by-night, bootlegging outfits—local women began smuggling jugs from outlaw fábricas in their skirts and surreptitiously selling them at village markets. This was mostly done by the distillers' wives, but it was also common for single women in the area, particularly widows, to support themselves or their families through the buying and reselling of mezcal. A number of those early mezcalilleras became significant players in the local economy.

Santa Catarina Minas is more widely recognized, however, for distilling its spirits in the type of earthenware alembiques that I had already seen at Florencio Sarmiento's fábrica when he was making pechuga. Although the village doesn't identify with an ethnic language group, it's strongly linked to the clay-pot distillation techniques that, we've seen, very likely evolved from pre-Columbian ingenuity. Graciela's family had been creating their mezcals in the fragile handmade stills for four generations, and she estimated that they typically went through around eighty alembiques per year as they continuously replaced ones that cracked from the intense heat used in the process. That can get expensive, so when she and her brother graduated from college and went into business with their father, they tried to convince him to upgrade to modern equipment.

"In school, they taught us that you have to be more efficient, and have more capacity, be more competitive," she said. "All these ideas that are completely Occidental and aren't thought of in terms of tradition or cultural preservation." But her father insisted that sticking to the old methods was a way, as she recalled him putting it, "that we producers in Santa Catarina Minas can still be identified by the rest of the world."

She explained that mezcal made in clay stills has characteristics that may not be shared with spirits crafted by other Oaxacan mezcal-making communities, such as Ejutla, Miahuatlán, or Santiago Matatlán. "When you start recognizing mezcals by their origin," she said, "the instruments used for their production become very important, and changing them doesn't make sense."

The signature differences also include what types of magueys are used in distilling the various interpretations of the drink. In Santa Catarina Minas, mezcals are created with several local agave species that historically have been used in and around the Ocotlán area. But other Oaxacan villages use the maguey types growing near them. Much like the many grape varietals that have been grown in European wine regions for centuries, agaves help define which mezcals are fabricated where in Mexico—joining forces with people to articulate geographically specific tastes. Because of the country's diverse landscapes and microclimates, distinctive spirits can be coaxed from different maguey species that habitually grow in and around villages only a few miles apart. It's as if the highly localized mezcals express dialects of languages slowly evolved over time—just like the many variations of Mixteco or Zapoteco.

The community identity expressed by each artisanal spirit is particularly important in Oaxaca, where individual villages are often known for a representative craft—say, the fine weavings of Teotitlán del Valle, the inventive *alebrije* animal figures carved in San Antonio Arrazola, or the shiny black pottery formed in San Bartolo Coyotepec. As Graciela put it: "It's not just language, clothing, food, or geographic situations that identify us—it's also what we produce. So when we ask each other, 'Where are you from?' the second question is always 'What do you make in your town?' And because you usually mention the elements that distinguish yours from the rest, the second answer might be, 'Oh, in my town we make mezcal!'"

The nuances of each spirit may vary from place to place in Oaxaca, but mezcal's traditional ceremonial use nevertheless remains consistent. "Mezcal is not just for consumption," she said, "but also for ritual." A classic example is when a Oaxacan man asks for a woman's hand in marriage. Mezcal is traditionally included in a gift basket offered to the prospective bride's parents—along with such presents as flowers, candles, and cigarettes, and such foodstuffs as bread, chocolate, a turkey, and freshly made mole. "When the two families sit down to talk about the interest of the man in marrying the woman, they *always* toast with mezcal," she said. "It's their way of sealing the commitment and also a way of blessing—a wish that the marriage will be a good one."

Quite often, the spirit is copiously consumed at the subsequent wedding celebration. In rural Mexican communities, this can be a major fiesta lasting several days or more. The lively, non-stop party of feasting, dancing, and ritual gift-giving—of housewares, furniture, and appliances—is commonly lubricated by a mezcal that's been especially distilled for the wedding, along with multiple cases of cold Coronitas. Mezcal is also poured at other milestones, such as first communions and christenings, and it plays a role at the beginning and end of life. "We use mezcal to toast when a baby is born and when someone dies," said

Graciela. "It connects our emotions and feelings, and helps us communicate with one another and speak about difficult things. This is because, when used in a collective way, mezcal is the link that one makes with others, so that everyone can be on the same *sintonía* [wavelength]."

Mezcal has other, holistic applications as well. Sometimes it's rubbed on sick children's bodies—or added to warm water to bathe them in (as I had seen Marcos and Imelda do with their infant son in San Luis del Río). It can be used for intestinal complaints; infused with herbs to treat rheumatism, bone pains, earaches, stomachaches, and colds; or heated up and rubbed on the chest as an expectorant. Graciela described a practice in which new mothers drink small amounts of mezcal for forty consecutive days after childbirth—which, she said, "takes the air out of their bodies" that they had "retained" during pregnancy, so that "the bones and pores close and the woman becomes thin again." It's common among the elderly to drink a little mezcal each morning as preventive *medicina*. And there's a long-standing belief, she said, that "when you're shocked or very surprised, your *alma* [soul] leaves your body—and the *only* way to get it back in is by drinking some mezcal."

The spirit is also consumed among Mexican artists to spur inspiration—the agave goddess Mayahuel playing a muse-like role similar to that of absinthe's *fée verte* (green fairy) in Belle Époque Paris. "Mezcal isn't hallucinogenic," Graciela said, "but it gives you another state of consciousness, makes your senses become more active, and awakens your creativity. So, if you like writing, you drink one or two ounces of mezcal, and you're going to start writing. Or, if you like painting, then it will help you concentrate and see things more clearly. That's one of the great things about it—when you're consuming an adequate amount, right?"

As Graciela described the drink's therapeutic and inspirational properties, it occurred to me that most of them would probably be news to the majority of agave-spirits drinkers outside Mexico. American consumers have been encouraged for decades to prove their bravado by eating the worm, and to anesthetize themselves with tequila that's either pounded in party shots or mixed into the frozen coping aid memorialized in Jimmy Buffett's song "Margaritaville."

Although mezcal was her family's livelihood, Graciela cautioned that the key to enjoying the spirit's benefits is respecting its alcoholic strength and imbibing it in limited quantities. "Drink mezcal carefully, because it's dangerous," she said. "The drink itself isn't bad, but it's important to know how to consume it in the right way. Obviously, someone who drinks a whole bottle in an hour won't be able to do anything—won't be able to paint, won't be able to write. He's simply going to be extremely *borracho* [drunk], no? Mezcal was never made for getting drunk. In the codices, one of the most prohibited items was alcohol, and, in our culture, originally, alcoholism was very frowned upon."

THE ANCIENT ONES would undoubtedly be appalled at how mezcal is often consumed in Mexico today. In Oaxaca de Juárez, I came upon many scenes of binge drinking where the spirit was basically being slammed. The city is filled with hard-partying college students and vacationing foreigners—and there are plenty of hip bars and clubs pouring a lot of mezcal to cater to them. There are also seedy cantinas in the town's shadier neighborhoods, where intoxicated men spend the day drinking excessively, groping women, singing maudlin songs, and getting into fistfights, until they pass out blind drunk. In either context, mezcal is mostly consumed to escape.

Of the city's innumerable celebrations, one of the wildest is the annual *Feria del Mezcal* (Mezcal Festival), a multiday extravaganza held each summer in July. The event takes over a large portion of the normally bucolic El Llano Park, downtown, and features dozens of tasting booths where brands give away mezcal. For a small admission fee, people can drink as much as they like—and many overdo it. When I stopped by the fiesta, the park's iconic statue of Benito Juárez loomed over an educational display of agave piñas, a millstone, a copper still, and a wooden tina—but no one was paying much attention to the artisanal aspects of mezcal. Instead, the focus was on the many stands serving free samples of añejos, reposados, and colorful cremas—mostly made by commercial distilleries and small brands in and around Santiago Matatlán.

The booths were arranged around a packed crowd dancing to lively banda music—fireworks launching high above them.

The fair's star attraction was *Platanito* (Plantain Chip), a famous Mexican clown, who came onstage wearing a loud orange suit and a bushy purple wig. Using roving cameras and a huge video screen behind him to poke fun at onlookers, he unleashed a torrent of salacious jokes at the drunken throng, accompanied by raunchy sound effects and dancing cowgirls.

Oaxaca's most famous celebration is the far more soulful *Día de los Muertos* (Day of the Dead), which also involves significant amounts of mezcal—the spirit playing a key role in honoring and connecting with the departed. During the annual event, which happens over three days, starting on October 31, deceased ancestors are remembered by their families with altars and graves that are beautifully decorated with old photographs and *ofrendas* (offerings) that might include marigold blossoms, fruit, candles, *calacas* (skeleton figurines), and skull-shaped sugar candies, as well as tamales, mole, copal incense, and bottles of mezcal. I saw the drink sipped in cemeteries, used as a toast before home shrines, and passed about inside a chapel in Teotitlán del Valle, where a group of old men sang a haunting song.

The yearly event also features huge public street parties in Oaxaca de Juárez and its many surrounding villages, where costumed revelers dance and parade around, many of them well lubricated with mezcal. Smaller private celebrations are held throughout the city. On the third day of the festival, a friend brought me to the annual "muertos" shindig thrown by a local crime-world figure. There, in an impoverished barrio clinging to a steep hillside, we found *jotos* (transvestites) and other party-goers dancing in the street while a band played before a lavishly decorated altar devoted to *Santa Muerte* (Saint Death).

The skeletal female figure—wearing a hood and bearing a reaper—is commonly associated with the Mexican underworld, and a burgeoning cult has developed around her. Even so, the party felt more like a church social than a devilish bacchanal. We were seated on metal folding chairs at banquet tables covered with bright white cloths, and we feasted on bowls of goat stew. As the evening progressed and the city lights twinkled below, the dancing became livelier, the host tossed wrapped gifts into the cheering crowd, and bottles of mezcal were passed around the tables and poured.

丬

MARKETING CONTRIBUTES NOT only to the abuse of agave spirits, but also to an overall lack of awareness of their traditional uses and cultural roots. In the U.S., tequila and, increasingly, mezcal are often associated with famous musicians and movie stars living the bling life—one that's extremely far removed from that of the people who traditionally work with maguey. But while celebrity actors and rappers launch their own brands—a cliché mined as a storyline in the HBO series *Entourage*—Graciela said that macho charro culture still remains the predominant motif for packaging the drink in its homeland.

"The symbol for Mexico," she shook her head, "that has been mined by the tequila industry and sold abroad has been the *mestizo* [mixed-race male] that dresses up with spurs, the pants with all the buttons, and the sombrero."

Although that iconic charro figure may be the typical image many non-Mexicans now have of a Mexican, Graciela said that mezcal actually "represents indigenous cultures that have endured attempts at eliminating them throughout the history of Mexico. It's the story of *los vencidos* [the conquered], and they have a very different identity from that of the charro." Whereas tequila, she said, has become associated with the concept of an independent Mexican nation, mezcal has not.

"It's been left in the wings, waiting for its moment to arrive," she said. "As mezcal emerges, it brings with it the *desharrapados* [downtrodden] of the country—the indigenous part, the campesino part—who had to kneel to the idea of the nation. But in the end they aren't really part of it. Well yeah, they're Mexican because they're in Mexico. But beyond that they're still Mixtec, Zapotec, and so on."

Rather than keep these diverse—and historically marginalized—cultures hidden offstage, Graciela hopes that the hardworking people who are the true guardians of mezcal-distilling traditions will instead be given starring roles. As agave and cultural stewards, they play as much a part in defining a spirit's essential character as the various types of maguey, terroir, and distillation techniques that many importers prefer to highlight—and a far greater role than the impresarios themselves. As Graciela put it, a maestro mezcalero's spirit creation is "the great connector" of his social world.

"We have lots of drinks that represent Mexico, because it's a mosaic of many cultures—so I wouldn't dare say that mezcal is the national drink," she said. "But I think mezcal is interesting *because* it represents all these different cultures. And in terms of taste, it's interesting *because* it's complex in its composition. It has a lot of different aromas and flavors that depend on a series of factors—biological, environmental, social, cultural, even economical. And it's a drink that's complicated not only as a spirit, but as a product of nature. So I think that for someone who's not interested in getting drunk, but in learning and discovering new things—or in experimenting with what you can obtain from the earth—it's an *essential* drink. It would be unforgivable for a cultured person not to know mezcal. I really think mezcal is drinkable art."

回

THANKS LARGELY TO Ron's success in almost single-handedly changing mezcal's profile, it's now common to find the drink discussed, like wine, as part of a cultivated and artistic lifestyle. Such a niche was once the realm of absinthe. In more recent memory, Absolut Vodka has worked at conquering the coveted demographic of moneyed sophisticates with advertisements showcasing acclaimed contemporary artists. In Mexico City and other cosmopolitan urban centers, small-batch mezcal has been adopted by what Graciela described as "*la moda*"—the fashion set. The spirit is poured not only at tony *mezcalerías* (mezcal bars), nightclubs, and restaurants, but also at gallery openings, fashion shows, and other elite gatherings. Likewise, pulque has also been re-"discovered," with new *pulquerías* (pulque bars) helping to quench thirsts for revised cultural identities by reconnecting with older ones. This is similar to the craft distilling and brewing movements in the U.S., where, until Prohibition, breweries and small-batch distilleries were widespread, and have now resurged in popularity.

"We Mexicans are lost in time," Berenice Acuña, a kindergarten teacher turned mezcal promoter, said to me in Mexico City. "We've forgotten what we have, and mezcal is a way of reconnecting with ourselves."

But this collective soul-retrieval comes with deeply rooted racial and class disparities that are often swept under the rug. "Fifteen years ago," said Graciela, "mezcal was considered a drink for construction workers, town drunks, and lowlifes. Now it's completely the opposite—it's 'in' and fashionable to drink mezcal. But that's where the sad part is: mezcal isn't a trend. Trends don't exist for five hundred years—they change each year, and mezcal doesn't. If you don't believe in and love the product, if you don't know how it's made, if you haven't smelled it, and lived it, or in any way experimented with it—you're just going to see it as a bottle that can be pretty or ugly, and sold as cheap or expensive."

Although some small-batch brands respectfully identify the maestros mezcaleros who make the spirits that they buy in bulk and later resell, it's usually difficult to learn much about the true provenance of what's really in a glass of mezcal. "I see a great irresponsibility on the part of the new mezcal *envasadores*," Graciela said of the new wave of bottlers. "They're seeing mezcal as a business, which is completely valid, but if there isn't any heart in what you do, it turns into something vile, because mezcal has a lot of spirit that comes from inside of the person who makes it. It's as if all these people who have money and contacts all around the world are empty. And mezcal is something that fills their lives—that gives meaning to who they are, and gives them an identity. But mezcal is more than that. I don't know one maestro mezcalero that conceited, and they're the ones who know—*everyone* else just learns from *them*. It just seems to me that in all of what's happening there's an absence of human understanding."

Mezcal brand names can be fanciful. Prominent ones include Los Amantes (The Lovers), Pierde Almas (Lost Souls), Vago (Lazybones), Los Nahuales (The Magicians), and one simply called Ilegal. And some community-distilled mezcals are presented by boutique outfits with folksy treatments that allude to their roots. But more often than not, maestros mezcaleros have little say in how their mezcals are repackaged, and the image-crafting for their drinks is coordinated by brand owners. The unpretentious people who actually made a spirit might keep it in a glass jug with a corncob stopper, or in a used container for orange soda, but a company might repackage it in an expensively priced bottle with a handmade paper label embellished with an artsy graphic. Such presentations may or may not reflect what maestros mezcaleros would do themselves if empowered.

Mezcal has also been described as drinkable folk art. Although using rustic design treatments to position mezcal in the context of other traditional Mexican arts and crafts takes it in the direction of folk art, the spirit isn't officially recognized or protected as a folk art genre. The International Folk Art Alliance describes folk art as "made by individuals whose creative skills convey their community's authentic cultural identity, rather than an individual or idiosyncratic artistic identity." Following that definition, a traditionally distilled mezcal would only qualify as folk art without a singular artist's (or brand owner's) vision imposed upon it. Such an interpretation would also be a fairly new development—just as the brightly colored yarn paintings created by Mexico's Huichol peoples are made using techniques first suggested to them by an American archaeologist, Peter T. Furst, in the early 1960s.

▣

WHEN SOMETHING IS appropriated, stripped of its origins, repackaged, and introduced into new cultural contexts, an emerging buzzword applies: "Columbusing." I first learned of the term in an NPR story by Brenda Salinas called "'Columbusing': The Art of Discovering Something That Is Not New." Examples include the Hawaiian *papa he'e nalu* becoming a surfboard, Buddhist meditation becoming mindfulness, and burritos becoming wraps—or "Whopperritos," in Burger King parlance. In New Mexico, the state government Columbused Zia Pueblo's distinctive, sacred sun symbol as an emblem for the state's flag and license plates. Salinas cites hummus, henna tattoos, and "Desi-inspired" color runs influenced by the Hindu Holi festival as examples.

"Columbusing," she writes, "is when you 'discover' something that's existed forever. Just that it's existed outside your own culture, nationality, race, or even, say, your neighborhood." But, she writes, there can be an "icky" feeling to this too. "When is cultural appropriation a healthy byproduct of globalization and when is it a problem?" she asks. Using an example of empanadas being reinvented as "hand pies," she writes that to "all the people who grew up eating empanadas, it can feel like theft." That, of course, means pretty much everyone in Latin America, and many people in the U.S.

"Admittedly," she writes, "cultural appropriation is an integral and vital part of American history. And one day, empanadas might become as American as pizza." However, she goes on, "the day when Latinos are considered as American as Italian-Americans, well, that feels further away." Such a sentiment is unsurprising at a time when politicians call for the deportation of undocumented Mexican immigrants and a wall along the entire U.S.–Mexico border. But Salinas uses Chipotle as an example.

The fast-food chain, she writes, "announced plans to print original stories by famous writers on its paper goods and failed to include any Mexican-Americans or Latinos on the roster. The American-owned chain can profit from Mexican culture while overlooking the harsh reality of how Latinos have been treated in this country." Rather than contribute to an ongoing pattern of

Americans turning a blind eye to the socioeconomic and cultural realities of others, Salinas suggests, potential Columbusers could "enter a new, ethnic experience with consideration, curiosity, and respect."

Food and drink items, traditional dishes, and heirloom recipes that are culturally specific to a place remain particularly vulnerable to being co-opted, because credit is rarely given to their true inventors. Because of the gray area created by *not* defining and protecting origin, contemporary fusion-style food entrepreneurs have been able to profitably cross-pollinate ideas and ingredients cobbled together from countless international sources. Sometimes this is because it's impossible to ascribe a specific dish to an individual—we think pizza originated in Naples, Italy, for example, but the Italian who invented it remains unknown. And we're often wrong anyway. General Tso's chicken is usually attributed to the Qing dynasty military official Zuo Zongtang, but the dish was unknown in China until it was introduced there in the second half of the twentieth century by Chinese-American chefs.

Although restaurant menus rarely provide details about the true authorship of a dish, they are commonly peppered with information about which local farm their lettuce came from and who grew it, suggesting that it's better for you to know this and that the cheaper, anonymously raised produce at the supermarket might be inferior. Certainly, by becoming more aware of the ingredients they're eating, consumers can take better control of their diets and nutritional needs—which, of course, is a good thing. But fostering feelings of inferiority in shoppers is also an effective sales tactic, and when farmers' market–style cuisine is more expensive and less accessible than mass-market fare, is it reasonable to make poor consumers feel inadequate for not being able to afford it themselves?

Farm-to-table marketing capitalizes on an anti-industrial yearning for authenticity. You can see the need met in everything from handmade, "lumbersexual" beard-grooming products to coffee shops festooned with reclaimed timber. When the market continues supplying goods, there must be a demand for them—so where are all these newfound cravings for bona fide authenticity coming from? In an article for *Lucky Peach* magazine called "The Problem of Authenticity," Todd Kliman takes a look at the phenomenon. "The emergence of the various interlocking food movements," he writes, "can be viewed as a reaction against the forces that threaten us—a kind of liberal turning-back-the-clock, a sentimental longing for a pre–World War II past when the food chain was not so ruthlessly efficient."

But Kliman views this as romantic thinking. "You can't take a big, mechanized society and return it to an agrarian, prelapsarian era," he writes. "You can't recapture the past. Perhaps that's what accounts for the profound nostalgia, the sentimental hunger, of the Slow Food evangelists, the do-gooding food writers, and the socially-conscious-seeming chefs who daily implore us, in one way or another, to get back to basics." Yet seeking the genuine can be problematic. "Authenticity," writes Kliman, "poses an even bigger challenge than locavorism and sustainability and seasonality. For one thing: how the hell do you define it?

For another: where the hell do you find it? And another: having found it, how do you know that it's, in fact, it?"

He cites the American chef, TV personality, cookbook author, and restaurateur Rick Bayless as a food entrepreneur who has enjoyed particular success hawking authenticity through what Kliman describes as trust-inducing "hyper-specificity." Bayless, he says, made "his reputation championing the regional cooking of Mexico," while also helping establish Oaxaca as "one of the great culinary regions of the world." But according to Kliman, there can be pitfalls to Bayless's positioning traditional Mexican food as being more authentic than, say, Tex-Mex. Kliman writes that "as biblical scholarship has shown us, the meaning of the prophet's words are often misconstrued by acolytes. So it seems to be with the legions of chefs, restaurateurs, and foodies who have enthusiastically followed in Bayless's wake." As a result, says Kliman, "Mexican regional food is now taken to be the gospel—the one and only true genre of Mexican cooking."

In his book *Taco USA*, the syndicated "¡Ask a Mexican!" columnist Gustavo Arellano also questions the dynamics involved when Bayless and others take it upon themselves to redefine American perceptions of Mexican food and drink. Arellano writes that "a succession of white authors and acolytes have prodded Americans out of their Mexican-food comfort zone, challenging the public to not only taste new dishes but also to prepare them at home themselves. In the process they introduced a fraudulent concept to the question of Mexican cuisine in this country: the idea that the food they documented was 'authentic,' while the dishes offered at your neighborhood taco stand or sit-down restaurant were pretenders to be shunned. Americans, arbiters of "authentic" Mexican. That smile Bayless always beams? P. T. Barnum approves."

When NPR ran a story in 2016 called "When Chefs Become Famous Cooking Other Cultures' Food," Bayless added a lengthy message to the online comments. "I invite you to criticize me," he wrote, "if you think I'm not talented at writing recipes, as a restaurant chef, or as a communicator on television. Criticize my work if you think it's not well researched enough, or if you think all the years I've lived and traveled in Mexico isn't enough to absorb the cuisine. But don't criticize me for being white, for falling head over heels for Mexico and its incomparable cuisine, and for wanting to share it with the world." In the comments that followed, several of the chef's fans cheered him on. But a commenter named "Nemophilism" left this thought:

"False equivalence. The key factor in discussions of cultural appropriation is distribution of power. Folks from an oppressed or colonized culture using aspects of the dominant or colonizing culture is not comparable to folks from the dominant or colonizing culture taking aspects of the oppressed or colonized culture."

回

IN MODERN ART, repurposing and appropriation can be traced to enfants terribles such as Marcel Duchamp, who famously signed his name on an industrially manufactured "readymade" urinal, and Andy Warhol, who recreated soup cans and soap cartons as artworks. In his book *Postproduction*, French critic Nicolas Bourriaud draws a comparison between contemporary art and modern deejaying. "Postproduction artists do not make a distinction between their work and that of others," he writes. Tracks by actual musicians—such as the soulful snippets of gospel singers sampled by Moby—are recontextualized into new musical creations. In the world of mezcal, many brands have now sampled Del Maguey's innovative, DJ approach of spinning choice playlists of traditionally crafted spirits created by handpicked maestros mezcaleros. Likewise, these brands also emphasize the artisanally crafted aspects of their products.

The underlying message for consumers is that by imbibing mezcal they are participating in a lifestyle in which drinking mezcal is both cool and somehow authentic. Such understandings of the spirit are partly defined by geography and language barriers—not everyone can travel in and to Mexico and knock on mezcal producers' doors. Americans may also be more comfortable with an intermediary defining the country for them. In 2014, when Anthony Bourdain showed up in Oaxaca to shoot a segment for his TV show *Parts Unknown*, he chose to sip mezcal with Ron, sitting atop a Monte Albán pyramid, rather than with a local maestro mezcalero. In a profile that ran in my local newspaper, the *Santa Fe New Mexican*, Ron described himself as "the godfather of mezcal," which might be news to Mexicans.

In 2014 and 2015, Ron was nominated as a James Beard Foundation Award semifinalist in the category of Outstanding Wine, Beer, or Spirits Professional, and he eventually won the award in 2016. A couple years earlier, he began importing a $200-per-bottle pechuga mezcal infused with free-range, acorn-fed ibérico ham supplied by the team of Spanish-born chef José Andrés. Andrés has been called "king" of small plates, other-wise known as tapas. The judges of the 2014 Ultimate Spirits Challenge awarded the drink the Chairman's Trophy, and it also won the award for Best New Product at the annual Tales of the Cocktail convention in New Orleans. But since Del Maguey's Ibérico mezcal cost more than the average monthly salary of many Oaxacans, it would be enjoyed by only a few of the people, if any, living in the region where it had been made.

Ron's unstoppable mezcal push might have been frustrating for pretenders to the throne, but they could have tried more origi-nal approaches themselves. Copying another artist's more suc-cessful model, however, is a long-standing Oaxacan tradition. Within each locally produced craft discipline—whether it's weav-ing, ceramics, or woodcarving—if one interpretation is ever seen as beginning to outsell another, imitators soon follow. Oaxaca's most famous living artist, Francisco Toledo—known for his dreamlike, figurative imagery of people and animals, inspired by Mexican mythology—is widely imitated by others.

According to Graciela Ángeles Carreño, maestros mezcale-ros should be not only credited for their spirits but also fairly paid for them—particularly because of the enormous amount of labor that goes into crafting agave distillates, which may be monetarily unquantifiable. "Mezcal is made by hand and pro-duced with less technical methods than tequila," she explained.

"The productions are on a smaller scale and homemade—more of a family business, not big businesses or empires. Each batch is different and you can't reproduce that. And the number of liters could be under a hundred in one production. A *tequilero* can produce up to fifteen thousand liters in a day, while a mezcalero could take a month to produce one hundred liters—and that's a lot of time."

And the imbalances aren't only in quantity. "The social sustainability and economic importance for the people who make mezcal is much greater than that of tequila sales for the national economy," she said, "because mezcal production is still, by at least 70 percent, composed of small families. But in the case of tequila, we're only talking about a few companies that produce vast quantities of liters, in which case the economic trickle down is obviously a lot less for the maguey producer, who is the only Mexican that participates in the chain of production, because nearly all of the profits that come from tequila sales are transnational."

In some situations, mezcal producers are asked to retain time- and labor-intensive production methods in order to protect the flavor and consistency of a particular mezcal—which may have originally been implemented out of necessity rather than choice. If a distiller actually *wants* to use wooden clubs to hand-mash his roasted agave, or to refine his mezcals in fragile clay alembiques, or to ferment his mash in an inverted cowskin trough, then those are legitimate artistic decisions.

But if a maestro mezcalero is leaving such archaic methods in place solely to preserve a middleman's notions of authenticity—when the producer's natural inclination might be to make things easier for himself with modern equipment—then he can find himself trapped in a cycle of continuously repeating the same recipe with the same methods year after year. This could be compared to an "outsider" artist being "discovered" by an art dealer, and then instructed to limit himself to "primitive" techniques to retain the market value of his brand. The dealer's justification, of course, would be that the artist would be better off financially than he had been before.

"I think it's difficult under certain circumstances," said Graciela, "to ask a producer to preserve their traditions if tradition is costing them their life. For 20 pesos a liter one can't survive. You don't need a gun to kill someone—you only need to keep paying less than what a mezcal is worth for a family to die of hunger. There are good mezcals and very good mezcaleros, but there is a rapacious market that pays them very cheaply for their products, and the producer can't put his own price on them because he's up in the mountains three hours from a highway, he doesn't have money, or a vehicle to leave town, and he has a family to support. Under those circumstances—if his son is sick, or his wife needs medicine, or he can't send his kids to school— then the *only* thing he can do is wait for a buyer to come, and whatever price they offer: *take it!*"

"This is an ethical problem," she continued, "because, in the end, the producer—the way things are today in the world— doesn't have any way to defend himself. There isn't an institution that defines the price—if the price is in the free market, it's made by the market. The maestro mezcalero has no idea about the economy—he doesn't know what inflation is, he doesn't know what taxes are—he only knows what it is to be hungry and to not have any food, and what it's like to have a sick child and not be able to take him to a doctor—that's everything he knows: that the survival of his family depends on him. So the decisions he makes are going to depend on his situation, and we can't ask them for more than that, because they've already been under those circumstances for over five hundred years."

"It's a very dangerous time for mezcal," she went on. "And sometimes I ask myself if exposing the maestros mezcaleros was the right thing to do, because all these people with money looking for a good business to invest in have shown up. Before that started, producers lived calmly in their communities—dying of hunger, if you wish—but calm. Not anymore—now people go out hunting with their garrafones to the pueblos, to see who they can buy mezcal from, and to look for their *own* producer."

"But 'my producer' doesn't exist," she continued, "because people don't have an owner. It makes me feel really bad when someone says 'my producer,' because I can't imagine myself being someone else's producer—it's like talking about 'my employee' in terms of possession—and it's as if the other person doesn't have any will because he only does what I tell him to do. Now it's a *trend* to have your own producer—what do you call it, neocolonialism? Now we're going to conquer all those barbarians that make mezcal, because they don't know about the market, and they need to better their processes because we're the people that know how to 'sanitize' them—and who knows what else that's disrespectful."

In the summer of 2014, an unnamed French wine-and-spirits collector paid $74,000 for a platinum-dipped crystal "art bottle" of "black" Oaxacan mezcal called the Shaman's Spell. The disparities between the cultures that traditionally produce mezcal and the drink's purveyors and consumers had grown even wider.

Late one night in Paris, in the fall of 2013, I stopped by a bar called *Candelaria* (Candlemas)—one of two places I knew of in the city that served mezcal. It was in the fashionable Marais district, hidden in the back of a nondescript taquería packed with attractive young people—the first taco stand I had ever been to with a bouncer out front.

I walked through the crowded eatery, opened an unmarked door, and found myself in a hidden, intimate lounge with dimmed lighting, groovy music, and a crowd pressed against a well-stocked bar. There, a couple of Parisian mixologists were shaking and stirring drinks like rock stars, occasionally to cheers of "*Bravo!*" and "*Formidable!*"

I was handed a cocktail menu listing several mezcals, but crediting none of the maestros mezcaleros who had made them. "I met the man who distills this!" I told one of the bartenders, as he poured me a shot. The Frenchman looked at me with a studiedly bored expression. "That'll be twelve euros," he said.

╚

AT THE END of the nineteenth century, the Viennese art historian Alois Riegl proposed that when viewers engage with art, they do so through their personal prism of experience, which then adds another dimension to the art itself: "the beholder's share." An artwork, therefore, remains incomplete until we bring something of ourselves to it. Certainly, no one is born thinking of mezcal as either a cheap drink or an exclusive top-shelf spirit. But if such impressions are the only experiences a consumer has with mezcal, that's the "share" they will bring to the table.

After listening to what Graciela had to say, I left feeling that my own beholder's share had just undergone a robust adjustment. It would be a false notion, I now realized, to romantically imagine that, because I consumed a traditionally produced alcoholic spirit that was a thread in someone else's communal web, I was somehow connected to that community myself. Part of my interest in mezcal, I recognized, was that I wanted to be part of something else. But since I wasn't a member of the cultures making the drink, I was out of context, my "authentic" experience inauthentic: I could only be a visitor passing through. And should I even be there at all?

I realized I was just another Columbuser, seeking out material for a book. This made me no less of an appropriator than the mezcal impresarios I had met, since I was hoping to cash in on the spirit, too. Furthermore, I was now acutely aware of how little I really knew about the drink. There are so many dimensions to mezcal that it may be unknowable—and perhaps it should be left alone. There would always be one more dirt road twisting into a hidden valley, where one more maestro would be distilling a mezcal. Or there would be more agaves to learn about, and other distillation techniques. How could I ever know it all? I could only bring my flawed beholder's share to mezcal.

Until then, I had mostly explored the realm of traditionally distilled mezcals. And I had found myself becoming uncharacteristically obsessive about ingredients, distillation techniques, and various other details—even though I never wanted to become an expert, a connoisseur, or a pundit who rates mezcals with points, like wines. Even so, I had become an elitist authenticity-seeker, a purist, when all I had originally wanted was to find out what that first amazing mezcal I had tasted in Santa Fe truly *was*. I had learned that maestros mezcaleros can be poets—deftly handcrafting traditional agave spirits from plants they've lived among for years. But now that I had experienced a bit of their realm, how would other parts of the mezcal universe appear?

Most aficionados would say it's impossible to create agave poetry on a grand scale, but if one accepts transforming maguey into mezcal as a creative act, then I found myself wondering if there should be a right or wrong way to go about it. Taste is highly subjective, and consumer culture shows us that not everyone wants or appreciates the best mezcals—especially when they are delivered in expensive packages. But if *all* mezcals—whether artisanally or industrially created—are ultimately expressions of plants, people, and place, is it fair to say that some agave spirits are more "art" than others? With these thoughts in mind, I decided to check out some of the commercial mezcal operations I had seen in and around Oaxaca de Juárez.

⌐

I STARTED BY visiting the Scorpion mezcal factory one morning. It consisted of a cluster of industrial buildings in a nondescript neighborhood near the Oaxaca de Juárez airport. The plant had originally operated as a textile mill producing table linens and bedspreads for export—"before NAFTA bankrupted us," as Douglas French, the American owner, put it. By cleverly cobbling together an 1883 wool-carding machine, an antique sugarcane press, and a variety of recycled parts salvaged from a defunct soft-drink factory, he had created an entirely mechanized Rube Goldberg contrivance for processing agave and distilling mezcal on a large scale. There was nothing artisanal about his products, some of which were almost as neutral in taste as commercially produced tequilas.

"My mezcal doesn't have the smoke flavor," French explained, showing me a big chamber that could steam nearly five tons of piñas at a time.

His spirits were predominantly distilled with espadín agave, but he also manufactured mezcals using "estate-grown" tobalá. He was barrel-aging a selection of reposados and añejos in floor-to-ceiling stacks along one of the factory walls. Scorpion's products may have lacked the "authentic" allure of other mezcal brands, but they were moderately priced and had received accolades from the Beverage Tasting Institute, *Spirits Journal*, and *Wine Enthusiast*. Although French expressed a deep admiration for the artistry of maestros mezcaleros, he was mostly concerned with delivering a product with wide appeal. He worked toward that goal with a refreshing lack of pretense, while also making it a point to employ women—many of them single mothers.

The scorpion that he included in each bottle was a marketing gimmick, he said, just like the worm. "It makes the stuff sell," he shrugged, showing me plastic barrels filled with thousands of dead scorpions sourced from neighborhood kids. He explained that to sanitize the scorpions for possible human ingestion, "we take the stinger out, wash out the guts, and neutralize the venom." French was one of a handful of mezcal businessmen I met who put his passion for agave sustainability and preservation into direct action. At the edge of his distillery's weed-filled junkyard, he had set up a nursery for tobalá maguey, which he cultivated for distilling as an alternative to harvesting the plants in the wild. He said he was growing many hectares of other agaves outside of town. French now also distills a "single barrel" whiskey in his facility. Called Sierra Norte, he makes it with native varieties of Oaxacan corn.

When I showed up for a tour of the far grander Casa Armando Guillermo Prieto factory, one of the largest agave-spirits plants in Mexico, I experienced a more corporate conception of machine-made mezcal. Set alongside Highway 190 near Teotitlán del Valle, with towering whitewashed walls, it reminded me of the eerie Fort Zinderneuf in the film *Beau Geste*. However, instead of dead legionnaires propped in its ramparts, there were white-coated workers inside, performing experiments in a glassed-in *Laboratorio de Calidad*. A polite, polished woman showed me around the rest of the otherwise unpopulated plant, which she said was in operation only a few months of the year.

She walked me past a gleaming manufacturing area containing an industrial-sized column still. There was also a formidable array of other sparkling stainless steel devices used to crush raw agave, extract its juice, and ferment it into mezcal products. Instead of horses, grindstones, and tinas, there was a stylish welcome center and tasting room screening a promotional video, a small museum with a fine collection of Oaxacan crafts, a temperature-controlled warehouse with multiple aisles of stacked-up aging barrels, and an outdoor tasting bar by a pond with a hippopotamus sculpture in it. There, I was presented with shots of proudly characterless products to sample. With the fake hippo for company, I sipped them while overlooking a broad, manicured lawn.

One afternoon I was given a tour of the elegant Destilería Los Danzantes in Santiago Matatlán. Looking like something out of an architectural magazine, it was beautifully built of locally quarried stone. There were stereo speakers over the tinas—used for playing Maria Callas arias to the mash during fermentation. Joel Antonio Juan, a maestro mezcalero from the mezcal-making village of San Juan del Río, distilled joven, reposado, and añejo mezcals for the brand's Los Nahuales line. But the company also distributes a curated selection of spirits crafted by maestros mezcaleros from several different Oaxacan communities under a separate Alipús label. These unaged *mezcales jóvenes* are from the villages of San Juan del Río, Santa Ana del Río, San Baltazar Guélavila, San Luis del Río, San Andrés, and San Miguel. The company also produces limited-edition bottlings with artist-designed packaging under its Arte Mezcal label. I was shown an unusual 2007 vintage distilled with tobalá, tepeztate, *cuishito*, *jabalí*, mexicano, and espadín agaves.

One morning, Ron took me to visit the master distiller Eric Adalid Hernández Cortés at his Místico fábrica, in Tlacolula. He made mezcal for the brands Los Amantes, Metl, and Ilegal. His engineering background was reflected in the three beautifully con-structed gas-fired alembiques that he had designed himself—two stainless steel, and one copper—their gleaming, curved surfaces like steampunk fantasies from the pages of Jules Verne. Other innovations included a tunnel into the fábrica's horno for effi-ciently delivering firewood, and an elaborate apparatus shaded by tall cacti that water-cooled his stills. After much experimen-tation with distillation temperature, Hernández discovered that, unless his spirits emerged from the alembiques at thirty degrees Celsius or below, they would lose some of their flavor. So, unlike in most palenques, he had fashioned his stills to trickle out spirits already quite cool to the touch.

He told us that he had recently purchased all of the prize-winning piñas at the *Día de los Magueyeros*—an annual trade exhibition I had attended in Tlacolula, where agave growers show off their biggest maguey hearts like pumpkins at a county fair. He had been busy distilling mezcals with them, and we tasted new drinks he had created with serrano, espadín, and *cirial* (*A. karwinskii*). He poured us one that he had made from four enormous arroqueño hearts—the biggest three hundred kilos—which he said had altogether delivered eighty-six liters.

As we sat around the fábrica and sipped, a dog suddenly bit Ron on his side.

"Just put some mezcal on it," said Hernández, and the artist-importer lifted his customary white smock, filled a shot glass with the spirit, and laid it over the bloody bite.

"*Está bien*," he said, lighting a cigarette.

Yet again, it seemed, mezcal could cure all.

Agave americana v. oaxacensis

PART FIVE

OAXACAN LEMONADE

B ACK IN SANTA Fe for a break, I was notified that a box of mezcal samples that had been sent home to me from Mexico had finally arrived. The shipper in Oaxaca had charged exorbitant "*rápido*" fees to ensure its fast, smooth delivery straight to my door. But instead it came several weeks late and appeared at the downtown post office. This was strange, because the USPS forbids mailing alcohol, yet the package had somehow fallen into its hands. Would I be arrested when I picked it up? Who cares, I thought. This was my beloved mezcal collection—the *only* choice was to go right there and get it.

When the postal clerk heaved the carton onto his counter, it was battered and wet, looking as if it had made its mysterious, seventeen-hundred-mile journey from Oaxaca to Santa Fe by mule train. "Smells kinda smoky!" he said, sniffing his mezcal-moistened fingers. I hightailed it before he could ask any incriminating questions.

But as my own hands sank into the mushy cardboard, I was relieved to find that, though a bottle or two had evidently broken in transit, the container still seemed about as weighty as it had on the sweltering day when I had lugged it across Oaxaca de Juárez by bus to the shipper. After I cut it open on my kitchen table, I found that three of the half-liter bottles I had packed were cracked and nearly empty, and four others had vanished. The missing spirits were particularly rare—had a savvy mezcal rustler jacked them? I could only hope that whoever stole the mezcals would enjoy transcendent moments similar to those I had experienced when sipping them myself.

Remembering those episodes, I opened a bottle and poured some mezcal into one of the jícaras I had bought at Abastos Market—carved with armadillos, rabbits, iguanas, and other local animals. The drink's flavors were the same as I remembered, but it felt strange to be savoring them by myself, far away from where the spirit had been crafted in Oaxaca. There, I had learned that the community distillate serves an important social purpose: allowing people to connect. "Mezcal is a pretext for being in the moment," Abel Iraizos, a Oaxacan aficionado, had once put it to me.

Although piercing rays of sunlight didn't always burst through the clouds when a mezcal distiller poured me his spirit, he would often look deeply into my eyes as I tasted it. Partly he was just expressing pride in his creation. But I would also feel that, by consuming his drink, I was somehow joining a constellation of other mezcal drinkers sharing a mutual catharsis through alcohol—perhaps a bit like the camaraderie of fellow fans drinking beer together at a baseball game.

There was something timeless about this experience that reminded me of when I had seen soulfully drawn prehistoric cave paintings in France, sharing sensations that other humans had felt for thousands of years. After returning to the U.S., I had looked forward to still feeling part of mezcal's connective network. I imagined that the maestros mezcaleros would continue telling me new things about their world whenever, wherever I

tasted their drinks, or that the spirits might return me to memo-
ries and emotions, as if I were leafing through old photographs
or smelling familiar scents.

Instead, as I sipped this mezcal, far removed from its original
context, I imagined that a figurative rope of agave threads was
now fraying, and it was this rope that had linked me to the spirit
through space, memory, and time. Here I was, drinking it on my
own, with no one around who could share what it meant. There
was no bonding, laughter, or emotional release. Like a sad sack
in a country-western song, I felt lonesome enough to cry. Then I
drank some more.

囜

I HAD OBTAINED the mezcals one by one in the villages where each
had been crafted—almost always at least an hour away from
where I was living in Oaxaca de Juárez, usually much farther.
The distillers had occasionally presented the spirits as gifts, but
they usually sold them to me at prices they deemed fair—typically
100 to 120 pesos (at the time, about $7.50 to $9.50) for each half
liter. I knew this was far more than many boutique bottlers were
paying per full liter in bulk, but, given the enormous amount of
care, time, and effort that goes into making fine traditional mezcal, I felt lucky to have it at any price.

I had transported each spirit back to my apartment in Oaxaca
de Juárez in a used plastic bottle. The maestros mezcaleros had
filled these either by tipping old jerry cans into funnels or by
siphoning from the ends of hoses stuck into battered plastic

barrels or stainless steel kegs. The repurposed containers some-times leaked during transit, and my weathered knapsack became a smoky scent map of roasted maguey: a little mexicano here, some arroqueño there, and espadín all over. As I would squeeze into a colectivo, sometimes the passenger beside me would sniff the air and ask, "¿Mezcal?"

I would decant the drinks into glass containers that I had found in a bottle shop around the corner from my apartment. I identified each mezcal with one of the fluorescent green labels I had purchased from a school-supply tiendita across the street, scribbling details in magic marker before placing it with other bottles on a sagging shelf. Although I was often asked if I was launching my own brand or investing in the mezcal business, I kept the samples for research and to occasionally share with friends.

As the collection grew, I lost interest in obtaining the spirit in any way other than straight from the maestros mezcaleros them-selves. By doing so, I was able to meet them and see their fábri-cas, learn about their methods and ingredients, and walk among their agaves—before tasting their creations right where they had developed them over time. Each mezcal had its own interesting story behind it, which made drinking it far more personal for me than buying a bottle with an unknown provenance or ordering a random shot.

But the vast majority of mezcal consumers will never have an opportunity to meet a maestro mezcalero, let alone visit a fábrica. They have to learn about the drink entirely from others, choosing their Mexican spirits from whatever brands are available at bars and liquor stores—a miniscule number compared with the many that are distilled. By the time those select tequilas and mezcals hit the shelves, they've already been curated to specific palates. Therefore, you taste them after they are sorted by go-betweens— from tequila brands launched by Justin Timberlake, George Clooney, and Sean Combs to mezcals represented by Toby Keith and Cheech Marin.

This is worth remembering. Taste is highly subjective, and the mezcal universe is so complex, obscure, and geographically challenging that it would be exceedingly difficult for *anyone* to attain a truly credible grasp of the drink. What does a famous entertainer know about agave spirits that you don't? Probably not that much. Mezcal is far more difficult to become knowledgeable about than Scotch whisky, or wine—which has an established educational system for sommeliers. Although some aficionados know a great deal more about mezcal than others, no one knows every mezcal, which means that no one has a truly comprehensive knowledge base to make recommendations from. There are thousands of traditional agave distillates still out there to "discover."

ロ

OF THE MANY "undiscovered" maestros mezcaleros, some might be happy to sell their spirits outside their communities, but few will have the resources to market and distribute their products themselves. At the same time, it's logistically daunting for the average consumer to head into the Mexican hills and buy directly from willing producers. Unless enterprising and empowered maestros mezcaleros are able to promote their spirits on their own terms, and consumers can make well-informed choices, the power to capitalize on and define mezcal will continue to remain in the hands of middlemen.

But not only can consumers ask questions about flavors, ingredients, and terroir; they can also inquire if producers were paid and treated fairly and if the agaves used for a spirit were sustainably grown—intrinsic issues to the mezcal story. How much of the $12 you just paid for that shot of small-batch mezcal went to the maestro mezcalero who distilled it? If enough bartenders are asked such questions, they may in turn ask them of brand owners, and increased transparency could result.

It's hard enough to find accurate information about mezcal outside Mexico, but even inside the country it can be difficult to find reliable answers. Maestros mezcaleros rarely have email and websites, let alone Facebook accounts or Twitter handles to tell you anything themselves. They have almost no voice—online or otherwise—in the mezcal world at all. In most of the new mezcalerías I've visited in the U.S. and in other countries, bartenders may be well versed in discussing the flavor particulars of a drink, but mezcal-tasting menus rarely say more than the name of a brand and the type of agave. Maestros mezcaleros are almost never identified. Even in Mexico City, I've found bartenders unwilling to reveal more than a few vague details about the uncertified, unbranded offerings they sell by the copa. Perhaps they don't want authorities cracking down on them for selling non-DO mezcals, or this secrecy helps them to prevent others from mining their "discoveries" themselves—as if they were gold deposits. But why not celebrate the maestros mezcaleros? Aren't they the most important part of all this?

ᗈ

DESPITE THE REGULATIONS for production standards and certification requirements in DO regions, mezcal is a logistically challenging trade to oversee. In mezcal-producing areas, the DO is commonly ignored altogether, and uncertified, untested agave distillates are frequently bought and sold quite openly. Things can get murky when a spirit changes hands after a distiller sells it. Uncertified mezcals might be blended or doctored and, though unlikely, could be unsafe to drink. Yet even if you live in a mezcal-producing region, it's difficult to know what to believe without going straight to the source.

In Oaxaca de Juárez, aficionados are regularly delivered unbottled and uncertified spirits in bulk, or *suelto* (loose), in plastic jerry cans brought straight to their doors from *el campo* (the country)—a fine arrangement if one truly knows what one's buying. Every now and then in the city, however, I would be invited into someone's home to try a *"muy especial"* mezcal—proudly poured from a tiny oak cask, perhaps—and my host would be unable to share more than a few uncertain particulars about the drink. "I have a guy who brings it to me," he would say confidently. "He knows." This made me curious to retrace the steps of one of these mysterious mezcals back to its maker.

Not long after I got to know the jolly proprietor of a hole-in-the-wall burger joint in my neighborhood, he offered me a taste of the mezcal his father regularly obtained from a local barber. When I expressed interest in learning more about it, and possibly visiting the fábrica where it had been distilled, he closed his grill lid, folded his apron, and took me down the street to the barbershop. There we found the luxuriantly mustachioed barber surrounded by sleepy-looking customers. While meticulously shaving an old man's neck, he told us his mezcal came from a village hidden deep in the mountains off Highway 190, on the way to the Isthmus of Tehuantepec.

"Do you think I could go there?" I asked.

"Too many narcos," he said, waving his straight razor. "*¡Es muy peligroso!*"

"What if I brought someone with me?"

"Pueblo Grande!" my friend joked. "If there are narcos there, the only way to protect yourself is to get one of these!" He lifted his grease-stained T-shirt to reveal a spooky Santa Muerte tattoo emblazoned across his broad back.

"Couldn't I just go with him since he already has one?" I asked the barber.

"*¡Imposible!*" the old man said. "You have to have one of your own!" Everyone sitting around the shop had a chuckle at that.

A seemingly easier opportunity materialized one morning as I emerged from the gate of my apartment complex. On the wildly uneven, earthquake-damaged sidewalk outside, I bumped into a father and son hawking "mezcal espadín" door-to-door from a ramshackle handcart. In the city, it wasn't unusual to come across vendors selling the drink in the streets. These two told me they had brought the spirit to town from their fábrica in San Juan del Río, about fifty miles northeast of the city. They offered me a sip from an old soda bottle. It tasted great, but I hesitated before buying it, and asked if I could visit them first and see their operation. They seemed taken aback by my request, but agreed to meet me in the village a couple of weeks later, by the community municipio.

ON THE APPOINTED day, I rode out in a colectivo with my friend Julio, who worked as a tour guide at Monte Albán. I had met him at a wild mushroom festival in the high mountain village of San Antonio Cuajimoloyas. There, after a morning fungus hunt in the surrounding cloud forest, a comida was served in a clearing. Long dining tables were arranged with hundreds of different mushrooms the group had gathered. A cook was stirring the few edible ones into a fragrant stew bubbling over a wood fire.

A lone woman, bundled in an embroidered wool shawl against the damp, ran a makeshift stand nearby. She was mostly selling candy, chips, and soda, but offered me some mezcal from a red plastic jug at her side. It tasted familiar.

"Is this mezcal from Santo Domingo Albarradas?" I asked.

"Yes," she said. "The family who made it is named Luis."

She sold me the container for 120 pesos, and I brought it to the dining tables to share with everyone. As a fine white mist descended into the clearing from a dark gray front coursing low overhead, the jug was slowly passed from guest to guest. It wasn't long before the Luises' spirit elevated the mood.

"*¡Qué chingón!*" (How cool!) Julio exclaimed. "I've never had mezcal like this before."

Although he had spent much of his life in Oaxaca, he knew very little about the regional drink. I had found this common among Oaxacans, most of whom have neither the resources to buy—or even try—re-bottled, micro-distilled mezcal at the prices it often sells for in the city, nor the free time to explore the region looking for it. And because they had never experienced anything different, many of the Mexicans I met viewed mezcal just as most Americans have: a crappy drink with a worm. This was common in Oaxaca, where billboards, factories, and tasting bodegas hawked lots of drinks with worms.

So when Julio expressed interest in learning more about mezcal, I invited him to come with me to San Juan del Río. After meeting up by the baseball stadium in Oaxaca de Juárez, we flagged down a colectivo driver. He was a heavily built young man named Daniel, who had recently returned home from the U.S. after the economy there turned sour. Like Julio, he said he also knew very little about mezcal and was curious to learn more.

When I asked Daniel if he would like to spend the day with us, he eagerly said yes. He usually spent his time shuttling passengers back and forth between the city and his home in Xaaga (near Mitla), which, he said, was "too full of *brujos*" (male witches) for his liking. "They've got black magic, white magic—you name it!" he shouted as we careened down the Pan-American Highway. "But I don't believe in that shit! They tell me we're going to do this or that—and I tell them: *fuck you, man!*" Like other enterprising local men I had met, Daniel had taught himself English by listening to rap, watching American TV shows, and playing video games.

回

NOT FAR FROM Xaaga, we left the main route and began winding our way into the rolling hills, heading toward the picturesque mountainside springs of Hierve el Agua, a popular tourist spot. Instead we followed a sign that read: VISITE SAN JUAN DEL RÍO, TIERRA DE MAGUEY Y MEZCAL. The road took us past an increasing number of sprawling, sun-baked agave fields before finally descending into the village itself.

The community was built along the banks of the same river that runs through San Luis del Río, due south, where Del Maguey called it *Río Hormiga Colorada* (Red Ant River). At the municipio in San Juan del Río I was told that it was locally called Río Tehuantepec. The village appeared far more prosperous than San Luis del Río, with many new-looking and well-maintained buildings. It had become a popular mezcal source for Mexican and American brand impresarios.

Unfortunately, the father and son I had met in the city were nowhere to be found. And when we asked inside the peach-colored municipio where we had arranged to meet up, no one there had even heard of them. Saying that your mezcal is from

San Juan del Río is a line one might feed an unsuspecting gringo, so perhaps they didn't want to explain that their product was from somewhere else—I'll never know. Later, I read an article in a U.S. magazine describing a Coke bottle of "top-notch mezcal" purchased on a Oaxacan street from a producer with the same name as the man I had met, who said he had crafted his spirit the day before from San Juan del Río agave.

But the day was not lost. After Julio, Daniel, and I fortified ourselves with some tasty chiles rellenos at the modest Restaurant Sheila, we headed out to explore a few of the village's many fábricas. Walking through town, we soon came upon a jumble of small distilleries lined side by side on the riverbanks. Magueyeros were splitting stacks of agave hearts, casting them into smoking hornos, driving horses that were pulling tahonas, refilling and emptying stills, and swigging freshly distilled mezcal.

The operations felt a bit like assembly lines to me—possibly because I knew that the men working in them were making spirits for brands rather than their community. And while many of the guys were friendly, others eyed us suspiciously, and some seemed drunk. Wondering aloud about their safety, I said it looked like a rough way to make a living.

"That's why all the homies bounce up to the U.S.," Daniel nodded. "Only now they're bouncing back."

By a small bridge, we encountered Don Joél Antonio Cruz, a dignified maestro mezcalero, who was taking an afternoon stroll. He told us that his family included four generations of mezcal producers and that the spirit had been made in San Juan del Río for at least three hundred years. He invited us into his home to sample his creations.

His son, Abel, and daughter, Judith, greeted us politely and sat us all down before the family shrine. Cruz poured us each a glass of the espadín mezcal he crafted for the Alipús brand. After we had tried that, he offered us tastes of two other spirits he had distilled, *sin marca* (unlabeled), made from maguey harvested in the surrounding hills.

He kept the clear drinks in large glass containers on the shrine, and looked deeply into my eyes as I tasted each one. The first was made from twenty-five-year-old tepeztate, and the second from *sierra negra* (*Agave americana var. oaxacensis*). I loved them both, and bought plastic bottles of each and slipped them into my rucksack. On the drive back, I asked Julio and Daniel what they had learned about mezcal that day.

"I didn't know the agaves could taste so different," said Julio.

"It's cool to meet the brother who makes your shit," said Daniel.

"Would you buy it from a brujo?" I asked him.

"Don't fuck with me, dude!" he exclaimed, nearly steering us over a roadside cliff.

卐

AT HOME THAT night in Oaxaca de Juárez, I decanted the two new spirits into glass bottles and added them to my collection. I felt tired and beat-up, as I often did after such excursions, especially when there had been lots of bumpy travel on remote, dusty roads—plus a steady stream of mezcal infusions. The next morning I tried to sleep in.

But when the pair of crazy old parrots living next door began barking like dogs to a pair of ornery curs that barked back, the Orquesta Primavera de Oaxaca that rehearsed in the garden right by me struck up the chords of "Eleanor Rigby" with brassy gusto, and the baseball players pumped up their boom boxes with high-fructose Mexican ballads, I gave up and headed to the neighborhood *gimnasio* down the street.

On the way, I ran the customary gauntlet of cordial greetings as I passed bodega proprietors selling used tires, Chinese trinkets, bread, auto parts, and Western wear. Then, in a spacious, second-floor exercise room filled with gleaming cardio equipment, weights, and flat-screen TVs blaring racy Latin music videos, I jogged on a squeaky treadmill. Through floor-to-ceiling windows, I could see a reclining cowgirl on a billboard across the street, her jean-clad hips jutting skyward.

Echoing her shape in the distance, mist-cloaked mountain ridges now seemed out of a dream. The view reminded me of the stunning places I had visited in Oaxaca, and the maestros mezcaleros I'd met. I had enjoyed the lack of smug sales intermediaries, those pompous little tasting cards with quotes and awards, and slick spirits packaging—all of which now seemed meaningless and absurd.

As a motley parade of ramshackle city buses rumbled up and down the busy boulevard outside—their proudly intrepid drivers seated under such individualized, hand-painted monikers as *CLANDESTINO*, *LA MAGIA DEL AMOR*, *PERVERSO*, and *QUIEN ES MI MADRE*—I noticed a fat, shaggy-haired, naked man ambling up the steep sidewalk down below. I had spotted him around town before—most memorably during the 2006 riots, when he had emerged from a puff of acrid smoke while police and demonstrators battled nearby. Now smeared black with filth, he began nonchalantly rummaging through a trashcan, appearing strangely invisible to the throng of pedestrians pressing by.

He's like the maestros mezcaleros, I thought—everyone knows they are out there, but until they are acknowledged, they will remain unseen. Wasn't it time to put some clothes on that naked man? Surely all people deserve to be recognized in their lives.

🔲

MY MUSTY CHAMBER at the Bourbon Orleans Hotel exhibited mysterious, crime scene–style carpet stains. In the courtyard swimming pool below my window, a pair of cackling, tattooed women were sandwiching an old codger who suckled an umbrella drink through a curly straw. It was July of 2011, and I had come to New Orleans to attend Tales of the Cocktail—an annual multiday booze marathon for spirits-industry professionals, mixologists, and the people who love them.

Ron attended the event each year to network, party, and hawk his mezcals, and he had suggested that I tag along and check it out. I was curious to see how the traditionally crafted Oaxacan spirit would fit into trendy U.S. bar culture, but Ron was also bringing a maestro mezcalero to the convention for the first time, Paciano Cruz Nolasco. I wondered how he would fit into that culture, too.

The convention's epicenter was located nearby at Hotel Monteleone, also in the French Quarter. So I left my air-conditioned room for the trash-reeking streets outside. It was just past lunchtime on a sunny weekday afternoon, but, in classic NOLA style, inebriated tourists were already staggering through the hot humid air like zombies. Just ahead of me, a drunk in an Orgasm Donor T-shirt lurched from a bar and collapsed on the grubby sidewalk. Further on, a trio of middle-aged, steak-faced men in Bermuda shorts and vomit-stained loafers were stumbling up Bourbon Street, tired-looking women halfheartedly shaking their rear ends at them from strip-club doorways.

By comparison, the dapper crowd of white millennial hipsters gathered in front of the Monteleone, on Royal Street, were party PhDs. They were ready to show the baby boomer weekend warriors how things were done—and lesson number one was looking damn cool while holding your liquor. The men sported fedoras, suspenders, chunky eyewear, and muttonchop sideburns. The women wore retro hairdos, vintage cocktail dresses, and lots of tattoos. A drinks cart served them cocktails made with the elderflower blossom liqueur St-Germain—a favorite ingredient in the mixology repertoire.

I went up the hotel front steps and inside its cacophonous, jam-packed lobby. Free copies of *Imbibe* magazine were stacked for the taking, and specialty cocktail shakers, muddlers, and other bar paraphernalia were displayed for sale. Farther on, tasting rooms had been set up throughout the building, promoting seemingly every possible spirit company on earth. If anything, the convention was a popularity contest where booze dreams could come true—perhaps even for Ron de Jeremy, a new rum brand spearheaded by the porn star Ron Jeremy, who was said to be in attendance.

I found Ron Cooper holding court on an upstairs landing, wearing his trademark duds. He was talking to a small throng by a station serving Oaxacan Lemonade—a cocktail made with basil vodka, lemon juice, agave nectar, cilantro, and Del Maguey's Chichicapa mezcal. As I sipped the first of what would be many, many cocktails over subsequent days, a spirited blond woman came up and gave Ron a hug. She worked for a leading multinational spirits company and had a bottle of "Eugenio Ramírez's" mezcal peeping out of her purse. "I've *always* got a bottle of Ron's tobalá on me," she winked. "It's just the way I roll!"

From a guerrilla marketing perspective, it was easy to see that the convention was a one-stop bonanza for Ron. He only had to move a yard or two before encountering yet another colleague from Booze World, and his mezcal devotees were constantly approaching him—at one point, a young mixologist pulled up his shirt to show off a large tattoo of one of Ron's artworks. The artist-importer clearly relished the attention, not seeming to mind being at least twice the age of almost everyone in the crowd.

I stepped outside the hotel with Ron so he could smoke a cigarette, and we bumped into Philip Ward, the rangy young co-owner of Mayahuel, a trendsetting agave-spirits-themed bar in Manhattan. He was carrying a bottle of Del Maguey's Minero mezcal in his shoulder bag—along with a set of Ron's signature clay tasting cups. He poured the three of us a taste.

"*Stee-chi-beu*," toasted Ron, saying a word he said meant "cheers," or "to your health," in Zapoteco. Ward dutifully repeated the toast. The word—pronounced "stee-chee-bay-oo"—may belong to a central-valley Zapoteco dialect used in Teotitlán del Valle, but it was unknown to Zapotecs I met from other parts of Oaxaca.

Although Del Maguey mezcals appeared to be the secret handshake of the convention, Ron wasn't the only one pushing pricey agave spirits. A glamorous woman, Bertha González Nieves, approached us. She was CEO of Casa Dragones, the tequila company she had co-founded with MTV founder Bob Pittman. She was carrying a $275 bottle of their drink in her shoulder bag, along with crystal champagne flutes. It tasted smooth, sleek, and weirdly healthy—like alcoholic mineral water.

A cavalcade of white Rolls Royce sedans purred up alongside the curb, there to ferry guests to an exclusive Beefeater Gin–sponsored shindig. None of us had been invited, but I followed Ron and Nieves into the backseat of one of the chauffeured vehicles. As we got in, a drunk woman draped herself across the hood with a Chihuahua, posing for photos. The driver slipped the car down St. Charles Avenue and deposited us at Gallier Hall, a historic Greek Revival building transformed for the gin event.

A phalanx of chesty male models stood guard at the front steps, wearing red beefeater outfits and kinky black eye masks. After stopping to say a quick hello to his friend Dale "King Cocktail" DeGroff, Ron breezed Nieves and me through a squadron of guest-list-brandishing public relations assistants. Inside, we passed a ballerina doing pliés inside a gigantic clear plastic beach ball, and entered a ballroom where an all-women string quartet in Marie Antoinette–style wigs was playing Vivaldi to beat-box thumps.

Red and blue gin concoctions were being served at the bar, but Nieves refilled our flutes with her tequila. As we reclined on a low-slung silver couch, Ron shared anecdotes from his mezcal adventures—which, of course, kept her occupied, instead of working the room with her competing tequila. As I watched people drinking, bumping, grinding, and drinking a lot more, I wondered what Paciano would make of the convention's bacchanalian flair. In San Luis del Río, spirits consumption is typically reserved for special occasions—well, other than when it's swilled by magueyeros in the local fábricas.

᠊᠊᠊᠊᠊᠊᠊᠊᠊ᴄ᠊᠊᠊᠊᠊᠊᠊᠊

BECAUSE OF A visa delay, the maestro mezcalero wouldn't arrive in New Orleans until the following day. I ran into him at Around the World, a cocktail event held at the Cabildo museum on Jackson Square. The eighteenth-century building is the former home of the Louisiana Supreme Court, and the landmark pro-segregation case *Plessy v. Ferguson* was decided there in 1896.

The Tales of the Cocktail party took over the entire third floor, and drink stations were set amid somber exhibits about the slave trade.

Paciano was there with Ron and Ron's friend Wyatt Peabody, a SoCal wine-and-spirits writer. I'd read a profile he had written about Ron in the *Los Angeles Times Magazine*, called "Free Spirit." Although Ron was staying at the Ritz-Carlton, he had booked a room at the more reasonably priced Monteleone for Paciano and Peabody to share. All of a sudden, a guy rushed up to the artist-importer and asked him to sign his T-shirt, shouting: "Del Maguey mezcal is in the house, y'all!" Several partygoers began cheering as Ron signed the garment with an artistic flourish.

It was Paciano's second trip to the U.S.—the first time had been with Ron to a much smaller event in Chicago several years before—and he said he would have preferred to be visiting his eldest daughter, in Indiana, so that he could meet his newborn grandchild. But instead he put aside his mezcal work and obligations as current village president to come and help promote Del Maguey. Like Ron, Paciano was wearing his trademark uniform—khakis and a lime-green T-shirt. Although he didn't speak or understand more than a few words of English, the spectacle of inebriated gringos needs no translation for any Mexican. But this was certainly a lot of them at once.

"*¡Híjole!*" (Wow!) he exclaimed, looking around at all the drunks.

Misty Kalkofen, a Boston-based mixologist, was whipping up a batch of a cocktail she called Bernardino's Bulleits. It was named after Bernardino de Sahagún, the Franciscan friar and chronicler of sixteenth-century New Spain—sometimes described as the first anthropologist. Before combining Bulleit bourbon, Fernet-Branca, fresh lemon juice, black pepper, simple syrup, and mango jam, she added a "rinse" of Paciano's San Luis del Río mezcal to each glass. "Just for the nose," she said.

"Look!" said Paciano, watching her drinks promptly get grabbed. "They're drinking my mezcal like mother's milk." Kalkofen chuckled and greeted him with a hug. A former Harvard theology student now turned agave-spirits enthusiast, she had been to Oaxaca to learn about mezcal and had visited the maestro mezcalero and his family in San Luis del Río. In 2013 she began working for Del Maguey.

Nearby, Andy Seymour, a mixologist from New York, was creating a *Grito de Dolores*—named after the legendary cry marking the beginning of the Mexican War of Independence, in 1810. It was made with Tanqueray gin, Paciano's Crema mezcal, "Eugenio Ramírez's" tobalá mezcal, Bittermens Xocolatl Mole bitters, and a grapefruit twist. Before a window overlooking the historic square, Bill Norris, a mixologist from Austin, was concocting the Immigrant Experience. His international set of ingredients was Tanqueray gin, Lillet Blanc, Amaro Nonino, Bushmills Irish whiskey, Paciano's Vida mezcal, Bar Keep Baked Apple bitters, and Luxardo cherries.

But with all that going on, I asked him, what did the mezcal add to it?

"Deliciousness," he said. "Funk and smoke and an earthy vegetal character that appeals to me. Mezcal grounds the other flavors in the real world."

At the other side of the room, Fred Sarkis, from Chicago, was mixing a drink he called Fair Trade. This one involved Tanqueray gin, Paciano's Vida mezcal, maple syrup, and Peychaud's bitters. "The mezcal brings in a little salt that plays with the minerality of the maple syrup," he said. Sipping some, a man slurred, "Wow, the maple syrup and the mezcal really *do* go together! Cool!"

A young Jamaican woman sidled up as I was trying yet another cocktail, this one made with only grapefruit juice, mezcal, and tequila. She didn't know much about agave spirits, she said, but had come to the convention in search of business partners for a new venture: birthday cakes in X-rated shapes, flavored with liquor.

"I want them to be beautiful and elegant," she said. "But also kinda sexy and boozy at the same time."

"You should put some mezcal in them!" said a square-jawed mixologist, handing her a drink.

"OK, honey," she giggled. "Maybe I will!"

As I left the building with Paciano later, a lively jazz band was playing in the square in front. A man in a colorful alien costume was madly dancing to the tune of "When the Saints Come Marching In."

"He looks like an alebrije!" the distiller laughed, spotting a reminder of home.

ㄹ

OVER THE CONVENTION'S remaining days, Ron brought Paciano to other tasting events. At some of them, the artist-importer poured Del Maguey mezcals himself. First, he would arrange an assortment of his bottles on a banquet table—along with their colorful baskets, stacks of his clay cups, and samples of caramelized roasted maguey hearts. "Mezcal education," he called it. More often than not, it was the first time many conventioneers had ever tasted an artisanal version of the spirit.

"Where's the worm at?" was a typical question.

"Good mezcal doesn't have a worm," Ron would patiently reply.

"Which one is your favorite?" a guy asked.

"Do you have kids?" Ron answered. "That's like asking which one is your favorite kid." He poured some mezcal for the man, who tasted it and said to his friend, "Wow, you gotta try this stuff. Tastes just like a campfire!"

"Actually," said Ron, "this is what you're tasting." He offered him a piece of smoky-flavored roasted maguey. The man bit into it uncertainly, chewed it, and spat it into a cup. "Nah, that's weird," he said. "I don't like that. Nuh-uh."

The learning curve for mezcal appreciation could be challenging at times. At an event called the Farmer's Bar, Ron brought along Gina Chersevani, a self-described "mixtress" from

Washington, D.C. She whipped up batches of an inventive drink she had created that combined Paciano's San Luis del Río mezcal, beet reduction, fresh pineapple, and Bittermens Burlesque bitters.

"Yuck," a woman grimaced after a sip. "Tastes like a smoked salmon cigar!"

But most attendees appeared to enjoy discovering a new and interesting drink. Paciano stayed in the background, watching the drunken throngs consume his handcrafted spirits. When Philip Ward showed up one day and began filling tasting cups and passing them out to eager hands, the maestro mezcalero beamed with pride. "It's like a *panadería* [bakery] for mezcal," he observed.

Indeed, thanks to Del Maguey, Paciano's mezcals were now reaching a broader clientele than the distiller ever could have imagined—but what were they doing with them? He was uneasy seeing his community's traditional distillate getting mixed into cocktails. "We don't do that in our village," he said, shaking his head. "But here I'm seeing people using ice and putting all kinds of things in it. We don't do this."

"Hey, when I drink it by myself," Ward assured him, "I only drink it puro!"

"That's the way," said Paciano, grinning and slapping Ward on the back. "Mezcal warms your body and warms your heart."

At the convention, however, mixology was the name of the game, and reputations could be made through creating snazzy new cocktails using mezcal. Ward served inventive drinks at two other events I attended. At a pairing dinner at Dominique's restaurant, he whipped one up called Faustino's Fault. Its ingredients were Del Maguey Chichicapa mezcal, jalapeño-infused Siete Leguas blanco tequila, St-Germain, and Dolin dry vermouth. At a tasting session billed as Last Call for Mexico, Ward stirred up another one he called the Short Rib—mixing jalapeño-infused Del Maguey Vida mezcal with pomegranate molasses and lime.

There were so many different cocktails competing for attention that it became difficult to imagine how anyone could remember much about what they had tried. The relentless spirits consumption didn't help, of course. It became increasingly rare to come across anyone even marginally sober, and I wondered what percentage of the conventioneers might suffer from alcoholism. The drug was highlighted at the New Orleans Pharmacy Museum, on Chartres Street, in an exhibit there called Aqua Vitale: The Spirited History of Alcohol as Medicine. It featured a display of early pharmaceutical elixirs, tinctures, spirits, and extracts.

回

ONE OF THE reasons Ron had brought Paciano to Tales of the Cocktail was to participate in an agave-spirits-themed panel discussion called "Before Man, The Plant." A few hundred people showed up in a Monteleone conference room to hear Ron and Paciano; mixologists Ward and Kalkofen; Iván Saldaña Oyarzábal, a biologist (who launched the mezcal brand Montelobos the following year); Steve Olson, a wine-and-spirits educator and consultant; and three tequila representatives— Tomas Estes, the owner of Tequila Ocho; David Grapshi, the tequila sales manager for the spirits supplier Sazerac Company (which now distributes Del Maguey, as well as Monte Albán mezcal); and David Suro-Piñera, the owner of Siembra Azul tequila, and president of the nonprofit Tequila Interchange Project. Only three of the nine panelists were from Mexico, which seemed odd given the subject of the event.

Flights of the brand owners' wares were placed before each attendee to taste, and Olson launched the proceedings with a general overview of tequila and mezcal, playing to an audience of enthusiastic mixologists. "Understand something, Americans," he said. "We represent 78 percent of the export of tequila from Mexico. We drink it, we serve it, we make cocktails out of it. So we are directly responsible for the future of this plant and for nurturing the education to make people understand what they're really drinking."

That made sense. But then, after scrolling through a series of slides projected behind him, he stopped at an image of a hefty-looking, round stone tahona lying on its side. "This dates back to two hundred years before the Spanish arrived," he said. "So we're guessing that maybe they had something figured out before those alembic stills showed up?" Moving on to an image of a rudimentary clay still, he asked: "Do you think the Spanish brought that? I'm guessing not!"

Although it now seems inarguable that distillation techniques were employed by pre-Columbian cultures in Mesoamerica, their only known use of the wheel was for toys—not heavy millstones. If the tahona in the photo had been in use before the Spanish

Conquest, what large animal could have possibly drawn it—a jaguar? But this sort of conjecture was evidently acceptable in Mixology World.

"It all began with this," Olson went on, pointing to a slide of an agave with a tall quiote jutting skyward. "Because up at eight thousand feet above sea level, where there is rain for two months of the year and static electricity in the air, this conductor is bringing static electricity down into the plant." Continuing to an image of a white, foam-filled jícara, he said: "And we have this—pulque. Or lightning nectar. The gift from the gods." The implication seemed to be that electricity coursing through a maguey somehow results in alcoholic beverages. This was a twist on the oft-told legend that Aztec gods revealed the plant's sacred aguamiel by striking one of them with a lightning bolt.

"So we'll start there," Olson went on. "The spirituality. The culture. The history. The heritage of the plant. And to do that, I'm going to introduce a man who knows a little bit about culture, being one of the most successful artists in the world—or most respected, is what I should say, actually, by his peers and by the art community. But most of us know him as the guy who brought us the Del Maguey Single Village mezcals. We also know him as the guy who almost single-handedly built mezcal as a category in the United States and now fortunately has a lot of really good friends, fans, and other producers helping to build that category so that we can benefit from it."

After receiving an enthusiastic round of applause, Ron apologized for being a "kinda shy" public speaker and said that he would read from a few things he had written over the years, instead. "There are many *dichos* in Mexico," he began. "A 'dicho' is a phrase. Before the Spanish Conquest it was called a *jade*. A 'jade' is jade, and meant a great saying. So there's a saying." He paused for effect. "You don't find mezcal, mezcal finds you." I had been hearing that line a lot in the mezcal world, though I never came across evidence of its historic use as a dicho. But it was certainly effective for putting a quasi-spiritual aura around the drink. Ron proceeded to talk about mezcal and its replacement of pulque as the ceremonial beverage of choice, before stopping to ask for some of the drink himself. Ward filled his cup with some tobalá mezcal, and Ron went on.

"The very first thing that happens at any fiesta," he said, "is that a judge is appointed—a *juez*—and the judge is responsible for serving everybody. So the very first thing the judge does is pours a cross on the floor, which is a salute to mother earth and our ancestors." He dribbled some mezcal onto the stage. "That being done," he said, "we can now begin to drink. So, stee-chi-beu!" He toasted the crowd and his fellow panelists, some of whom replied "stee-chi-beu" in earnest, reverential tones. "That, by the way, means 'to your health,' to the health of your friends and the life of the planet. It's Zapoteco, Paciano's first language. So here we go!" And he took a sip.

"Mmm," he said. "OK—that's done."

He began talking about Hermes, and the Greek god's association with enclosed spaces like walled gardens and nuns' cloisters: "We could say that in the ancient walled garden, as in the alchemical vessel, new metals get formed as the old ones melt. Enjoying ritual space is an intimate and imaginative act—and a transformational act. One rarely sees mention of the most important early inventions—distillation, the great alchemical art of transformation used in the search to understand the essence of existence. Aside from alchemy being the basis of modern science and industry, the transformation of human beings brought on by the imbibing of distilled spirits is of great interest to me. So," he paused, "I just had a sip—I'm in another place."

"Hopefully," he went on, "every man and every woman on this planet is on the road from the law to the legends. The legends stand for the moist, the swampish, the wild and untamed. The legends are watery when compared to the dryness of the law. A work of art is successful to me if it transforms the viewer, the experiencer. The mezcal that we're involved in is a living, breathing, transformational art. These mezcals tap into the mythical past, and they retain the ancient mysteries. They embrace the notion of intoxication from the maguey as a gift from the gods. They are 100 percent organic, unblended, made the four-hundred-year-old handcrafted way—from the heart of the maguey and the soul of the village." At this point, he was reciting lines straight from Del Maguey marketing copy.

He spoke for a while longer, touching on the unique nature of the mezcal buzz, Ayurveda ("the ancient yogic science"), and the mysticism he said surrounds the drink. "There's a high reverence," Ron said, "for this magical liquid and its ceremonial, social, and medicinal uses among the villagers. There's obvious pride regarding the mezcal's power. There's also great disdain for the cheap, diluted, chemically altered liquids sold commercially. The way mezcal affects your palate—and the way it warms your chest, throat, and mouth—is quite different from any other spirit." And then, for a grand finale, he couldn't resist adding: "And Del Maguey transcends all others."

When Ron began introducing Paciano as the next speaker, I was curious to hear what the maestro mezcalero's own take on the spirit might be. After all, he had lived and breathed it, and had been working hard for decades to support his family with it. What would he have to say? In his introduction to the seminar, Olson had said, "We have actually brought for you one of the greatest growers and distillers of agave from Oaxaca, as well, to join Ron, and to tell us more about the culture, the spirituality, the origins of this plant." But Paciano didn't speak or understand English, and no one had been translating for him while he was sitting with the panel onstage.

When it was Paciano's turn at the podium, Ron seemed to have a hard time with sharing the spotlight. He repeatedly interrupted Paciano, and provided uneven translations of the maestro mezcalero's words. Finally, after coaching Paciano through what he called a Zapotec blessing, Ron told him in Spanish: "Paciano, our time is short, so thank you." And that was that. "One of the greatest growers and distillers" had been given an airtime of about three minutes.

I TRAVELED BACK to Oaxaca with Paciano. At the New Orleans airport, we ran into one of the panel members, who, as his fellow panelists were leaving the stage, had testily said for all to hear: "Ron is not the only one making mezcal. He doesn't own mezcal!" Indeed, Del Maguey was the sole mezcal brand represented at the event and it had all felt quite clubby. The panelist took me aside. "I was somewhat disturbed," he said, "by the way no one was translating for Paciano."

Although he hadn't understood much at the seminar, Paciano had witnessed the mixologists' rabid enthusiasm for Ron and mezcal. As a result, the maestro mezcalero was leaving NOLA with a fresh take on the long view of things. Changing planes in Houston, we killed some time in the departure lounge. "They're going to put Ron on a throne," he said excitedly, and "make a museum for him when he dies. They love him, don't they? I see that they really love him! Everyone loves him. Finally something has been achieved! How many years? Sixteen years of working so very hard . . . and not to achieve it?" He shuddered at the thought.

"The world is crazy right now," he added. "It doesn't know what mezcal is and what tequila is. But by making it known what a fine mezcal is, people are going to understand."

The key, he said, was educating the public about the spirit's "cultural and artisanal" aspects when compared to commercially manufactured tequila. "From morning until night they make thousands of liters, and we can't do that," he said. "We need a month to make two thousand to three thousand liters. A month!

But not them—in twenty-four hours they have thousands. So we can't even compare them." But he was undeterred. "They might have a bigger market, but we're going to get it for sure," he said. "We're going to show the whole world what mezcal is, and that's how we have to succeed. We have to teach them," he joked, "so everyone drinks it like Diet Coke!"

Still, the prospect of achieving this vision was daunting—he was living with limited resources in a remote village. The cocktail convention had been exhausting, and Paciano was tired and ready to go home. He struck up a conversation with a woman from Oaxaca sitting near us. She was returning home to be with her family, after working for a time as a cleaning lady in the U.S. Listening to her stories, he looked around at his fellow countrymen waiting to board. "There sure are a lot of Mexicans here," he said quietly, "and they've all been working like burros."

We flew high over the wilds of his country, tall, snow-capped volcanoes appearing in the windows below us. The terrain was mountainous and rugged, with precipitous, roadless valleys looking impenetrable and perhaps untouched. Soon after we landed at the Oaxaca de Juárez airport, Paciano slipped into the pitch-black night, climbing into a colectivo headed down the Pan-American Highway toward his village.

He had a lot of work to do there.

回

NOT LONG AFTER the New Orleans trip, I went back to Santo Domingo Albarradas for their annual fiesta, generously invited by the Luis family. Armando met me in Santa María Albarradas, and we followed the long track out to the village in his pickup. It was early August, and the hills were now lush and green, the clear blue skies streaming with fast-moving puffy white clouds. When we came to the community, fireworks were soaring into the sky from the church, where mass was being held under a billowing red-and-white-striped awning out front. I remembered the first time I had come to the village, which had also been during the fiesta—it looked just the same.

At the Luis family compound, Armando's mother, Concepcion, ushered us into her kitchen, offering me a jícara of chocolate atole. This was soon followed by a steaming bowl of red chicken mole, which she served with hot tortillas fresh from the comal. The annual fiesta also functioned as a family reunion, and three of her daughters had come home from Oaxaca de Juárez for the occasion. Everyone had some extra work to do this time, however, as Ron and Steve Olson had just called to say they would be bringing a vanload of American mixologists to visit the next morning. "I'm worried about what to feed them all," fretted Concepcion. Finally, they decided to kill a goat and make *birria*, a traditional spicy stew reserved for special occasions.

"A goat is worth 200 pesos," said Armando. (At the time, about $16.) "I hope the bartenders like it."

I followed him down the steep mountainside to the goat pen, where he roped one of the bleating animals and handed me the length of cord. I slung it over my shoulder and dragged the goat uphill, Armando pushing and shoving the reluctant creature from behind. Finally, when it dug in its hooves and refused to budge, we grabbed it by the legs and carried it the rest of the way up the path to the house. There, Espiridion emerged from the kitchen, sharpening a knife.

As Armando pressed the goat's head to the ground, I held a rope lashed round its legs, and his father deftly plunged the knife deep into the base of the animal's throat, quickly dispatching it. One of his sisters held a plastic bowl under the wound, filling it with dark red blood. Then Armando and I held up the goat's legs as Espiridion went about skinning its body, finally slicing the hide from its lips, eyes, and ears, before yanking it all off and revealing glistening pink flesh beneath.

As Espiridion carved up the carcass and set the organs aside in buckets, the women laid the skin on the ground and began curing it with salt. "We'll sell it for making huaraches," Concepcion explained. No part of the valuable animal would be wasted. Meanwhile, under a bare lightbulb in the kitchen, her daughters busily chopped up peppers, cloves, garlic, oregano, *chiles guajillos*, thyme, and onions, mixing them together in a blue plastic mixing bowl. Later they would combine the ingredients with the goat meat in a galvanized steel trough, and place it over a wood fire on the dirt kitchen floor to simmer overnight.

We could hear the lively sounds of the fiesta nearby, and Espiridion and I walked into the village to check it out. Under the awning in front of the church, dancers wearing white costumes and masks were performing the traditional *Estrella de Guzmán* (Star of Guzmán) dance, named after the village saint—Santo

Domingo de Guzmán (Saint Dominic). Before becoming the patron saint of astronomers, the Spanish priest had founded the Dominican Order—the order of preachers—in the Middle Ages. Among other things, he taught that spiritual power is attainable through deprivation.

Down by the municipio, a brass band from Santa Catarina Albarradas—one of the two neighboring villages sharing the same Zapoteco dialect—was playing on the second-floor balcony. Below them, ramshackle carnival rides ferried happily screaming children, and traveling vendors manned makeshift stalls. Meanwhile, several farmers were leading powerful bulls down ramps set in the backs of trucks. They tethered the gigantic, snorting animals to a high metal fence set up in a ring. It had been erected for the *jaripeo*, a bull-riding event traditionally practiced in indigenous communities all over Mexico.

When the jaripeo originated there in the sixteenth century, riders literally rode their bulls to death. The Spanish had brought horses and cattle to the New World but forbade the natives from using them. As a result, bull riding emerged in the shadows as a form of resistance, a show of rebellion by the conquered against their oppressors. Now the bulls are ridden by *jinetes* (horsemen) until they are either subdued from bucking or the riders fall off. It's dangerous stuff, and the nearest hospital was very far away—too far, in fact, if anything serious were to happen. But that dark edge was partly why a crowd was now gathering around the fence.

Another brass band came marching up to the arena, with two girlishly costumed boys wearing masks and wigs dancing out front. They entered the ring and performed a raunchy dance for the crowd. Then Espiridion climbed through the fence to join some *topiles* (officials) in the center, gathered to consecrate the bullring with mezcal. After saying blessings in Spanish and Zapoteco, they sprinkled mezcal on the ground before toasting each other with copas of the spirit.

A man circled the ring offering cold Coronas to onlookers, and clowns hurled apples and passed out sugarcane stalks and candy. Finally, it was time for the riding to begin. One after another, young men straddled the bare backs of their bulls, reaching one hand behind them to grasp the end of the animal's tail, while waving the other high in the air. They held on for dear life as the vigorous beasts bucked, stomped, and occasionally bolted around the ring, smashing their riders against the fence. And, one after another, each man tumbled to the dirt in a dust cloud, clowns drawing the riled-up bulls away from the fallen riders by waving old blankets at the animals. The band played, the crowd grew drunk on mezcal and beer, and the jaripeo continued into the early evening, the setting sun casting an eerie glow. Luckily, no one was seriously hurt.

Back in the Luises' kitchen, Espiridion sat me down at the worn wooden dining table and poured me some of his mezcal from an old plastic bottle into a chipped glass. He then filled one for himself, and spilled a few drops on the floor as an offering. The first drink was followed by another, and then another yet again—the distiller keeping our copas full as the two of us drank into the night. His family gathered around the old man, as the alcohol took over his mind and he grew sentimental. Tears streaming down his face, he asked God to continue helping him support his beloved family. He mourned his decades of toil, and tunneled deep into the past—remembering his younger days of boldly riding bulls in the annual jaripeo. For a while, he seemed to go a bit mad.

But expressing such emotion was nothing to be ashamed of here—drinking the mezcal with the comfort of his family around him provided a safe, supportive arena for Espiridion's soulful catharsis. He could no longer ride bulls, but he could still have an inner jaripeo—facing the demons of imminent death, while, for a sweet moment, transcending the many difficulties of life. At our feet the birria simmered, awaiting the arrival of the American mixologists. They were coming to meet the producers—and learn about the local terroir and how they could flavor their cocktails with it.

Agave cupreata

PART SIX

THE TURNING OF THE WORM?

I N *THE BOTANY of Desire*, Michael Pollan explores the idea that cultivated plants such as potatoes, marijuana, tulips, and apple trees may be opportunistic. "We automatically think of domestication as something we do to other species," he writes, "but it makes just as much sense to think of it as something certain plants and animals have done to us, a clever evolutionary strategy for advancing their own interests."

Have agaves, too, been manipulating us?

At first, their hearts supplied us with food and drink, and their leaves gave us threads for rope and cloth, as well as sharp points for weapons and tools. Later, we began farming maguey to produce nectar for sweeteners, and fibers for twine, dartboards, and carpets. We keep finding new uses for the plants—in 2016, the Ford Motor Company partnered with Jose Cuervo to explore using leftover agave plant fibers for bioplastic car parts. And magueys are increasingly harvested for their high concentrations of inulin, a polysaccharide used in foods and for medical purposes. We also like the looks of them—the striking shapes of agaves can be found livening up traffic islands and ornamental gardens around the world. And sometimes they inspire us—at the contemporary art space SITE Santa Fe, I came across a maguey cleverly sculpted from embroidered, decommissioned Border Patrol uniforms, by the El Paso–based artist Margarita Cabrera.

In exchange for all this, we've kept agaves around instead of removing them as thorny nuisances—an extraordinary gain for the plants at a time of large-scale species extinction. But their biggest contribution by far has been supplying an effective materia prima for our alcoholic drinks. Indeed, Pollan writes that intoxication "is a human desire we might never have cultivated had it not been for a handful of plants that manage to manufacture chemicals with the precise molecular key needed to unlock the mechanisms in our brain governing pleasure, memory, and maybe even transcendence."

But this relationship can be problematic for agaves when we demand too much of them. Unlike coffee and cacao trees or grape vines, which trade seeds and fruit for life, a maguey is gone for good once it's harvested. So what could agaves be up to? Certainly, a successful strategy might be for them to be farmed in enormous numbers. But that doesn't always work out: A. *tequilana* became a victim of its own success when the surging demand for tequila spurred a problematic monoculture of cloned plants.

To ensure the genetic diversity that's essential to their survival, it's much better for agaves to be left to their own devices and propagate freely, their future health determined by natural selection. But when non-farmed magueys are unprotected they become vulnerable to another threat: overexploitation. This is a rapidly growing problem. As more consumers seek out obscure small-batch mezcals distilled from agaves silvestres, such as tobalá, arroqueño, *barril* (A. *karwinskii*), madrecuixe, mexicano, and tepeztate, the increasing demand for these rare "varietals" requires that more plants be gathered from nature.

Significant blows have already been dealt to wild tobalá populations. There are efforts to cultivate the magueys in Oaxaca—such as the nursery Douglas French showed me at his Scorpion distillery. Other mezcal brands have been experimenting with raising agaves such as barril and madrecuixe from seeds, and then planting them in their natural habitats—the semi-wild plants becoming semi-cultivated. But some agaves used for mezcal refuse to be tended by man, and others, such as tepeztate and arroqueño, can take decades to mature. Mezcals made from these increasingly sought-after types are some of the most lucrative for brand owners, although high prices keep them out of reach for most consumers. Yet without long-range conservation strategies, several agave species could easily disappear if their supply is over-harvested to meet the growing demand.

If we consider the possibility that it is magueys, not we, who are in the driver's seat, then perhaps they are addressing their mismanagement and overexploitation by calling attention to the burgeoning numbers, and variations of, the alcoholic drinks we distill from them. In the U.S. the popularity of Mexican spirits continues to skyrocket. According to a 2016 article on Bloomberg.com, "Global sales of mezcal rose to a record $80 million last year, according to International Wine & Spirits Research. In the U.S., Pernod Ricard and Diageo have benefited from the rising popularity of tequila amid slower vodka sales. From 2010 to 2015, combined sales of tequila and mezcal rose 30 percent by volume in the U.S., more than any other alcohol category except cognac, according to data from Euromonitor

International." Those figures translate into the distillation of hundreds of millions of *A. tequilana* magueys per year alone.

Agave spirits are also gaining popularity in Asia, Australia, and Europe, and a new range of non-DO distillates is being produced in India under the brand name DesmondJi by the company Agave India. Their spirits are manufactured with methods similar to those used for tequila, from a maguey species that's long been grown in the Deccan Plateau, perhaps introduced there by British colonialists. In 2011, Railean Distillers, in Texas, began making a 100 percent "Made in USA" agave spirit called *El Perico* (The Parrot), which the company has described as "perfect for Authentic Texas Margaritas." And the artisan distiller St. George Spirits has begun cultivating *A. tequilana* in southern California for small-batch distillates.

At the Tales of the Cocktail seminar I attended in 2011, biologist Iván Saldaña Oyarzábal was already warning of the overharvesting of wild-grown Mexican agave. "When you drink mezcal, you're drinking plants!" he said. His message to the audience of mixologists was clear: fewer wild magueys will mean fewer esoteric heirloom spirits to sell. A study of mezcal agaves in the Tehuacán-Cuicatlán Valley, published in *Economic Botany* in 2015, states that a "total of 37 agave species are extracted from forests of Mexico for producing mescal. This activity has caused decline of numerous populations, and their sustainable management is indispensable for preventing species extinctions." The study's "viability analyses" suggest that unmanaged populations would "decrease 30 percent to 90 percent in thirty years," and that "at least 30 percent of reproductive plants should be left to ensure seed provision for natural and assisted populations' recovery."

Bartenders, of course, can always hop on the next worldly booze train. That might be French agricole rums one day, and Italian amaro digestifs the next. Likewise consumers have learned that drinks, as with songs and dishes, can offer magic carpet rides from a bar stool, and that mixologists can be the genies who make them fly. But maestros mezcaleros remain highly vulnerable to the effects of losing their valuable materia prima. Mezcal is not only an important thread of their cultural identity; their entire livelihoods can depend on it. While harvesting and distilling the neighborhood agaves silvestres for fast cash might work as a short-term strategy, it's untenable over time. But when people need to feed their families, it's hard for them to think about the future. Even so, there are farsighted communities in Mexico that have been planning ahead.

回

AT A COMIDA and tasting event at the Real Minero distillery, in Santa Catarina Minas, I met Nils Dallmann, a German architect living in Mexico City. On the side, he exported a selection of artisanal mezcals to Berlin through a small company, Mezcalería. He told me about a brand he was interested in called Sanzekan, distilled by a large cooperative in the state of Guerrero called Sanzekan Tinemi (Nahuatl for *Seguimos Juntos*, or "Onward Together"). The group was using sustainable methods to produce papalote (butterfly) mezcal, which is traditionally made with wild-grown *A. cupreata*.

The papalote maguey can be more challenging to cultivate than other agaves because it doesn't produce clones, which are easy to transplant. Instead, it reproduces sexually, by seeds. But the Sanzekan organization had figured out that by raising the magueys in nurseries, they could replant the baby agaves in plots, like crops, as well as in their natural habitats. Now, for each maguey harvested, many more are grown for reforestation projects, as well as for future distilling—the medium-sized agaves taking from seven to thirteen years to mature. Dallmann said that some of the Sanzekan maestros would be attending an upcoming forestry festival in Mexico City—would I like to come and meet them?

The event was held at Centro Banamex, an enormous convention center overlooking Las Américas racetrack. After making my way past an endless array of polished displays featuring everything from cutting-edge tree-trimming equipment to regional foodstuffs, I found the Sanzekan Tinemi booth in a remote corner of a cavernous hall. It was homespun—a few maestros mezcaleros were hanging out in front of a large mural depicting the many activities associated with growing agaves and making mezcal from them. The entire marketing effort was only themselves and the carefully hand-painted picture.

A polite young man, Juan Pedro Teliz, showed me the important details in the painting. "Here we can see hummingbirds and butterflies drinking from the maguey flowers," he explained. "And on this side some bats are pollinating them at night under the moon. And this is the nursery with the *plántulas* [seedlings].

And there you can see men and women replanting the baby papalotes in the mountains. Here a magueyero is harvesting a mature one with a coa. And below him you can see a maestro mezcalero mashing some piñas with a wooden mallet. This woman is bringing a burro loaded with firewood to these men preparing an horno. And over here you can see the quality-control inspector in his laboratory." Finally, Teliz pointed out two men at a table who were clinking glasses of mezcal. ¡¡SALUD!! was written in black letters above them.

Teliz explained that Sanzekan Tinemi was a large-scale collective based in Chilapa de Álvarez, a small town a few hours south of Mexico City, in the low central mountain region of Guerrero—above Acapulco. The organization worked with mezcal-making communities spread over four municipios: Chilapa de Álvarez, Zitlala, Ahuacuotzingo, and Tixtla. He said that about four dozen maestros mezcaleros were participating, each one distilling a unique papalote mezcal from *A. cupreata*. The maguey is endemic to the mountainous basin of the upper Balsas River, a major waterway known locally as Río Mezcala, after the Mesoamerican Mezcala culture of southwestern Mexico.

Teliz said that, above all, Sanzekan Tinemi was a societal organization. In addition to its maestros mezcaleros, hundreds of other members were performing the tasks shown in the mural, as well as many others. He showed me a paragraph on a bottle label: "Neither agave nor mezcal has meaning without its people and its culture. That's why we take care that the profits from our product go to our communities and contribute to strengthening our cultural heritage."

In the interest of fairness, no distiller was to be advanced over another. This solidarity was emphasized by the brand name: Onward Together. Every bottle of Sanzekan mezcal was 48 percent ABV and was given the same label: a bright green papalote maguey with a rainbow of colors fanning out behind it. But some differences among the spirits were identified on the backs of the bottles, where the name of each producer, his village, the batch number, and the vintage year were inscribed. Like paintings, every bottle was individually signed by its maestro mezcalero.

Marketing the mezcals could be challenging, however. For the average shopper, seeing all the different, yet identical-looking, Sanzekan mezcals lined up together was like checking out a set of baseball cards for an unfamiliar team. Without being led in particular directions by tasting notes and spirit-award emblems, consumers were left to themselves to decide which papalote mezcal they might prefer. Although this was refreshingly egalitarian, I could see that tasting all of them would be daunting for even the most enthusiastic aficionado, including me.

Luckily, before I needed to choose which one to try first, Ciro Barranca Bello, a genial old maestro mezcalero from the village of Santa Cruz, poured me some of his. It was complex, the roasted *A. cupreata* providing a sweeter, richer flavor than, say, espadín or tobalá. Ciro introduced me to another producer, Refugio Calzada Hernández, who was from the village of Tetitlán de la Lima. Refugio said he was descended from four generations of distillers and had been making mezcal since the age of fourteen. He poured me some of his spirit, which tasted slightly different but was also superb. Soon I was sipping mezcals crafted by other Sanzekan maestros, living it up in the polished majesty of Centro Banamex. Maybe I *could* taste them all!

"Why don't you come visit us in Chilapa?" Teliz suggested.

◲

NOT LONG AFTER, I hitched a ride from Mexico City to Guerrero with Catarina Illsley Granich, the biologist and agave expert who had written several interesting articles about mezcal and magueys. She was part of the nonprofit advocacy organization GEA (Grupo de Estudios Ambientales) that had been founded in 1977 to address environmental concerns in Mexico. According to its website, the group valued "cultural diversity combined with bio-diversity and agro-biodiversity, as well as the ancient and modern contributions of indigenous and campesino cultures, so we encourage dialogue between traditional and scientific knowledge."

Although Granich was no longer directly involved with Sanzekan Tinemi, she had been instrumental in working with them to plan and set up the mezcal cooperative in the early 1990s. She was now primarily focused on other farming and natural-resource projects around Chilapa de Álvarez, where the mezcal-making organization is based. As we made our way down Highway 95D, by way of Cuernavaca, she explained that the original concept for Sanzekan was to bring new jobs and sources of income to Guerrero, one of Mexico's poorest states.

The biggest city is Acapulco, the popular tourist destination, but it and much of the rest of the region have been struggling economically while suffering high rates of drug-war violence, as well as such natural disasters as hurricanes, earthquakes, and floods. In fact, when I was in Mexico City right after my visit, the powerful Zumpango earthquake, with a 6.5 magnitude, shook my room at the Hotel Milan for about a minute, and shut down the power in the surrounding Colonia Roma neighborhood. The epicenter had been one hundred miles away in Guerrero. With so many challenges continuously facing its inhabitants, the state was one of the top for generating migrants who head to the U.S. for work. But they also travel to other parts of Mexico to earn a living. As we drove through a barren and mountainous landscape, we passed a line of orange-colored buses that Granich said were surely filled with families on their way to pick grapes and tomatoes in the states of Sonora and Nayarit. She speculated that the workers would likely be gone for months, their children taken out of school for the duration.

"If making mezcal allows for pride in what you do and allows people to stay and not migrate, that's a big difference," she said. "But at the same time, the carrying capacity is important—at what point can you keep making mezcal without draining the local resources, which include firewood as well as agave?" Those problems don't have easy answers, but she said the ethnic groups of the area, which include the Amuzgo, Nahua, Mixtec, and Tlapaneco indigenous peoples, as well as a group of Afro-Mexicans descended from African slaves, are known for being very resourceful, having been marginalized and left to their own devices for centuries.

Guerreros (warriors) are also known for having a strong sense of community identity. They express this through traditional fiestas, where dancers wear spectacular costumes and masks. One of the most famous events is the annual *Tigrada* (tiger) parade in Chilapa de Álvarez. Every August 15, hundreds dress up in eye-catching yellow-and-black jaguar outfits and hand-painted wooden masks, and march through the streets of the city. They both honor the Virgin of the Assumption and pray for rain and a bountiful harvest from Tepeyollotl, the Aztec "jaguar god" who protects the local mountains.

After driving about three hours from Mexico City, we left Highway 95D just before Chilpancingo de los Bravo, the state's capital and its second-largest city, and then followed Highway 93 for another forty-five minutes to Chilapa de Álvarez. This is a dusty, unpretentious town, founded by the Aztecs in the fifteenth century, and locally known as the Gateway to the Mountains. The main attractions are its regional market and a gray cathedral on the plaza, where a beloved mechanical figure of Juan Diego, the first indigenous saint, emerges from a spire.

Granich dropped me off at an inn near the edge of town, and the next morning I was met there by Juan Pedro Teliz and two other Sanzekan associates, Alba and Melquiades. For the next few days, the companionable trio showed me around the area, bringing to life the many details of the hand-painted mural I had seen at the forestry convention. We began with a visit to the nondescript two-story headquarters of the Social Solidarity Society Sanzekan Tinemi. There, in an upstairs meeting room, I was told the five basic principles of the organization: autonomy, pluralism, democracy, self-management, and mutual aid. Then I was seated in a yellow plastic chair and shown a well-crafted documentary from 2006: *Papalote Mezcal of Chilapa: From the Mountain to the Bottle*.

Several maestros mezcaleros were featured at the beginning, including Ciro and Refugio, whom I had met at the forestry convention. A longtime magueyero named Gabriel Vázquez was also interviewed. Wearing a white shirt and straw hat, he was filmed standing on a steep mountain slope dotted with short palm trees and squat green papalote magueys. Their leaves were broad, the edges serrated and thorny. "The custom of mezcal doesn't belong to just one person, it belongs to everybody here," he said. "The tradition has been passed down to us from our *abuelitos* (grandparents) who left us a long time ago. And because it's a tradition that's been passed down, it's become a custom that hasn't been lost."

Mezcal remains an important social connector in the region, as it still does in Oaxaca and in many other parts of Mexico. In Guerreran communities, the drink plays a prominent part in annual fiestas and life milestones such as weddings, christenings, and funerals. One local celebration takes place on the third of May, the day of the Holy Cross. Vázquez pointed to a large mountain looming in the distance, known locally as *El Volcán* (the Volcano). He said that every year on the holiday, men and women make a pilgrimage to its conical peak, walking to the "music of the wind." They carry *chiquihuites* (baskets with headstraps) filled with mole, tamales, and bottles of mezcal. When they reach the top, they dance at the foot of the *Cruz de Mayo* (May Cross).

The documentary went on to explore some of the rebellious roots of Guerreran mezcal. A middle-aged maestro mezcalero named Albino Tlacotempa was interviewed. He had been instrumental in founding Sanzekan Tinemi, and had passed away several months before I saw the film. "Mezcal was produced clandestinely by our ancestors and grandparents," he said. "It wasn't allowed and was prosecutable by law. But it never lost its importance." The camera cut back to Vázquez, who elaborated on the prohibition period, which I had heard about from Graciela Ángeles Carreño. "At that time it was a very tricky situation," he said. "From 1954 and before. The poor producers were making mezcal in hiding from the government. They would look for a secluded *barranca* [ravine] . . . and between a mountain here and a mountain there they would find a space, and that's where they would put their fábrica."

Distilling in secret allowed the maestros mezcaleros to avoid federal inspections, taxes, and onerous bribes. When local officials were spotted en route from a nearby town, word was quickly spread to the producers that a shakedown was imminent. A common punishment was having their wooden tinas filled with gasoline, which would make them unusable. "At night, if you heard dogs barking, you would think that the government was coming," recalled Telésforo Calzada, another old maestro mezcalero featured in the film. "It was a touchy time—you knew they would seize everything you had." Even worse, if your mezcal was confiscated, it was likely to be drunk by the rats who nabbed it. "It's different now," Calzada said. "You can work as you like. Now they don't suffer like we did. Yes, we suffered a lot."

Although the Sanzekan Tinemi mezcal project was founded in 1990, the collective originated ten years before to address a lack of such basic food supplies in the impoverished rural area as corn, rice, and beans. Now, aside from managing its agave and mezcal production chain, the group runs a handicraft enterprise, oversees soil and water restoration projects, helps to resolve community conflicts, and addresses many other local concerns. The idea is to encourage economic development without losing the traditions of sustainability that have historically been part of the region's cultural identity.

On its website, Sanzekan stated that its reforestation programs plant up to 1.5 million *A. cupreata* seedlings per year. This not only helps maintain healthy populations of papalote agaves, but also addresses problems caused by deforestation, such as erosion, as well as water pollution and loss. To further conserve local resources, biofilters are used in the fábricas to treat wastewater, and the leftover mash from distilling is plowed into fields as a fertilizer. I was told that all the Sanzekan mezcals I tried were organic.

Catarina was also interviewed in the film. "For hundreds of years, the campesino resistance has kept mezcal alive as a resource that generates income and employment in the communities," she said. "Now we are beginning to catch a glimpse—and the members of Sanzekan already see this clearly—that it is coming back as a catalyst for regional development." It seemed that, in Guerrero, agaves had figured out ways of ensuring their future by linking their destinies with man.

ㄹ

I PILED INTO a white Chevy SUV with my trio of escorts, and Melquiades drove us out of town to visit Sanzekan Tinemi's biggest agave nursery. We soon passed a funeral procession that was moving slowly alongside the road. Some men had shouldered a polished wooden casket and were following an empty white hearse as a brass band played a sorrowful tune under the hot sun. A windy route took us through limestone hills covered with scrubby oak trees and the short, broad-fanned palms that are used for weaving baskets. The fronds are also laid across piled-up piñas in hornos, protecting roasting agave from the dirt that's heaped on top.

As we entered the small village of Santa Cruz, we found Ciro standing by the road. He was dressed in white, eating a cone of mezcal-flavored nieves that he had just bought from a vendor. He hopped in to join us for the ride. We passed a rugged limestone cliff with a cave entrance opening over a wide ravine. He said a large colony of *murciélagos* (bats) lived inside the chamber. They are crucial for pollinating the local papalote agave flowers, so the magueyeros need to be careful to leave some quiotes untouched, allowing the plants to reproduce and providing the bats with nectar to drink. The flowers bloom for four months, from early September into late December.

When a papalote maguey enters its reproductive state, which is known as *velilla*, Ciro said, the pencas in the center turn a light shade of green, an indication that the quiote is about to sprout. When the stalks are then removed from the magueys, the plants are often left in the ground for another year or two, in order to concentrate the sugars inside their piñas. This form of "pre-aging" can significantly add to a mezcal's flavor. A de-sexed agave is called a capón, which means "castrated rooster," and caponization is often performed on the roosters as well, to improve *their* flavors. Sometimes a bottle label will include information about the length of time maguey capones have been aged. The longer the better, and mezcals distilled solely from capón agaves can be highly prized.

Near Tecoanapa, Melquiades parked just off a hillside road above the Sanzekan *vivero* (nursery), and from there we walked down a sloping path. On the way, Ciro noticed a writhing ball of daddy longlegs on a cliff. He showed me that, by moving closer, I could hear the spiders clashing their limbs in tiny clickety-clacks. Then he picked a small purple fruit from a nearby vine and gave it to me to taste. Below us, about forty workers were tending baby agaves in a large plot. There were at least a million plants, I was told. The field was irrigated from a nearby spring via long lengths of black plastic tubing.

At the bottom of the path, a woman was squatting under a shade tree. She was building two small fires to cook a comida for the field hands. A breeze rustled through some palms as two boys mounted a lively swordfight with broken sticks. Nearby, a man and two women were sitting on unfolded raffia sugar sacks that were spread on the ground. A large pile of seedlings was heaped in the dirt before them. One by one, they prepared them for planting, pinching off the roots to encourage new ones to sprout.

The baby papalote agaves are initially kept inside for eight or nine months, until they are hardy enough to relocate to the plots outside. There, they spend from one to one and a half years exposed to the elements, but are regularly watered and well-protected from cows and other animals that like eating them. When they are eventually transferred to Sanzekan's reforestation projects in the surrounding countryside, other native species are planted alongside them. This helps to combat deforestation, which often occurs when too much firewood is gathered for distilling, cooking, and other uses.

On the way back to Chilapa de Álvarez, Ciro invited us to stop by his fábrica in Santa Cruz. It consisted of a deep, narrow horno and a low brick building with a tin roof. There were rows of tomato plants in a field outside, as well as peach, avocado, plantain, and plum trees. A spring provided fresh *agua dulce* (soft water), which was used for fermentation and for cooling his stills. Inside the structure were six large wooden tinas and one small one. A wooden grinding trough, called a *canoa* (canoe), had been sunk into the concrete floor. Ciro picked up a big wooden mallet and showed me how he uses it to hand-mash his roasted agave. He had two copper alembiques, which were topped with the conical, sloping sombreros of the Michoacán style. A low-slung bed had been set up by one of the stills. "I can lie there and watch my mezcal come out!" he said. The maestro was seventy-five and had been making the spirit for fifty-two years.

Ciro told me about some of the traditional rituals that are followed in the local fábricas. After the last shovelfuls of dirt have been heaped on top of an horno, a small cross is always stuck into the pile, in order to bless the agave baking below. When distilling begins, the first few drops to emerge from an alembique are thrown into the still fire as an offering. Each fábrica has a mythical "owner," and other rules must be followed to keep this being happy, or bad luck will follow. One edict was not to be greedy and ask for too much mezcal from a still. Another was that visitors must be offered some of the spirit to drink. Ciro generously presented me with a rare bottle of espadín mezcal. He had crafted it from some agaves that had been growing nearby. Instead of signing his name on the label, he had made an ink thumbprint.

Over the next couple of days, we visited other Sanzekan maestros mezcaleros, and I learned that each of them also used highly individualized production techniques, their fábricas tailored to meet their particular styles. One distiller was Moisés Calzada Rendón. He had a distinctive, hexagonal tin roof over his horno, which was wide and shallow, and inside his fábrica the still fire was set in the opposite side of his alembique, which was encased in concrete. But not every choice had been a personal one: lurking on one side was a huge stainless steel autoclave, which had been provided as part of a government program. "They told me that it would make the flavor better and be more economical," he said. "¡Al contrario! They were thinking like Jalisco, which is very industrial. But we're artisanal—we use agaves silvestres, as well as palm fronds and tools that are made from wood." He jokingly called the unused, dust-covered machine "*mi aeroplane*."

At his one-still fábrica, tucked into a lush hillside hollow beside Tetitlán de la Lima, Refugio offered me a jícara of pechuga mezcal he had created with papalote agave. He distilled only eighty liters of the spirit per year, using a family recipe passed down through four generations. He said that before he distilled the drink for the second time, he had fed the breasts of eight "*gallinas del rancho*" (free-range chickens) into the mouth of his copper alembique, along with a mixture of almonds, raisins, cinnamon, peppers, and cloves. It was the most delicious pechuga I had ever tasted, and it wasn't for sale. "I make this one for fun," he shrugged.

Although the Sanzekan team did their best not to promote any distiller over another, it was apparent that everyone held a special reverence for the mezcal-making skills of Benigno Sánchez Gatica. "Don Beni" lived with his wife and son in the hills above El Peral. When we stopped by to visit, the maestro was off feeding and watering his mules and burros. We waited for him in the dirt courtyard beside his adobe house. Chicks pecked around our feet, and I noticed an armadillo shell hanging on an outside wall. The son told me that a special tea had been made from the animal to treat his mother's asthma, a common ailment of people who cook over wood fires.

Don Beni soon appeared, wearing a big cardigan sweater and a white shawl wrapped tightly around his head. His deeply tanned face was wizened and good-natured, and he had an easy laugh. He brought us into a storeroom that was filled with large glass jugs of his papalote mezcal. He emptied some into a jícara, and then sucked it up into a venencia. He showed me the cordón of perlas, which he said indicated a 46 to 47 percent ABV, and passed me some of the spirit to taste. It was sweet and silky, like ethereal, slightly cinnamon-flavored, liquid honey. Magic, I thought.

"After I've cut the quiotes, I always wait another two years before I harvest the magueys," he said. "That makes the mezcal taste much sweeter, because there's more sugar in the piñas. I grow my magueys in *tierra negra* [black earth], which has a lot of iron that gives them more flavor." He said that he also used special *piedras negras* [black rocks] to heat his horno, which he handpicked from a nearby river. "Our mezcals taste less smoky here than they do in Oaxaca," he said. "This is because we put a cap of palm fronds on top of the horno that allows more steam to come up from below. 'I'm breathing!' the maguey always tells me!" After roasting the agave for three to five days, Don Beni would hand-mash it in a canoa and then ferment it for seventy-two hours in oak tinas. He distilled only five hundred liters of mezcal per year, in March, April, and May.

He invited us back for breakfast the following morning. It was an annual feast day in the village, one that celebrates the Immaculate Conception. We gathered around a table covered by a blue oilcloth, in a semi-enclosed room with clay-plastered walls, a tin roof, and a concrete floor. His wife served us huge earthenware bowls of steaming chicken *pozole* (hominy stew), a regional specialty, and smaller bowls of chopped onion, chile powder, limes, oregano, salt, and chicharrones. Don Beni brought out some mezcal, and as we began sipping it we heard fireworks exploding and a brass band starting to play.

We walked downhill to the plaza in front of the village church, where a troupe of dancers were whirling in the *Danza de los Diablos* (Devil Dance), one of the many traditional dances of Guerrero. An expression of resistance, the Devil Dance is rooted in the colonial period, when African slaves were brought to work along the Pacific *Costa Chica* (Little Coast) shared by Oaxaca and Guerrero and Spanish missionaries were evangelizing local indigenous peoples. The devil dancers, representing the underworld, wore dark clothing and black masks with huge red ears and swinging gray tassels. Each dancer waved a red bandana as he moved in and out of formation. A boy dressed as a woman danced among the others, carrying a fake baby and wearing a white mask and a long red skirt. There were many onlookers, and a juez offered us plastic cups of locally made mezcal.

Before we left the village, Don Beni took us to his fábrica. It was clean and simple—redbrick walls, a single copper still, two tinas, and a wide canoa sunk into the floor. He showed me the clear *manantial* (spring) that he used for water, and then a beautiful ammonite fossil that was sitting on a pile of bricks by the door. "Come back sometime, and we'll eat *venado* [deer]!" He warmly patted me on the back. "You remind me of the *rubio* [blonde gringo] who fell out of the sky in that movie *Okey, Mister Pancho*!" He doubled over with laughter.

I was able to see the film later. Released in 1981, it was a slapstick comedy starring the actress María Nicolasa Cruz. She had also cowritten the story, which features a recurring character she had invented called "La India María." Reminiscent of Charlie Chaplin's "Little Tramp," María is an amiable underdog—a naive indigenous woman who gets tangled up in ridiculous situations that often involve racist and classist dynamics. In *Okey, Mister Pancho* we find her living in a rural Mexican rancho with her grandfather, along with a burro, a parrot, and a chimpanzee. A small plane crashes in the surrounding forest, and she rescues an American from the wreckage. She names him Mister Pancho, falls in love with him, and highjinks ensue when she gets suckered into a diamond-smuggling ring and crosses the border to Houston. Although the film makes it clear that rubios mean trouble, Don Beni didn't seem to hold it against me.

My hosts brought me to one last, very important spot. In 2007, Sanzekan Tinemi finished erecting a massive storage-and-aging repository for the collective's mezcals. The cavernous building was constructed with thick concrete walls to maintain a constant temperature inside, where there was enough space to store up to sixty thousand liters. Long, high rows of industrial shelving were loaded with large glass containers of aged mezcal, and thousands of empty bottles were stacked in the back, waiting to be filled.

With so much liquid knowledge at hand, the storehouse was also an archive for tasting research. To demonstrate what happens when a clear "joven" mezcal is aged in glass, I was poured two spirits distilled by Ciro. The first was from May 2005 and had a lyrical, citrusy taste. The second was only a few months old and tasted much greener. When we tried mezcals crafted by other distillers, the aging had refined and condensed the flavors, making the spirits progressively smoother and their complexities more delicately articulated. There were subtle variations among distillates made with papalote maguey grown in different microclimates, or hand-crushed in canoas rather than processed through mechanical grinders, or aged in the ground as capones. Clearly the possibilities for expression were endless.

The mezcal collection was a treasury of mezcal authorship, as well as a proud monument to cultural identity in an uncertain and slippery world. For the people of the region, merely seeing the grand building provides an affirmation of who they are. Returning to Chilapa de Álvarez later, we passed a large canvas circus tent on the outskirts. In the town center, a gaily painted trailer, two bored-looking tigers lounging in cages on its back, was parked in the middle of a busy roundabout to promote the circus.

As we drove around the circle, the magnificent cats languidly flicked their dust-covered tails as they impassively watched us whiz by. Their wild potential thwarted, the caged animals made me think of some of the maestros mezcaleros I had met in Oaxaca, who had been distilling the same spirits for mezcal companies year after year. They hadn't seemed as free to innovate and express their creativity as the Sanzekan distillers. Things felt more agreeable here without brand owners hogging the scene with their carefully cultivated personas, their producers treated as authentically colorful background extras in The Mezcal Rush.

回

BUT THERE WERE some Oaxacan mezcal makers who were determined to produce and sell their drinks entirely on their own terms and with as few middlemen as possible. Not long before I left Oaxaca de Juárez for the last time, I received an email from a young entrepreneur, Elisandro González Molina. He wrote that he and his cousin, Edgar González Ramírez, had started their own mezcal brand in the village of San Cristóbal Lachirioag. It was called *Tosba*, which Elisandro said means "just have *one*" (but with a wink) in the local Zapoteco dialect. Edgar was the maestro mezcalero, while Elisandro focused on their business and marketing, spending much of his time in the U.S. Would I like to come and visit their fábrica? On the map, I could see that their community was in the remote Villa Alta district of the mountainous Sierra Norte. It looked as if it would be at least four hours away from Oaxaca de Juárez by colectivo or bus. But Elisandro happened to be visiting his parents in the city, so I rented a car for us to drive out to the village together. The only vehicle left at the rental agency was an immaculate white Volkswagen Jetta. "It might get a little dirty," said Elisandro. "But it'll make it."

Because some roads had been washed out by heavy rains, we took a lengthy and circuitous route that brought us down the Pan-American Highway to Mitla, and then into the mountains by way of Ayutla, before continuing through the villages of Tamazulápam del Espíritu Santo, Santa María Tlahuitoltepec, and San Andrés Yaá. On the way, Elisandro told me more about himself and Tosba. He was thirty, and his parents were teachers.

In 2000, when he was nineteen, he used a fake driver's license to cross the U.S. border from Tijuana. He headed to San Jose, where an uncle, Tomás Gonzalez, had migrated many years before. At the time Elisandro spoke very little English, so Tomás immediately enrolled him in an ESL program. When Tomás had first come to the U.S. himself, he had worked long hours as a laborer in nurseries, and had learned that speaking English allows for greater opportunity. He now co-owns, with Edgar's brother-in-law, chef Manuel Martinez, a Latin-inspired restaurant and agave-spirits bar in Redwood City, called LV Mar, that proudly serves Tosba mezcal.

After spending about eight years in San Jose, learning English while supporting himself busing tables and working in tax preparation and real estate, Elisandro returned to Mexico to study business and marketing at the University of Guadalajara. While there, he waited for an adjustment of his U.S. immigration status, which he had applied for while in Mexico and took four years to sort out. When I met Elisandro in 2011, he had recently been working for a food-and-agricultural agency affiliated with the United Nations called PESA (Proyecto Estratégico para la Seguridad Alimentaria). But in 2012, soon after our trip to San Cristóbal Lachirioag, he was able to return legally to San Jose, where he worked as a restaurant server and bartender while launching Tosba.

Edgar had also lived in San Jose for several years, from 2000–2006, working as a roofer and in a variety of restaurant jobs. Sharing a sparse room with little more than their sleeping bags and what they could fit in their backpacks, the two cousins were excited by the enterprising spirit of Silicon Valley. Edgar made sandwiches at Subway for a variety of tech entrepreneurs, and Steve Jobs would come for dinner at Brigitte's, a French restaurant in Santa Clara where Elisandro worked under the sommelier François Gallet. As Elisandro put it, the cousins were inspired to build "our own innovative bridge from Oaxaca," and decided to launch a mezcal brand.

"We want to do with mezcal what Steve Jobs did with computers," Elisandro said. He wore New Balance sneakers, a conscious nod to the Apple co-founder.

The odds were heavily stacked against the two cousins fulfilling that dream. They had no financial backing and would need to depend entirely upon their wits, talent, resourcefulness, persistence, and determination. They also had very little experience in business management or finance, let alone in making mezcal. But they very much wanted to be their own bosses and bring much-needed jobs to San Cristóbal Lachirioag. The once-thriving village had become more of a ghost town after many of its inhabitants migrated to El Norte for work. Although agaves grew in the region, along with coffee trees and sugarcane, mezcal was no longer distilled in the surrounding area. The men had grown up hearing stories about a legendary mezcal that had once been produced in the nearby village of San Francisco Yatee, but the tradition had been lost decades before after the family who had crafted it moved away.

The cousins began sending home any extra money they made, and Edgar's father, Felipe González Cruz, started planting espadín agaves on some of his plots of land outside the village. He liked to tell the story of when he had first bought two thousand maguey seedlings, and expected them to fill a truck bed, but they were so small they actually filled only a bucket. After several years, when enough agaves were growing, the men built their fábrica. First they salvaged an expansive metal structure that had once covered the village market, and erected it over the mezcal production site. Next they dug an horno outside it, and recycled an old copper still that Felipe had formerly used to make aguardiente from the local sugarcane. Later, they bought another copper still, as well as a grinding machine. A local carpenter built them four large wooden tinas with pine from the nearby mountains. Finally, there was only one thing left to do—learn how to make mezcal.

Although Felipe had previously distilled aguardiente, they found, after a great deal of trial and error, that distilling agave spirits was a very different ballgame. So they brought in a consultant, Delfino Martínez Cruz, a maestro mezcalero from Santo Domingo Albarradas. After learning the ropes from him, and then experimenting some more, they finally decided that they had a mezcal worth selling. In fact, it tasted so good that a prominent American importer made them an offer of thirty pesos per liter in bulk. Although that was in the range of the going rate, the cousins didn't think it was fair—the importer sold his mezcals for nearly fifty times that much in the U.S. Why should he nab all the profits? Instead, Edgar and Elisandro decided to purchase a bottling machine and design their own website, labels, and packaging. They had come this far on their own—why stop now? They registered Tosba with the CRM under the categories of producer, bottler, and commercializer.

ꔮ

AS ELISANDRO AND I followed a dizzying route up into the mountains, the slopes became lusher and greener. At one point, we stopped at an overlook to take in a thick bank of clouds that was sweeping into the beyond. When we left the main route and began traveling on dirt roads, there were times when the car barely made it through the narrow, muddy tracks that clung to the edges of precipices, some of which had been almost entirely washed out in recent storms. When we finally reached San Cristóbal Lachirioag, the once-white Jetta was almost entirely brown.

Just before entering the village, Elisandro told me to park alongside the road. "The palenque is just down there," he said, pointing straight down the mountainside. As we walked down a steep track, a deep, beautiful valley opened below us, a wide river coursing through the bottom. Most of the terrain was covered with trees, but here and there were telltale patches of bluish-green espadín. Elisandro said they had around seventy thousand of the plants, and each one could be transformed into as many as seven liters of mezcal. We soon entered a plot of their agave, where we came upon Edgar and his father. Edgar was using an axe to pry a mature maguey from the soil. After finally rocking it back and forth to unearth it, he quickly sheared the spines off the plant with a machete.

"We learned that by cutting the pencas very close to the piña, less methanol will be produced in distilling," he said, wiping sweat from his forehead. "And removing the lower part of the quiote, where it goes into the piña, also affects the flavor."

He helped his father strap the shorn white piña to the back of a burro. With Felipe leading the pack animal ahead, the four of us continued walking downhill. We soon passed a clear spring bubbling up from below a tangle of thick tree roots clinging to the slope like talons. "Agua dulce," nodded Felipe. The distillers used the water for fermenting the maguey and for cooling their stills. He filled a bottle and passed it to me, and it tasted sweet and delicious. The river below provided another crucial resource: firewood. Every year during the rainy season, flash floods would leave huge piles of dead trunks and branches on the banks, which the men would gather to heat their stills.

"We're trying to do things as sustainably as possible," Elisandro said.

They used the leftover ash, along with the spent mash from distilling, to fertilize a small nursery of baby agaves, as well as a vegetable garden where they grew onions, peppers, beans, string beans, squash, and tomatoes. Papaya, mango, banana, orange, coffee, guanabana, and passion fruit trees surrounded the fábrica, providing some of the wild yeasts that fermented the roasted maguey. A high, expansive, tin-roofed structure sheltered the two copper stills, the grinder, and the four tinas. The setup was at an altitude of around twenty-six hundred feet, which was about fourteen hundred feet below the village. They didn't have a vehicle at the time, so the men had to carry everything in and out by hand or use their burros. Edgar's commute up and down the steep slope to and from the fábrica was similar to strenuous day hikes in the Grand Canyon, except that he was making mezcal in between his long walks. The name of the fábrica dog was *Quebradita* (Broken), after the crack it got in its leg bone from chasing a rolling piña downhill. In later years, a second dog was also named Broken after a jaguar broke its leg in a tussle.

The two cousins took me down to the river, which was about fifty yards across at its widest and filled with large gray boulders. In a lush ravine nearby, a beautiful waterfall cascaded down a series of cliffs. A flock of wild turkeys was hurrying through the trees, and Edgar said he would occasionally shoot one and eat it, although the most delicious-tasting local animal was the *tepezcuintle*, a spotted lowland paca that can grow as large as twenty-six pounds. "If you find one in its burrow, you can spear it with a long stick," he said. "We use it to make barbacoa, and it has the most tender meat, even better than venado." They invited me to come back and try it someday.

We made our way back uphill in the dusk. The half moon lit up Felipe's white clothes as he walked ahead of us, and I could hear the river raging farther and farther below. When the four of us drove into the village, Elisandro told me to park by a modest brick storefront. It was a tasting room the cousins had built for Tosba, with large windows revealing an elegant display of mezcal bottles neatly arranged on shiny white shelves. Inside, they showed me their expensive new bottling machine in an adjoining room. They used clear glass 750ml wine bottles, and narrow black labels with borders reminiscent of Greek key patterns, which Elisandro said were actually inspired by the fine stone carvings at Mitla. He poured me some Tosba and the three men watched me intently as I sipped it. Their mezcal was crisp, clean, and citrusy, with hints of papaya and vanilla, and reminded me somewhat of the spirit the Luises distilled in Santo Domingo Albarradas. In fact, the two villages shared the same river, the Río Cajonos.

Edgar invited me to spend the night at the home he shared with his parents. It was near the village center, and from their house I could see a large white church illuminated by a streetlight, and the silhouette of Yiawiz, a conical peak looming in the distance. His mother, María Elena, served us a delicious meal of black mole, beef with onions, and gigantic tortillas. She said I wasn't the first foreigner to visit—a Dutch anthropologist had lived with them many years before, while working on his dissertation about San Cristóbal Lachirioag. "His girlfriend was a supermodel," Edgar remembered fondly.

He insisted I use his bedroom, which contained a gigantic four-poster bed built from a reddish local wood. It was covered with a thick blanket that had a large pink rose on it. The rest of the room was completely bare except for one book: a well-thumbed copy of The Tequila Lover's Guide to Mexico and Mezcal, by Lance Cutler. I opened it to a section called "Visiting Mezcal Palenques," and read: "Most palenques are literally backyard affairs, so you'll meet the whole family when you visit."

Generally, I had found this to be true. But Cutler also wrote: "Fortunately, palenques share many similarities. In other words, if you visit one palenque you've pretty much visited them all." To me, each mezcal fábrica is a proud bastion of individuality, so I couldn't have disagreed with him more. The limitless differences among them were the best part.

At dawn the next day, Edgar's mother was already baking the day's tortillas on her comal. Outside, roosters crowed and peppy banda played from tinny loudspeakers erected around the village to keep people entertained while they performed their chores. Over breakfast, I noticed that Edgar and Elisandro had identical burn scars on their right forearms. They got them while carrying *torito* (little bull) fireworks over their heads at the village fiesta. I imagined them in the raucous dark, spinning below the explosions with the same fierce determination that had gotten them this far with Tosba.

When I was back in the U.S., Elisandro kept in touch. He began spending more time in San Jose, where he lived with his American wife, Jessica, a language instructor, and their young son, Emiliano. After years of cutting through red tape, he was eventually able to begin importing Tosba from Mexico to California. The going was tough, and sometimes he felt discouraged. But every now and then he would share another small victory with me. The mezcal won a tasting competition in Santa Barbara, and a radio correspondent came to San Cristóbal Lachirioag and produced a story for NPR about the two cousins. He spoke about mezcal at a symposium at the California

Academy of Sciences, and Tosba was mentioned in the *New York Times*, *Los Angeles Times*, *Huffington Post*, and by Reuters. It was slowly becoming available in more bars, restaurants, and liquor stores in California. Edgar began distilling pechuga and tobalá mezcals, while Elisandro worked at developing their business, which included building its website, using social media for marketing, and networking with bar managers and mixologists. And in between his restaurant hours, he kept pouring Tosba, turning on one convert at a time.

匚

MEANWHILE, THE THIRST for mezcal was spreading around the globe. Bartenders dressed up in nurse outfits were serving the spirit in a 1970s ambulance in London, and mixologists were shaking it into fancy cocktails in Hong Kong. One sunny fall day in Barcelona, I checked out a new mezcalería called Oaxaca. It was on the ground floor of an old stone building by the port, and had opened only a few weeks before as part of an "authentic" Mexican restaurant. Inside was a cool old jukebox, sofas and armchairs upholstered in spiffy cowhide, papier-mâché Day of the Dead figures, and potted agaves. At the carved wooden bar, a server showed me a menu listing dozens of mezcals. I could order everything from a 30ml glass of espadín for three euros ($4) to a bottle of pechuga for 340 euros ($425).

"Wow, that one's expensive!" I said.

"Don't worry," he said. "You can write your name on it and keep it in here."

He showed me a sturdy black safe, its shelves loaded with rare bottles of pricey mezcal. Here in Spain, it was hard not to see the Mexican spirits as colonial bounty. Like birds in a cage, the drinks looked sad. I remembered a conversation I'd had with the mezcal expert Ulises Torrentera, across the Atlantic Ocean in Oaxaca de Juárez. He had written several books and articles about the drink, and eventually opened a popular mezcalería in the city called *In Situ* (On-Site). "Mexico is a synthesis of pre-Columbian and Spanish cultures," he had told me, "and the roots of mezcal and Mexico share the same belly button."

But the maestros mezcaleros, he said, are "the least favored" in the business, and "the commercializers" reap the greatest benefits. "These people don't always respect the traditions of the mezcaleros," he explained. "They want mezcal to compete with tequila and other drinks like rum and whiskey. And the only ones helping the mezcaleros are themselves, as it's always been throughout the history of mezcal. During the colonial period the Spanish wanted to eradicate mezcal so people would buy aguardiente from Spain instead. And during much of the history of Mexico, mezcal has been persecuted. There was a bishop in Jalisco who'd excommunicate people who drank mezcal."

"But even," he went on, "with all the laws and regulations the government has made to control mezcal, the palenqueros will keep making it as they've always done. And even if there's a lot of money involved, I don't think traditions will change much because most of the land here is communal, and big distilleries can't buy large plots of land for themselves to grow agaves because communities aren't going to let them have it. Each mezcal producer has his own formula inherited through generations, and he supposes that his is the best one. He gives part of his production to the local fiesta that celebrates the patron saint, and the people consuming it are of the same community and aren't going to drink one from somewhere else. So I don't believe laws and money will change things much. The CRM has the Norma, but the producers don't really care. Everything's against them, but they're going to keep going and survive no matter what."

Losing their tradition of mezcal-making would mean losing their community identity along with their individual voice. "They've received teachings from their parents and ancestors," said Ulises, "and they know about the cycle of agave, the environment, and sustainability, and through preserving the environment where agave grows, they've created a culture, and when you preserve a culture you're an artist. I compare them to alchemists, because beyond the scientific and technological aspect, they make mezcal with a lot of care and in a magical way." They may not be able to express how they do this in Spanish, he said, but "you can see it when you spend time with them."

"It's only recently," he went on, "that any importance has been given to mezcal. Its history and production methods are still not very well known, or the many different types of processes used in the various regions of Mexico. This is understandable because mezcal is made in a different way in each part and with different agaves. A lot of people don't know about this differentiation, and that creates confusion. But people are going to discover new worlds in mezcal, in the senses of both flavors and places. Each town has its own drink that you can identify it with. And because there's such a great variety of mezcal and agave, the tastes are almost infinite, because of the many types of agave and the magical hand of the maker. A single producer can create many types of flavors, and that makes the richness of mezcal all the greater."

Ulises said that when tasting a mezcal, you should first examine the perlas and slight coat of oiliness on the surface, before putting a little on your hand to smell the flavor and then taking a small taste and playing around with it in your mouth. "It's like trying to find the roots of a culture," he said. "How did this community come to make this drink? By tasting it you can identify the character of a village. Knowing mezcal is knowing what connects everything in Mexico. It's very strong like our ancestors were very strong." The drink is already aged, he said, because the agaves used to make it are so old. It doesn't make sense to add anything to it, because "you lose the authentic taste of the agaves used to make it. Once you know mezcal and how it's made, you realize that it's a product of nature and irreplaceable."

Looking at the expensive mezcals stored in that Barcelona safe, and thinking about the unheard stories behind them and how little the maestros mezcaleros who had created them had likely been paid, I thought of an economic concept known as the Agency Problem. A conflict of interest occurs when an agent acts in the interests of a principal and the agent's interests are different from those of the principal. A CEO might find ways to thwart the takeover of a company out of fear of losing her job regardless of the best interests of shareholders. A mezcal brand owner might not want to pay producers more for their mezcals because his personal gains would be less.

I left the bar and walked to the nearby harbor. Seagulls squawked, and overhead I could see the iconic *Teleférico del Puerto* cable cars slowly traversing the empty blue void between Barceloneta and Montjuïc hill, buffeted by the wind. I remembered a scene from *The Passenger*, when Jack Nicholson leans out from a window and flaps his arms over the dark blue sea like wings, with a chuckle and a grin. It reminded me of how I had felt when I first drank mezcal, and I wished I could feel that way again.

ᗷ

BY 2016, THE spirit was sold in forty-two countries, according to the CRM, and mezcal bars had opened all over the place. During a visit to British Columbia, I took a walk along the Malcolm Lowry Trail in Cates Park, in North Vancouver, where the British author worked on *Under the Volcano* in a "squatter's shack" overlooking Burrard Inlet. Then I crossed the bridge to Vancouver and stopped by La Mezcaleria, a bar on Commercial Drive. A red neon sign outside read MEZCAL, and PARA TODO MAL, MEZCAL, PARA TODO BIEN, TAMBIEN! was inscribed on the glass front door. Inside, bartenders poured drinks from a selection of certified agave distillates, dozens of which are now available outside Mexico.

In the course of a day in Brooklyn, I saw a *tequilana* agave perched on a rocky outcrop in the Desert Pavilion at the Brooklyn Botanic Garden and then, in the Brooklyn Museum next door, a clay sculpture from Jalisco—circa 100 BCE to 300 CE—of a seated couple sharing "a bowl containing an unknown beverage" before I stepped into a lively mezcal bar called Leyenda Brooklyn Coctelería and shared a flight of three distillates—sotol, bacanora, and raicilla, listed as "The Mexican Outliers"—with a fun trio of French flight attendants. And in my old stomping grounds in Baltimore, where I had first tried mezcal, I visited an atmospheric new mezcalería called Clavel, which occupied a sparsely chic space in the Remington neighborhood that felt airlifted straight from Oaxaca de Juárez, but had been reinvented from an old-school joint called Corky's Grill.

A few blocks from the historic plaza in Santa Fe, a touristy town where it sometimes appears as if margaritas run from faucets, a tequila-and-mezcal bar opened as part of a new Mexican restaurant called Sazón. They sold two-ounce pours of Del Maguey Chichicapa and Minero mezcals for $25 each, and a two-ounce pour of Del Maguey Pechuga for $65. A 750ml bottle of mezcal is 25.36 ounces, so twelve two-ounce pours would equal around $300 of Chichicapa, and around $780 of Pechuga—quite a profit margin for bottles with retail prices of around $70 and $200 each.

The Sazerac Company now distributes over a dozen different Del Maguey mezcals, as well as three from the industrially produced Monte Albán brand. In an article for the *New Yorker*,

Ron Cooper told the writer Dana Goodyear: "I converted people one person at a time, nose to nose. I created this whole market, and until three years ago I owned the whole fucking deal." A gallery in Taos put on a show of some of his found-bottle artworks, in an exhibit called Irony and Enigma. In a business profile in the *Taos News*, Ron told the reporter that his mezcals are "fair trade," that Del Maguey is the "No. 1 exporter of mezcal from Mexico," and that in 2015 the company "sent" Paciano Cruz Nolasco "$900,000."

When asked if, when traveling around the world, he identified as an artist or a "mezcal purveyor," Ron said: "Well, this started out as an art project, and I still call it my liquid art. So it's all art to me. I'm not as famous as Richard Serra or Jeff Koons or a lot of the artists. But I'm fairly well known for being one of the originators of the California Light and Space movement in the '60s. So my mezcal buddies say Ron Cooper is an internationally known artist. And vice versa. I realized as a young artist that art should be an adventure. It's not over. This Del Maguey is really paying for itself, and it's paying me now." An announcement for a book deal on the website Publishers Marketplace described Ron as the "architect of the artisanal mezcal renaissance."

When the *Taos News* asked for his thoughts on art as a business, he said: "You buy materials, manipulate them, transform them, and hopefully sell them. But you don't go into art to sell stuff. It's just a beautiful thing. I didn't start the mezcal project to make money. I did it because I love the art of it. Now it's really become a sustaining thing for these 10 families and about

400 other people." The reporter asked Ron if his success in business translated to success in art, and he said: "A work of art is successful for me if, in the making of it, a question is generated and answering that question becomes the next work. That's one aspect. Another is that art must have that aha moment to be successful. I don't care if it's a nude or a sunset or a landscape or a pile of trash or words. It doesn't matter, as long as it transforms the viewer. Mezcal is really successful because it transforms the imbiber. You have these wonderful, humorous thoughts going on it your head. So it fits my criteria for a work of art."

In an emailed newsletter to the "Del Maguey Family" in July 2016, the artist-importer was pictured wearing his shiny new James Beard award around his neck. Another photograph showed him driving his 1920s Ford Roadster on a beach, announcing his participation in an upcoming "automotive carnival" called The Race of Gentlemen. At the bottom of the email was a "Drink of the Month," a mezcal cocktail invented by Mattia Cila, a bartender at a restaurant called *Drogheria*, in Licata, Italy. He called his drink *El Cartello* (The Cartel).

ㄹ

ONE MORNING IN the summer of 2016, I paid a visit to Elisandro González Molina in San Jose, California. I hadn't seen him since we had visited San Cristóbal Lachirioag in 2011, and he had just returned from spending two months in Oaxaca. He had been busy there working on a variety of projects, from making mezcal with his cousin, Edgar, to overseeing an updated label design for their brand. A doctor in Washington had invested in the business, and they had also received a government subsidy. Elisandro showed me a photograph on his smartphone of a new white truck with TOSBA painted on the side. Edgar drove it to work instead of walking up and down the steep mountainside.

The cousins now had four magueyeros working with them, and they had installed four new stills and ten new tinas and constructed a new cooling tank. They had also transferred their bottling machine to the production site, and erected a small building that housed a kitchen and storage room. And Edgar had fabricated a molino Egipcio with rock and cement to replace their mechanical grinder. A new bathroom used gravity-fed water from the spring, and solar panels provided electricity. Elisandro showed me pictures of masks that Edgar's father-in-law had created to decorate the new building, which was painted in earth tones and with the patterned border from their bottle label. A gilded church altar from the village of Talea de Castro had been repurposed into a tasting bar, and a low fence outside the building was embedded with the Tosba insignia. The cousins were developing plans for events and workshops at the site, and they had hosted tours led by an American mezcal advocate, Clayton Szczech.

The Caltrain from San Francisco to San Jose was packed with fresh-faced tech workers heading to work at Apple, Google, and other corporate campuses. Elisandro and his wife, Jessica, picked me up at the San Jose train station in their silver Prius, and we got on the freeway. It seemed as if just about every other car was

a Tesla. We soon got stuck in traffic next to a large truck emblazoned with advertising for Casamigos tequila. An entire side was
plastered with a gigantic photograph of George Clooney and his
business partner Rande Gerber. They were both wearing jeans
and dark shades, riding motorcycles past a field of tequila agaves.
OUR CASA IS YOUR CASA was written below.

"Me and Edgar should do one like that for Tosba, but with
burros," Elisandro laughed.

He dropped off Jessica at a secondary school where she was
teaching French and Spanish. Then we stopped by LV Mar, the
restaurant in Redwood City co-owned by his uncle. Bottles of
Tosba were displayed on a shelf behind the bar. The brand's
espadín mezcal was retailing for around $50, its pechuga for
around $80, and its tobalá for around $100. "We've been planting papalote, tepeztate, tobalá, karwinskii, and mexicano,"
said Elisandro. "And we've got around one hundred thousand
plants now." He had just become the company's importer, and
Tosba mezcals were now being sold beyond California, in Texas
and Washington. The company's four new stills could double
their capacity to twenty-four thousand liters a year, although
they were still making an average of five thousand. As more
magueys matured and required harvesting, they would make
more mezcal.

Elisandro estimated that from the price of each bottle of
Tosba, approximately 30 percent went to the retailer, 30 percent
to the distributor, and 40 percent to the brand, which had to
absorb the expenses of shipping, marketing, storage, overhead,

and other costs, in addition to taxes. "Instead of being paid 30 pesos per liter if we were to sell it to someone else," he said, "we decided that it makes more sense to earn closer to 450 pesos a liter. We can actually make more money by importing it to the U.S. and selling it here instead of in Mexico, because the taxes on mezcal are so high there."

As empowered mezcaleros, Edgar and Elisandro were extremely rare—the "unicorns" of mezcal, in Silicon Valley lingo. "We were only able to do this because I migrated and have a foot on this side of the border," said Elisandro. "I've had opportunities for education, and to have access to the market, which are opportunities that most mezcal producers don't have. The reason why maestros mezcaleros, just as in any other underdeveloped country, haven't been able to enter the economy is because they lack access to resources like education and money. And at the same time, people who do have access to those resources come and take advantage of them, which is more than unfair, it's unethical."

"I like mezcal, of course," he said, "but ultimately I see it as a valuable resource for the economy and culture of San Cristóbal. So one of the reasons I'm doing this is to benefit the community with more employment and a greater sense of pride. Already in the region people are talking proudly about Tosba, and that's maybe giving them the hope and inspiration they need to do their own projects with maybe coffee or sugarcane, just like we're doing with mezcal. Getting the Villa Alta-Cajonos region on the map is just as important as getting mezcal on the map."

Leaving the restaurant, we returned south to San Jose, with Jane Birkin and Chuck Berry playing on the car stereo through Elisandro's smartphone. He took me past a nondescript apartment complex he had lived in when he first came to the area. Then we drove through Santana Row, a high-end mall where there were two Mexican restaurants he had worked at over the years, Consuelo and El Jardín. Nearby was a Tesla showroom, alongside Tumi and Gucci boutiques. "When Edgar and I first started thinking about this," said Elisandro, "we would tell our friends, 'Hey, we're gonna make mezcal and sell it on Santana Row!' And everyone would make fun of us, saying things like, 'Oh yeah? You want to sell that stuff with some tamales, too?' We used to daydream about it, but now they're selling Tosba over there at Consuelo."

"I often think of what we're doing with Tosba as a political statement," he said. "My fellow indigenous peoples look great in pictures, but I want my people to have access to the technology, education, and financial services that would help them to get ahead. We're a lot more things than just images in magazines. Tosba could not only be used as an economic source to combat poverty and lack of employment, but also to help uphold our strong cultural values, and our traditional respect for the land and the community." As we left Santana Row and continued driving through San Jose, the dry brown mountains ahead of us shrouded in smog, Elisandro looked somewhat wistful.

"Living in California is allowing me to hopefully live in Oaxaca again," he said.

In San Francisco mezcal was everywhere, and when I returned to the Mission District that evening I ordered "mezcal steamed savory clams" at the Range restaurant on Valencia Street. But Elisandro said the spirit was a tougher sell in suburban San Jose, where tastes generally run more conservative. "They'll embrace innovation like Tesla," he said, "but mezcal is more challenging." However, he parked outside a restaurant in downtown San Jose that was actually called Mezcal. He said that until a few years ago, it'd had more of a tequila focus, although the vision of the owner, Adolfo Gomez, who was from the Oaxacan village of San Pedro Apóstol, had always been to have a full-scale mezcalería. The bar manager, Marsella Macias, was helping to fulfill that dream.

Inside the restaurant, the bar shelves were loaded with dozens of mezcals distilled from a broad assortment of agave varietals that had been crafted by a wide variety of maestros mezcaleros. "We now have about eighty mezcal expressions from around twenty-six different brands," Marsella told us. An enthusiastic aficionado, she frequently traveled to Mexico to learn more about the spirit, and was enrolled in a four-part educational program in Oaxaca called *Mezcología*, in which she was learning about the history, science, production methods, and cultural aspects of mezcal. She said that she would be the first person in the U.S. to have a *Mezcólogo* certification. "I'd like to be able to educate people further about the drink," she said, "so they can take their appreciation to a whole new level—because mezcal deserves it."

She said that she came across new facets of mezcal on every visit to Mexico. She showed me a photograph on her smartphone of a highly unusual alembique that she had just seen on a trip to the state of Puebla, where the DO had recently been expanded. The still combined a large clay olla encased in adobe bricks, a hollowed-out tree trunk of palo blanco wood, a clay condenser, a short wooden sluice, and a metal cylinder containing a copper coil that finally passed the mezcal into an earthenware vessel. She was about to return to Oaxaca for the third part of her course, and she later shared that she had met a 101-year-old maestro mezcalero in the village of Santa María Ixcatlán, in the Mixteca region, who had distilled papalote mezcal for sixty years. "He hand-mashed his agave in wooden canoas," she said. "And he fermented the mash in rawhide."

Elisandro opened his backpack and brought out samples of mezcal made with tepeztate and madrecuixe that he had just brought back from the villages of San Cristóbal Lachirioag and Miahuatlán in Oaxaca. He poured us each a sip. "These are very interesting expressions," said Marcella thoughtfully, her palate referencing them with many hundreds of others she had tasted. I asked her how she felt about the current state of affairs in Mezcal World. "It bothers me that there's a lot of repression in the business," she said. "The people who should be benefitting aren't. I'd like it if we could have more single-family owners. What I'd love to see a lot more of is single-*family* mezcal."

GLOSSARY

(Please note that some of the following translations are colloquial.)

a granel: in bulk

abocado: a mezcal with additives

ABV: Alcohol By Volume

aguamiel: agave nectar

alembique de cobre: copper still

añejo: an "aged" mezcal

bagazo: agave mash

cabeza: the "head" of a distillation

canoa: trough used for mashing agave

capón: castrated maguey

coa: implement used for harvesting agave

cola: the "tail" of a distillation

colectivo: shared taxi

comal: wood-heated stove

copa: cup

cordón: ring of bubbles in a *jícara* (see below)

CRM: Mezcal Regulatory Council

cuerpo: the "body" of a distillation

DO: Denomination of Origin

fábrica de mezcal: mezcal distillery

garrafone: jerry can

horno: pit oven

jícara: gourd cup

joven: a "young" or unaged mezcal

maestros mezcaleros: mezcal distillers

maguey: agave

magueyero: an agave or mezcal worker

marca: brand

mazo: wooden club used for mashing agave

molino Egipcio: "Egyptian" millstone fabricated from rock and cement

NOM: Official Mexican Standard

olla de barro: clay still

palenque: mezcal distillery

palenqueros: mezcal distillers

pechuga: mezcal distilled with meat, usually poultry

penca: agave leaf

perlas: bubbles in a distillate

piñas: agave hearts

quiote: flowering agave stalk

reposado: a "rested" mezcal

tahona: millstone

tina: fermentation vat

venencia: cane tube used for aerating mezcal in a *jícara*

CITED WORKS

Arellano, Gustavo. *Taco USA*. Scribner, 2012.

Asimov, Eric. "A Year of Acquired Tastes." *New York Times*, December 27, 2011.

Bourriaud, Nicolas. *Postproduction*. Lukas & Sternberg, 2002.

Bowen, Sarah. *Divided Spirits: Tequila, Mezcal, and the Politics of Production*. University of California Press, 2015.

Bruman, Henry J. *Alcohol in Ancient Mexico*. University of Utah Press, 2000.

Contreras, Tigram, director. *Papalote Mezcal of Chilapa: From the Mountain to the Bottle*. Universidad Autónoma del Estado de Morelos, 2006.

Cutler, Lance. *The Tequila Lover's Guide to Mexico and Mezcal*. Wine Patrol Press, 2000.

Gentry, Howard. *Agaves of Continental North America*. University of Arizona Press, 1982.

Godoy, Maria, and Kat Chow. "When Chefs Become Famous Cooking Other Cultures' Food." NPR, March 22, 2016.

Goodyear, Dana. "Mezcal Sunrise: Searching for the Ultimate Artisanal Distillate." *New Yorker*, April 4, 2016.

Hooks, Cody. "Getting Down to Business with Ron Cooper." *Taos News*, June 17, 2016.

Huston, John, director. *The Night of the Iguana*. Metro-Goldywn-Mayer, 1964.

——. *The Treasure of the Sierra Madre*. Warner Bros., 1948.

Illsley Granich, Catarina. "Keys to Savoring Mezcals." In *Mezcal: Arte Tradicional*. Translated by Jana Schroeder. Artes de Mexico 98. Artes de Mexico, 2010.

Kaplan, Jennifer, Thomas Buckley, and Andrea Navarro. "Tequila's Smoky Cousin Gets Push From World's Biggest Distillers." Bloomberg.com, September 26, 2016.

Kliman, Todd. "The Problem of Authenticity". *Lucky Peach* (Summer 2011): 82–92.

Lawrence, D. H. *The Plumed Serpent*. Alfred A. Knopf, 1926.

Legorreta, Alejandro, and Gustavo Rivera Loret de Mola. *Corrupcionario Mexicano*. Grijalbo, 2016.

Lowry, Malcolm. *Under the Volcano*. J. B. Lippincott, 1947.

Mitchell, Tim. *Intoxicated Identities: Alcohol's Power in Mexican History and Culture*. Routledge, 2004.

Pollan, Michael. *The Botany of Desire*. Random House, 2001.

Pool-Illsley, Emilia, and Catarina Illsley Granich. "El Papel de los Activos Culturales en las Dinámicas Territoriales Rurales: El Caso de Tlacolula y Ocotlán en Valles Centrales de Oaxaca, México." *Grupo de Estudios Ambientales*, 2012.

Puche, Mari Carmen Serra and Jesús Carlos Lazcano Arce. *El Mezcal, una bebida prehispánica. Estudios etnoarqueológicos*. IIA-UNAM, 2016.

Reed, John. *Insurgent Mexico*. D. Appleton & Company, 1914.

Sacks, Oliver. *Hallucinations*. Alfred A. Knopf, 2012.

Salinas, Brenda. "'Columbusing': The Art of Discovering Something That Is Not New." NPR, July 6, 2014.

Sanneh, Kelefa. "Letter from El Salvador: Sacred Grounds: Aida Batlle and the New Coffee Evangelists." *New Yorker*, November 21, 2011.

Siegel, Ronald K. *Intoxication*. E. P. Dutton, 1989.

Tolstoy, Leo. "Why Do Men Stupify Themselves?" In *Recollections & Essays*. Oxford University Press, 1937.

Torres, Ignacio, Alejandro Casas, Ernesto Vega, Miguel Martíez-Ramos, and América Delgado-Lemus. "Population Dynamics and Sustainable Management of Mescal Agaves in Central Mexico: *Agave potatorum* in the Tehuacán-Cuicatlán Valley." *Economic Botany* 69, no. 1 (2015): 26–41.

Vanderbilt, Tom. *You May Also Like*. Alfred A. Knopf, 2016.

Wija, Tantri. "James Beard Award Finalist Turns Mescal into a World-Class Liquor." *Santa Fe New Mexican*, April 15, 2014.

Zizumbo-Villareal, Daniel, Fernando González-Zozoya, Angeles Olay-Barrientos, Laura Almendros-López, Patricia Flores-Pérez, and Patricia Colunga-García Marín. "Distillation in Western Mesoamerica Before European Contact." *Economic Botany* 63, no. 4 (2009): 413–26.

ACKNOWLEDGMENTS

I WOULD LIKE TO thank: my superb agent, Joy Tutela, and the David Black Agency. My fine editor, Rolph Blythe. My old friend Jack DeLap for his agave artistry. Jack Shoemaker, Kelly Winton, Bethany Onsgard, Megan Fishmann, Nick Gomez-Hall, and everyone at Counterpoint Press. Also Jennifer Heuer, Megan Jones, Barrett Briske, and Matthew Hoover. Daniel Barsotti for his photograph. Editors Alex and Susan Heard for helping me to shape and develop the book. Sue N. Greene for her keen and unerring eye, and Jack P. Greene and J. Megan Greene for their wise counsel.

Most important, I would like to particularly thank the following maestros mezcaleros and their families for their gracious hospitality—this book wouldn't exist without them: Espiridion Morales Luis, Paciano Cruz Nolasco, Florencio Carlos Sarmiento, "Eugenio Ramírez," Faustino Garcia Vasquez, Felipe Cortés, Elisandro González Molina, Edgar González Ramírez, José Garcia Pacheco, Joél Antonio Cruz, Benigno Sánchez Gatica, Ciro Barranca Bello, Refugio Calzada Hernández, and Moisés Calzada Rendón.

I would also like to thank Ron Cooper and Arturo Ramírez Zenteño of Del Maguey. Graciela Ángeles Carreño and Real Minero. Ulises Torrentera, Sanzekan Tinemi, Silvia Philion, Marco Ochoa, Douglas French, Julio César Zárate Olmedo, Marsella Macias, Nils Dallmann, Abel Iraizos, Eric Adalid Hernández Cortés, Destilería Los Danzantes, Zignum, Berenice Acuña, Misty Kalkofen, Philip Ward, Andy Seymour, Bill Norris, Fred Sarkis, Steve Olson, Gina Chersevani, Iván Saldaña Oyarzábal, and Daniel Martinez.

I am also grateful to: Henry Shukman for his ongoing input and title suggestion, and Michael Anft, John Thorndike, Stephanie Pearson, Baylor Chapman, and Devon Hawkes Ludlow for their thoughtful reads. Indiana Christov Moore, Jenny Sanborn, and Rodolfo Juárez for their translations. Sarah Meghan Lee for her camera tutelage. Jack Parsons for his photo editing advice. Barend and Claudia van der Vorm, Tom Melk and Sarah Potter, and Anatol Yusef, Elspeth Bobbs, Barry Ellsworth, and the Meem Library staff at Saint John's College for memorable writing spots.

I appreciate the help I received from: Hannah Hughes, Donald S. Lamm, Sean Moody, Susan Thornton, Andrew Gellatly, Clare Dunne, Maxime Guillon, Edward McLoughlin, Lara Streatfield, Alexander Neumann, Tyler Rothamel, C. Edward Peartree, Molly E. Moore, Morgan Lee, Anne Johns, Rick Stevens, Alexandra Eldridge, Antonio Melchor, Joanna Hurley, Amy Zavatto, Joseph Garcia, Louis R. Levin, Yan Yang, and John Ellsberry.

Authors I have cited are: Sarah Bowen, Patricia Colunga-García Marín, Catarina Illsley Granich, Emilia Pool-Illsley, Brenda Salinas, Tom Vanderbilt, Dana Goodyear, Daniel Zizumbo-Villarreal, Fernando González-Zozaya, Angeles Olay-Barrientos, Laura Almendros-López, Patricia Flores-Pérez, Gustavo Arellano, Henry J. Bruman, Howard Scott Gentry, Kalefa Sanneh, Lance Cutler, Leo Tolstoy, Malcolm Lowry, Michael Pollan, Nicolas Bourriaud, Oliver Sacks, Rick Bayless, Ronald K. Siegel, Tim Mitchell, Todd Kliman, Eric Asimov, Tigram Contreras, Maria Godoy, Kat Chow, Cody Hooks, John Huston, Jennifer Kaplan, Thomas Buckley, Andrea Navarro, D.H. Lawrence, John Reed, Tantri Wija, Ignacio Torres, Alejandro Casas, Ernesto Vega, Miguel Martínez-Ramos, América Delgado-Lemus, Alejandro Legoretta, and Gustavo Rivera Loret de Mola.

Finally, I would like to honor and remember three wonderful people mentioned above who contributed to the evolution of this book but are sadly no longer with us. In addition to her translations, Jenny Sanborn offered many helpful insights and comments. Lara Streatfield provided logistical support in Oaxaca de Juárez. Nick Gomez-Hall was a kind and able presence at Counterpoint Press. The world was a better place with them in it.